D1553885

HISTORY *and*
MAGICAL POWER
in a Chinese Community

HISTORY *and* MAGICAL POWER
in a Chinese Community

P. Steven Sangren

STANFORD UNIVERSITY PRESS

Stanford, California

Stanford University Press
Stanford, California

© 1987 by the Trustees of the
Leland Stanford Junior University

Printed in the United States of America

CIP data appear at the end of the book

Published with the assistance
of the Andrew W. Mellon Foundation
and the Hull Memorial Publication Fund
of Cornell University

Preface

This study is intended to interest two audiences: first, experts in the study of Chinese institutions and, second, scholars concerned with general problems of relating institutions and culture in complex civilizations. Ideally, the interests of sinology and social theory ought to be dialectically complementary. That they are not always perceived so is a mark of anthropology's failure to come to terms with the social and cultural dynamics of the world's largest non-Western civilization and of sinology's sometimes unselfconsciously empiricist specialization.

Although I defend a unity of sinological and anthropological interests, I do not expect all readers to find the same parts of the following text of equal interest. Sinologists may find some of the theoretical discussions too abstract and speculative, and those mainly interested in social theory may find some sections too full of ethnographic and historical detail. The detail is justified because, just as I make frequent use of data discussed by authors whose interpretative strategies are quite different from my own, I expect that some sinologists will make similar use of the ethnographic information documented here. However, the value of documentation must be balanced against the tedium of excessive detail, and no attempt to balance argument and evidence can hope to satisfy everyone. I suspect that Parts I and II will be of most interest to sinologists; Part III is more theoretically ambitious and addresses debates of wider interest in social theory.

During my stay in Ta-ch'i, Taiwan (from January 1976 to August 1977), I had the good fortune to meet many knowledgeable, open, and generous people. (Wade-Giles romanization is used throughout the text.) Without their active cooperation, I would have been unable to learn enough to write this book. I am particularly indebted to my assistant, Wang Ch'un-hua, whose enthusiasm, intelligence, and talent for ethnographic interviewing helped to compensate for my own shortcomings. Huang Mei-ying was equally energetic and helpful in assisting me on a shorter research trip during 1984 to famous Ma Tsu cult centers. I would also like to express my appreciation to the Institute of Ethnology, Academia Sinica, for granting me status as a research associate (1976–77) and as a visiting fellow (July 1984).

Arthur P. Wolf and G. William Skinner, my teachers at Stanford University, encouraged and sustained my interest in China through a rather lengthy apprenticeship; this book's intellectual debt to them is self-evident. Charles O. Frake and Michelle Z. Rosaldo inspired me to broaden my anthropological horizons. Many conversations with Fred R. Myers and David H. Holmberg have been important in developing the positions outlined in Part III. Bernard Faure, Davydd J. Greenwood, David Hess, Sarah Miller, Robert J. Smith, Terence Turner, and Deborah Warner read and commented on drafts of parts of the manuscript. The reviewer for Stanford University Press was particularly helpful, providing more than ten pages of detailed criticism. My thanks to them all.

Financial support for fieldwork in Taiwan from June 1976 to June 1977 was provided by a Fulbright-Hays Fellowship and a grant from the Social Science Research Council. The SSRC also provided six months of dissertation write-up support. Additional write-up support was provided by a grant from the Mabelle McCleod Lewis Memorial Fund. A grant from the Mellon Foundation administered by the American Council of Learned Societies provided time for research on pilgrimages (1983–84), and a grant from the Hu Shih Memorial Foundation funded research in Taiwan (July 1984). The Hull Foundation provided funds to help underwrite the production of the book. Much of Chapter 2 was published in somewhat altered form as "Social Space and the Periodization of Economic History: A Case from Taiwan," *Comparative Studies in Society and History* 27:532–61 (May 1985).

Finally, I wish to thank my wife, Li Chung-ying, whose emotional support sustained me through periods of loneliness and self-doubt; it is to her that my debt is the greatest.

P.S.S.

Contents

Eight pages of photographs appear following page 60

Tables, Maps, and Figures

HISTORY *and*
MAGICAL POWER
in a Chinese Community

If *ch'ien* and *k'un* [yang and yin] are obliterated,
there would be no means of seeing the system of Change.

I Ching

Introduction

This book is a case study of history and culture in a Taiwanese town and the group of rural villages that constitute its standard marketing community, to use G. William Skinner's (1964) phrase. However, its scope goes beyond those of most community studies. I attempt to construct a holistic view of aspects of Chinese culture from an analysis of the relationship between history and ritual in a particular locality. In other words, I try to present a synthetic view of the whole from the position of a part or periphery.

This undertaking, if not entirely iconoclastic in anthropological circles, is unconventional in anthropological studies of Chinese society and culture. For one thing, it assumes that at some level Chinese culture is holistic, that there is a logic of symbolic relations that underlies manifest differences in social institutions across class, region, and time. This crucial assumption has sharply divided scholars over such issues as whether or not there is a "Chinese religion" (e.g., A. Wolf 1974b; Watson 1976; Freedman 1974), and over the relationship between the so-called great tradition and little traditions (Sangren 1984a). More fundamentally, I assume that pervasive cultural contrasts, especially those related to what I term "structures of value," transcend variations in local institutions and practices. This assumption runs very much against the grain of the sociocentric, structural-functional methodology that has defined Anglo-American sinological anthropology to date. In this latter, still dominant perspective, "culture" is explained as a product or reflection of local social structure.

Even among scholars inclined to view Chinese civilization holistically, discussion has consisted mainly of asserting or documenting the pervasiveness of a limited set of categories of thought (e.g., bipolarity, "associative thinking," the five elements, and so forth) or values (especially filial piety and hierarchical subordination). The discovery of such universals, however, falls short of explaining their persistence and their relationship to the social institutions (e.g., the family, community, state) that are presumed to embody them.

In my view, the task of describing how categories of thought are reproduced in Chinese institutions and, dialectically, how Chinese institutions reproduce Chinese categories of thought is essential to deepening our understanding of the processes that pattern both Chinese thought and Chinese institutions. In conventional anthropological parlance, culture (whether it be thought of in terms of "collective representations," values, worldview, or symbolic system) and society (what people do, the institutions in which they live and interact, "social structure") cannot be analyzed separately.

To put this assertion more concretely, I argue that Chinese collective representations, to use Durkheim's terminology, are at once products of social institutions and their preconditions. In other words, social institutions and collective representations are dialectically connected in the process of social and cultural reproduction. Moreover, although I concentrate on dimensions of community identity, this characterization is true of institutions ranging in scale from the family to the state.

I am well aware of the conceptual slipperiness of terms like "dialectics" and of the difficulties involved in realizing in analysis what sounds plausible in abstract theory. Nonetheless, I attempt to describe this dialectical process through analysis of key cultural concepts like *ling* (which can be translated variously as "spirit" or "magical power") attributed to supernatural entities such as ghosts, gods, and ancestors. In my analysis of the symbolic logic that constitutes *ling,* I argue that it can be fully understood only as a product of the reproduction of social institutions and as a manifestation of a native historical consciousness.

In addition, I attempt to illustrate how the cultural construction of relations among history, social relations, and magical power played an important role in the remarkable ability of the traditional Chinese state to incorporate and, to some degree, "co-opt" popular religious cults. I argue that history, by means of its important role in authenticating and legitimating both the magical power (*ling*) attributed to territorial-cult deities and the virtue (*jen*) of the hierarchically ordered imperial state, performed a crucial ideological function in disguising contradictions in the structures of legitimacy of local and state institutions and of patterns of authority.

In this regard, my examination of the semiotics of religious symbols is aimed at developing a model of the structures of value that legitimate social institutions. Using, broadly speaking, structuralist techniques, I compare the structure of value embodied in the notion of *ling* with that embodied in the Confucian notion of virtue. I argue that although these two structures of value differ in important respects, they can nonetheless be contingently reconciled. The key to my analysis hinges on a logic similar to what Louis Dumont (1980a) terms "the encompassing of the contrary." Simply put, in Chinese thought, history is capable of simultaneously authenticating contradictory models of power. The way this contradiction is ideologically disguised in Chinese religion has been a crucial element in the reciprocally legitimating relationship between state and local institutions and patterns of authority.

This analysis is particularly complicated because the two structures of value in question are present in both state and local institutions, albeit with differing emphases. It is important to stress that my analysis rejects any easy separation on the order of "elite/folk," "text/ritual," or "great tradition/little traditions" at the level of structures of value (Sangren 1984a). Elements of both Confucian or "high" culture and "folk" belief inform all Chinese institutions and are not uniquely ascribable to social classes. This idea is the basis of my attempt to develop a holistic view from ethnographic evidence taken from a single locality. Although I make reference to the broader sinological literature on history and philosophy, my perspective remains that of an anthropologist. It is, no doubt, an unbalanced perspective, but given the nature of the arguments I make, I hope that it will occasion appropriate corrections from those who know the fields into which I trespass.

I am led to these perhaps overambitious arguments first by an analysis of religious symbols. Here my inspiration comes from such "structuralist" writers as Claude Lévi-Strauss, Louis Dumont, Marcel Granet, and Edmund Leach. Yet my argument attempts to cross the epistemological boundary between structuralism and more historically oriented approaches, by taking into account the growing interest in "practice" or "social reproduction" in current theoretical discussion (see especially T. Turner 1977a, 1977b, 1979a, 1984; Ortner 1984; Sahlins 1981; Merquior 1979; Bourdieu 1977; and Augé 1982).

The structuralist portions of the argument, particularly in Chapters 7 and 8, challenge structural-functionalist interpretations of Chinese religious symbols as straightforward projections of social categories into a

supernatural world. In structural-functionalist treatments, Chinese supernatural symbols are viewed as entities that "represent" mundane social
categories; the pantheon mirrors society, and since society is "real," it
must explain the structure of the pantheon. Although in some contexts
this is precisely how the Chinese pantheon appears and is described by
informants, the relation between religious and social categories is more
complex. More sense can be made of the seemingly endless complexity
of Chinese religion by viewing supernatural categories as mediators between order and disorder in an extremely wide variety of contexts, rather
than as cosmological reflections of society.

In my view, this structuralist approach can explain more of the ethnographic facts, contradictions, and trivia that constitute the cultural
logic of Chinese religious behavior and symbolism than can the kinds of
arguments offered to date. This is a difficult position to argue because it
means that no given supernatural entity means the same thing all the time;
the nature of its power and meaning depends upon the ritual context in
which it is addressed, who is worshiping it, in what role the worshiper
addresses it (as individual, officeholder, member of a family or community, and so forth), and with what other supernatural entities it is being
implicitly or explicitly contrasted.

I rely extensively on examples to demonstrate this point, but the complexity of Chinese religious symbology necessarily renders my analysis
far from exhaustive. Generalizations about the meanings of Chinese
supernatural categories can always be challenged, because the contexts
that define those meanings are so variable. The Chinese pantheon is not a
static "model of and for" the social world, but a complex language for
speaking about and (re)creating social relationships. In short, deities,
ghosts, and ancestors must be understood as cultural and social operators
as well as symbolic entities. The fact that informants consciously conceive
supernatural power in the form of entities is part of the process by which
the connection between cosmology and social institutions is mystified.
To legitimize social institutions and the relations among categories of insiders and outsiders, magical power must be conceived as emanating from
sources outside these institutions.

The examples I provide in attempting to illustrate this point are intended to promote an open-ended reappraisal of our understanding of
Chinese "folk religion." So-called folk religion constitutes a much more
sophisticated medium for expressing complex philosophical and social
paradoxes than either Western analysts or some traditional Chinese elites
have acknowledged.

My argument goes beyond conventional structural analysis of symbols, however, and attempts to reincorporate the undeniable connections between religion and social institutions. Social institutions do, as structuralists emphasize, embody basic symbolic contrasts and values; religion does constitute, in Marxist parlance, an ideological support for structures of social authority; and religion does, in structural-functionalist terms, reflect social categories. But it is not enough to show how institutions embody the values constituted in the logic of symbols; one must describe the process by which institutions and collective representations constitute a larger reproducing system. It is this problem that motivates the discussion of the cultural construction of history and the social construction of identity in Chapters 9, 10, and 11. Marx's oft-cited insight that history both makes us and is made by us is an important theme of these chapters. Of particular importance is the special role of history as ideology; both local institutions like community festivals and the Chinese Empire itself depended upon a particular, culturally constructed vision of history as a form of legitimating rhetoric.

In sum, my analysis attempts to avoid the pitfalls of functional explanations without denying the important functional links between collective representations and social institutions. In this regard, it participates in what I perceive as "function's" qualified return to legitimacy in anthropological theory (e.g., Augé 1982). However, in the process of recapturing legitimacy, attention to function is undergoing a radical transformation from its incarnation as the building block of Radcliffe-Brown's "structural-functionalism." In a word, Radcliffe-Brown's radical (and now notorious) separation of function and history, science and "pseudo-causal" explanations (1952: 3), has been replaced by a more temporalized vision of function in social process (be it conceived as "practice," "action," or "history").

Both structuralist and historical-materialist critics have pointed out one of the major shortcomings in structural-functionalism (shared with other "functionalisms")—namely, its failure to distinguish causes and effects. Social institutions like ritual may be shown to produce increased reproductive fitness, individual psychological well-being, social solidarity, or reproduction of class interests. But can these effects be taken to "explain" the meaning, existence, or persistence of ritual? In attempting to illustrate how *ling* is best understood as both a cultural logic of symbolic relations and a material logic of social relations, I attempt to show that the answer to this question is "No." Identifying integrating effects is only the beginning of social or cultural analysis. In addition, we ought to investigate not only how such effects are produced, but also how the institutions that produce them are themselves perpetuated in the encompassing process of social reproduction. However, this is not to say that institutional effects are irrelevant to sociological explanation. On the contrary, they may ultimately bear a great deal on processes of social and cultural reproduction and change, but they are always conveyed through the cybernetics of the total social/cultural system (Augé 1982; Bourdieu 1977).

Stated in such general terms, this proposition is hardly controversial. Disagreements arise mainly because it is very difficult to describe the complex matrix of social and cultural institutions that structures the ways in which "effects" are fed back (to borrow a metaphor from systems theory) and converted into causes. When one speaks of the cybernetics of cultural and social systems, one is not speaking of anything as straightforwardly intelligible as, say, the cybernetics of natural selection.* Not only is culture not tied to individual organisms, but the very institutions that reproduce culture are themselves, at least in part, culturally constituted. Culture and society are aspects of a program that continuously rewrites itself in transmission from one generation to the next and in transformation from one institutional context to another.

Marshall Sahlins (1981; 1982; 1983) makes this point most eloquently, but he is suspicious of the utility of the notion of reproduction, preferring to stress transformation. For example, he argues that "the deployment of a received structure in a new context produces no simple or stereotypic reproduction, but rather assigns new functional values to old oppositions and thereby orders an unprecedented course of events" (1982: 91). One can agree with Sahlins's emphasis on the transformative potential of historical processes without abandoning the idea that there is a more general reproductive process by which "structures" are received.†

If all cultural and social systems evolve their own evolutionary logics (what Marxists term "laws of motion"), then neither clear-cut determinisms nor simple-minded cybernetic models can succeed in describing them. Thus anthropological theory is probably destined to remain more

---

*Bateson's (1972; 1979) abstract discussions of logical-type hierarchies in cybernetic processes suggest some of the pitfalls associated with oversimplified models of natural selection. For example, a rather rigid orthodoxy especially prevalent among some sociobiologists insists that the only relevant level of selection pertains to the "inclusive fitness" of individual organisms. By denying the possibility of relevant cybernetic processes at molecular, group, and ecosystem levels, such a model sacrifices encompassing explanatory power for parsimony.

†Sahlins (1981) writes of a dialectics of "intentional values" (individuals "practicing" according to varying social positions) and "conventional values" (something like collective representations, structure, or even culture) as the motor of historical transformation. However, his examples of transformation (in Fiji, New Zealand, and Hawaii) all involve European—and hence "external"—interventions. His eloquent discussions of "structures of conjuncture" thus serve rather poorly as illustrations of the conceptual advantages of "transformation" over "reproduction." Uncontacted Polynesian societies emerge from Sahlins's descriptions still somewhat cold.

abstract than theory in the natural sciences, becoming a kind of meta-theory for the various theories that anthropologists construct for particular societies.

At this admittedly abstract level, "history" is increasingly viewed as the necessary corrective to shortcomings in functional analyses. Change is inherent in the Western notion of history, and this upsets synchronic functional models that assume homeostatic equilibrium. Few anthropologists would still defend Radcliffe-Brown's (1952) excommunication of history from the arena of proper anthropological concerns. Nonetheless, understandings of the nature of the much-touted fusion of anthropology and history are widely divergent.

Most at issue are two sometimes conflated understandings of "history." On the one hand, there is increasing interest among Western historians in the "history" of nonelites, tribals, and peasants (e.g., E. Wolf 1982). "History" in this sense is a conventional, post-Enlightenment notion of an all-encompassing, causally connected sequence of events leading from past to present. This essentially objectivist view of history has been increasingly challenged in recent years because of the growing interest not only in what happened, but in how people at any particular historical juncture made sense of events.

This shift to what might loosely be termed an "emic" approach to history has seen both anthropologists and historians resort to broadly structuralist methods of cultural analysis. An example is Sahlins's recent writings (1981; 1982; 1983) on the early period of contact between Europeans and Polynesians. Sahlins draws on a combination of French structuralist and American culturalist ideas to insist that we must appreciate both native and European constructions of events to make sense of what appears either serendipitous or unintelligible in earlier historical accounts. Embedded in Sahlins's writings is a critique of unconscious ethnocentrisms in historical analyses, which thus neglect the very concrete social effects of actors' understandings of the meaning of events. One might include in this category not only theoretically naïve historiography, but also Marxist and other perspectives that see history as the product of objective forces and participants' perceptions as irrelevant, distorted, or mystified visions of these objective realities.*

Along with this interest in what might be termed "culture in history"

---

*Terray (1978) makes an interesting argument to the effect that preexisting social formations (including their superstructural or cultural aspects) determine the meaning or transformative effects of external events on a social formation's internal development. Terray's position, somewhat more cognizant of culture's role in patterning change than some Marxist arguments, is thus similar to Sahlins's, but he is much more of an objectivist; that is, he assumes that historical reality includes but is by no means limited to participants' constructions of it.

is an interest in history as culture. The historian's traditional sources are no longer viewed merely as reservoirs of fact from which the irrelevant and erroneous must be purged in order to construct a version of the historical truth. Rather, they are seen as "texts" from which to decipher the underlying, unstated, but culturally fundamental assumptions that defined their production. (Clearly, Michel Foucault has been most influential in this regard.) Not the least of these assumptions concerns the nature of "history" itself.

Historians of China, for example, have long noted that the purpose of historical writing there has always been quite different from its purpose in the West. As Tu Wei-ming (1979: 250) puts it:

The historian, in the classical Confucian sense, assumes responsibility for the continuation of human excellences in culture. The act of historical writing is as much a message for the future as a memory of a selected past. The legitimizing authority of the historian so conceived does not derive from a political system, but from a much broader supply of symbolic resources, in which the worth of politics is itself determined.

Attempts to separate fact from myth in the "historical" writings of exotic cultures may construct an objective view of history only at the expense of the value of such documents as cultural productions—and, more to the point, at the expense of the cultural significance of the native historical consciousness they exemplify.*

Western historians of China's intellectual "great tradition" have increasingly attempted to strike a balance between treating such materials as sources of historical fact and as examples of cultural forms, but in the arena of social history, such discretion is less evident. In a laudable broadening of attention to nonelite society, social historians are often prone to neglect culture in favor of the "hard realities" of polity and economy. The world of the peasant is no longer dismissed as timeless.† Nonetheless, even recent studies of peasant culture often view it either as a watered-down version of the "great tradition" or as a proletarian reaction against it. Although there is growing recognition of the important role of peasant rituals, arts, and performances in communicating important cultural values and categories, there has been little attention to how such idioms may constitute a native historical consciousness.

---

*Of course, no "objective" work of history is politically value-free. Consequently, the Confucian historian might even be said to be more forthright about the values that inform his work than many modern Western writers are.

†Even the once-prevalent view of so-called primitive societies as "tribes without history" is no longer respectable. Studies like Renato Rosaldo's *Ilongot Headhunting* (1980) make clear not only that tribal societies are aware of change over time, but also that their sense of social identity is profoundly informed by the way they interpret their pasts.

There is more at stake here than mere oversight; lack of attention to native historical consciousness fundamentally diminishes our understanding of culture and its historical operations. In the case of China, it is particularly important to emphasize that a sense of history was not limited to the restricted circle of Confucian scholars. Indeed, communal rituals and institutionalized pilgrimages in China constitute a type of historical consciousness almost completely overlooked by Chinese and Western scholars. This historical consciousness played a role in the reproduction of Chinese institutions that was just as pivotal as the historiography codified in Confucian writings. In other words, China's "little traditions"—the social organization and culture of villages and market towns—depended as much on a native historical consciousness as did imperial institutions.

In sum, more is required than simply adding social-science theory or methods of cultural analysis to the practice of historical description, or adding attention to time and change to functionalist theories. In accord with observations of a number of other scholars (e.g., Rosaldo 1980), this book shows that history, social structure, and culture cannot be neatly compartmentalized into either disciplines or mechanical, functional models. Time must be treated as more than the temporal dimension within which social processes unfold. We must also account both for the ways in which culture constructs time and for the dialectical effects of these constructions on social processes.

In an effort to lend substance to these assertions, I make frequent reference to theoretical literature, but in light of the scope of the task, it is only possible to provide glimpses of the larger social processes that I seek to identify. Consequently, let the reader be forewarned of promises unfulfilled; this book must remain in large part a speculative one. I hope it will be accepted in the spirit in which it is offered—as an attempt to introduce new integrating frameworks in anthropological understanding of complex civilizations in general and of the integrating processes of Chinese culture in particular.

The book is divided into three parts. Part I is a social and economic history that outlines in standard narrative fashion what one might term an objectivist or positivist view of Ta-ch'i's history; that is, it attempts to document social and economic developments in causal terms, with a view toward describing events "as they were," regardless of the perceptions of local participants. This material is presented as a conventional "background" to the synchronic sociological analysis of local territorial cults that constitutes Part II. It is also a kind of yardstick by which to compare Ta-ch'i's history as a Western social historian might view it with what the Taiwanese themselves, through the idiom of territorial-cult rituals, make of it. A straightforward objective view of history is displaced but not disregarded in Part III, where the idiom of *ling,* a kind of magical power, is shown to underlie Taiwanese constructions of history and identity, defining what might be termed a privileged arena of symbolic production (Sahlins 1976) in Taiwanese culture.

This sequence of presentation is entirely conventional in ethnographic writing. In a sense, history provides the context for a description of social organization and institutions, which are then shown to embody assumptions and values of an essentially cultural sort. Yet I attempt to present a more complicated picture of the relationships among history, society, and culture in Ta-ch'i. In brief, I assume that the object of historical, sociological, and cultural analysis developed in separate parts is in fact the same entity—Ta-ch'i society.

The vantage points developed in each part thus provide some insights while obscuring others; none can claim to exhaust the reality of its object.* More to the point, it is important to restore some degree of unity to this object even in analyzing it. Consequently, although each part constitutes an autonomous argument to some degree, each part is also relevant to the other two. For example, the local impact of exogenous historical forces outlined in Part I is mediated by the general cultural structures analyzed in Part III to produce the social institutions described in Part II.

In attempting to develop a synthetic and novel view of Chinese culture and civilization from the perspective of local history and ritual, I open my argument to the charge that some of its assertions are overspeculative and less than thoroughly documented. But in my view a degree of license is justified in this regard, if only to move sinological anthropology more into the mainstream of contemporary social theory. After all, Chinese civilization constitutes the largest and most complex non-Western society in the world, yet (perhaps because of this very complexity) its study in the West has had a relatively minimal impact on social theory.[†]

Let me attempt to anticipate another potential objection—that Taiwan, a relatively recently settled frontier periphery of China, can hardly be considered "typically" Chinese. A Dutch colony for part of the sixteenth century and considered an administrative headache by the ruling Ch'ing

---

*Bateson makes essentially the same point in his classic ethnography *Naven* (1958), but his three vantages are social institutions (or social structure), "eidos" (culture as collective representations), and "ethos" (in his usage, "a culturally standardised system of organisation of the instincts and emotions of the individuals").

[†]It is noteworthy that Weber's *Religion of China* (1951), usually considered one of his minor works, is little discussed even by sinologists. China's greatest impact on anthropological theory has been through Lévi-Strauss's use of Marcel Granet in his *Elementary Structures of Kinship* (1969b: 311–70). It is a mark of the shortcomings of sinological anthropology that it seems to have been little affected by the latter work.

dynasty during the seventeenth, eighteenth, and nineteenth centuries, Taiwan was never a center of Chinese "high" culture. Moreover, between 1896 and 1946 Taiwan was a Japanese colony, and today the island is governed separately from the Chinese mainland.

Without denying the effect of these special circumstances on the development of Taiwanese society (indeed, Part I documents their role in shaping economy and society in Ta-ch'i), I argue that the people of Ta-ch'i are every bit as Chinese as those living in the imperial capital. The justification of this assertion lies in the body of subsequent argument; where appropriate, I make reference to the wider literature on Chinese culture and civilization, but in the long run, the value of my approach must be judged for the insights it produces.

Similarly, much of the evidence used in my analyses of Chinese ritual and iconography was obtained during the period of my fieldwork in Ta-ch'i between 1975 and 1977, yet I make assertions regarding the relationship between official ideology of imperial times and current local religious practice. Let me acknowledge from the outset that this methodology does present problems unless the reader is convinced by my arguments that, despite important changes, the major features of late-traditional Chinese cosmology persist in the social and religious life of contemporary Taiwan. Moreover, as already noted, contradictory structures of value embodied in Confucian ideology and in aspects of local religion persist together to some degree in local religious practice. I offer some hypotheses in an attempt to account for this persistence, but it remains a problem that can be fully addressed only by analyzing new forms of the state religion in Taiwan (Feuchtwang 1974a) and its relation to local practice. This latter project goes beyond the scope of the present study. However, I believe there are sufficient reasons to suppose that an altered but still characteristically Chinese pattern of mutually authenticating local and state cults is emerging in Taiwan.*

*In my study of important Ma Tsu cult centers in 1984, for example, it seemed to me that the government had changed its attitude toward such shrines. Where once it had viewed them with ambivalence, if not hostility, it now seemed willing to accommodate them as an ideologically acceptable form on the basis of their historical associations with Chinese heroes like Koxinga.

Part I

An Objectivist Perspective

I begin with an assumption, inspired by work in "regional analysis" (especially Skinner 1964–65, 1976, 1977a,b; Smith et al. 1976a,b), that social systems and human interaction are hierarchically patterned in space and time. This assumption informs my attempt to discern order in the historical development of society and economy in Ta-ch'i. More concretely, I attempt to demonstrate that the appropriate regional context for analyzing the "external forces" that have shaped developments in Ta-ch'i varies over time.

To locate these forces, the historian/social scientist must be prepared to shift focus in spatial terms from one level to another. Taking the spatially hierarchical structure of economy (and social interaction in general) as an object of empirical study provides a methodological "zoom lens" for this analytical endeavor. By operating on the premise that urban hierarchies and exchange networks define nested hierarchies of economic interaction, vague terms like "local," "regional," and "global" can be given concrete spatial specification. Moreover, these shifts in the relevant arena of economic change mark the most important historical watersheds in development at the local level; hence, they form the basis for my periodization. In other words, attention to the spatially hierarchical pattern of economic organization underlies my approach to the temporal patterning of economic development.

Applying clearly defined spatial and temporal boundaries around the units of analysis allows me to employ analytical insights from a variety of more general theoretical orientations without implying the universal truth or validity of any of them. Their respective utilities are limited to particular, specifically defined contexts. But by the same token, the bounded contexts of the analysis provide a limited forum for evaluating the claims of general theoretical orientations in particular applications.

Ta-ch'i's economic history can be divided into four periods marked by three major transitions in the structure of regional economic integration.* The period from roughly 1750 to 1850 was one of traditional frontier expansion. This period ended with Taiwan's incorporation into the expanding capitalist world system. From 1850 to about 1920 Ta-ch'i enjoyed a commercial heyday that ended with the modernization and restructuring of Taiwan's transportation system. The following period of stagnation lasted until the onset of Taiwan's rapid industrialization, which began about 20 years ago.

Before proceeding with my analysis of these transitions, I wish to specify in more detail the relationship between Part I's "objectivist" history and the book's larger themes. Although Part I relies on insights developed in Skinner's "regional systems" approach to the study of Chinese society and history, the book is intended to both modify and complement Skinner's essentially sociological perspective by attending to ways in which actors' constructions of the cosmos affect their construction of society. In this regard, it is important to clarify a potentially confusing point of terminology. The notion of "nested hierarchy" that underlies the regional-systems approach of Part I, and to some degree my analysis of territorial-cult hierarchies in Part II, is somewhat different from the logical relation of hierarchy among cultural categories (e.g., yang and yin, order and disorder) developed in Part III. This latter notion of hierarchy is inspired by Louis Dumont (1980a; see also T. Turner 1984). The notion of hierarchy utilized in regional analysis refers to patterns of social interaction in spatial, behavioral terms, whereas the notion of hierarchy developed in Dumont's work and evoked in Part III refers to a logical relation that is cultural. Moreover, in this latter, cultural sense, hierarchy is also a structure of value.

One of the important contributions of Skinner's work on the hierarchy of regional systems in China has been to show how localities were economically and administratively linked to form a society of unprecedented scale. One of the aims of this book is to complement Skinner's work by

---

*Ramon Myers (1972a,c) periodizes Taiwan's economic history at the island-wide level. Apart from the period of stagnation that was specific to Ta-ch'i and a few other towns, his economic watersheds align with mine. Myers's work here and elsewhere is clearly formalist or neoclassical in tone. Consequently, although he notes the importance of foreign trade and exports in Taiwan's economic development, his emphasis is on the internal development of capitalist commercial institutions.

augmenting its essentially sociological perspective with one that incorporates ways that cultural factors have played an important role in the integration of Chinese civilization. Thus Part III shows how the notion of hierarchy embodied in culturally constituted structures of value fits the pattern of spatially nested regions in the "hierarchies of local systems" that Skinner describes.

Given the seminal importance of Skinner's work in this regard, it is worth reviewing some of his central insights. Skinner's early work, in particular, is in part a reaction to community studies that treat villages in agrarian societies as "microcosms" of the total society, as representatives of all other villages in the society, or as "closed corporate communities" only minimally integrated into society as a whole. The shortcomings of such studies are now generally recognized and need not be reiterated. Skinner's regional-systems approach attempts to overcome these deficiencies by studying the institutions and patterns of behavior that join localities into wider social systems.

For anthropologists, one of the practical consequences of this heightened awareness of how local-level communities are embedded in higher-level ones is a shift in ethnographic focus from villages, lineages, and hamlets to marketing systems and regions. Skinner argues that what he terms the "standard marketing community" (that is, a market town and its surrounding rural hinterland) is a more appropriate unit than the peasant village for studying what Robert Redfield (1956) termed great civilizations' "little traditions." Moreover, Skinner's analyses of the spatial organization and temporal dynamics of late traditional Chinese administration and economy constitute an elegant and convincing model of how such "little communities" are functionally integrated into a single civilization of unprecedented scale.

In most essentials, this study lends support to Skinner's arguments. Part II's study of local and regional social organization in northern Taiwan reveals that hierarchies of ritual organization and social identity correspond closely in spatial terms to the nested hierarchies of economic regions, just as Skinner predicts. However, the perspectives developed in Parts II and III must be seen as both complementing and modifying some of Skinner's assumptions.

In his analyses of China's hierarchy of central places, Skinner (1964–65; 1977c) insists that economic and administrative organization and functions be rigorously distinguished. He consistently argues that the spatial structure of economy emerges, more or less "naturally," out of the maximizing decisions of peasants and merchants. In contrast, China's administration, motivated to maximize very different values, was imposed from the top down.* As a result, despite forces tending toward convergence, administrative and economic hierarchies never align perfectly. Some district capitals were established in cities of minor economic importance, and some economically dominant cities served no or only modest administrative functions.

Of greatest relevance here are Skinner's discussions of the lower levels in these two regional hierarchies. In imperial times the lowest-level administrative unit directly administered by a government bureaucrat was the county (*hsien*). But the *hsien* was much too large for the county magistrate and his staff to carry out directly all the functions associated with government.† In practice, magistrates relied a great deal on local leaders and the various organizations they headed to maintain order and to disseminate values amenable to the government.

In Skinner's view, the patterns of economic exchange defined by marketing logic determined the dimensions of sub-county-level social organizations. In other words, below the level of the *hsien,* the distinction between "natural" and administered social organization disappears. Although elements of Skinner's suggestions regarding the social and cultural correlates of marketing behavior have been both substantiated and challenged by other scholars, a thorough ethnographic evaluation has yet to be attempted. What seems to be required—and what I attempt in Parts I and II—is a combination of historical and ethnographic analysis focused on the standard marketing community. To anticipate my conclusions, Skinner is essentially correct in arguing that patterns of marketing behavior and social organization are correlated, but he may overestimate the causal priority of marketing logic in the historical process through which this correlation is achieved.

For example, I argue that a particular cultural construction of social space played an important role in patterning concrete social relations in the history of Ta-ch'i's development as a community. This cultural construction of social space takes form in a nested hierarchy of territorial cults and pilgrimages. Ritual organization thus constitutes a third hierarchy of regional systems that must be added to the economic and administrative hierarchies Skinner describes.

Even more generally, I argue that the historical processes through which cultural, economic, and exogenous political forces interact in the shaping of local communities defy the assignment of straightforward

---

*Skinner (1977c) implies that the elegantly fine-tuned administrative arrangements he reveals (in contrast to the emerging economic ones) must have evolved over the long course of Chinese history in part by a kind of adaptive, trial-and-error process.

†This well-established insight dates back at least to Weber (1951).

causalities. In brief, it seems to me that Skinner's elegant treatments of aggregate behavioral interaction patterns ought to be complemented by examining how actors' understandings inform their behavior—in other words, how culture creates as well as reflects community. Part III is devoted to developing the theoretical and ethnographic arguments necessary for this synthetic project.

1

Ta-ch'i

Ta-ch'i (Big Stream) is located on the Ta-han River, south of Taipei in northern Taiwan. The river, a major tributary of the Tan-shui, has played a decisive role in the town's history. Ta-ch'i first came to prominence as a river port, and the town's marketing area is essentially defined by the river's upper watershed.

A visitor to the upper reaches of the Ta-han River would find it difficult to believe that one of the world's most densely populated and industrialized regions lies only a short 40 kilometers to the northwest. The river begins among 3,500-meter mountain peaks in the northern part of Taiwan's central mountain range. Precipitation is heavy, and the mountains are covered with luxuriant vegetation. Frequent mists and innumerable waterfalls complete a wilderness scene evocative of Chinese landscape painting.

Only three roads traverse Taiwan's rugged mountains. The northernmost of these cross-island highways begins in Ta-ch'i and follows the gorge of the Ta-han River for much of its length. The narrow dirt road is often obstructed by landslides, and some sections are literally carved out of the cliffside a thousand feet above the torrent below. In winter the mountains are lost in ceaseless heavy mists and drizzle, and summer thunderstorms and typhoons add to the seemingly inexhaustible volume of water. At between 1,500 and 2,000 meters in elevation, these mists and rains water forests of giant cypress trees, relatives of California redwoods. Everywhere huge ferns and creepers struggle with larger trees to reach the light. At lower elevations the cypresses are replaced by hardwoods.

One of these, the camphor laurel, yields a substance of considerable value, used to make mothballs and, formerly, celluloid.

The upper reaches of the Ta-han valley are still inhabited by descendants of Taiwan's earliest settlers, the aborigines. The aborigines are Austronesian speakers whose ancestors probably first came to Taiwan at least 10,000 years ago. The northern portion of Taiwan's central range has been inhabited in historical times by the Atayal tribe (T'ai-ya *tsu*), swidden agriculturalists and hunters once noted for their headhunting and military prowess.

The scattered Atayal villages of the upper Ta-han River basin are administratively part of Fu-hsing township. In 1977 the township was still a restricted area; to go there nonresidents were required to obtain a special permit. The policy of restricting access is justified primarily as protecting aborigines' rights and mountain resources. It is argued that without such protection, the aborigines would quickly lose what land remains to them to the more commercially astute Chinese. The history of alienation of aborigine lands in Taiwan's more accessible and fertile areas lends considerable credibility to this argument.

Access to the mountains is also restricted to protect important natural resources. The demand for wild animal products for use in Chinese medicines has already resulted in the virtual extinction of several native species (e.g., bears, deer, wildcats). More important are the island's forests. The government is aware that without stringent controls the demand for forest products will quickly deplete what remains of Taiwan's mountain forests, with devastating effects not only on the forestry industry itself, but also on Taiwan's lowland agriculture, in the resulting deterioration of watersheds and consequent floods.

The Ta-han River leaves the mountains a few kilometers upstream from Ta-ch'i (see Map 1). At Shih-men (Stone Gate) the river once passed through a narrow cleft in the cliffs. A large dam stands there now, supplying the Taipei Basin to the north with electricity and the T'ao-yüan Plain to the northwest with water for irrigation. Below the dam the river takes a sharp turn northward and cuts a deep, terraced valley through the alluvial T'ao-yüan Plain. The upper reaches of this valley and the bordering plain form the most fertile and populous portion of Ta-ch'i's marketing area. The town itself is located on the first of three terraces ("steps"; *ts'eng*) that flank the east bank of the river. Behind the terraces to the south and east, about three kilometers from town, the foothills begin.

Ta-ch'i is the first settlement of any size in the seaward course of the Ta-han River. Intensively irrigated rice paddies cover most of the geological terraces on either side of the river. The foothills to the east of town are

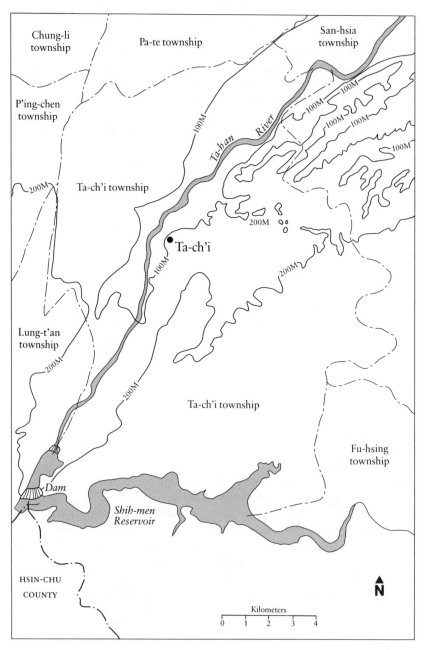

Map 1. Physical features of the Ta-ch'i area

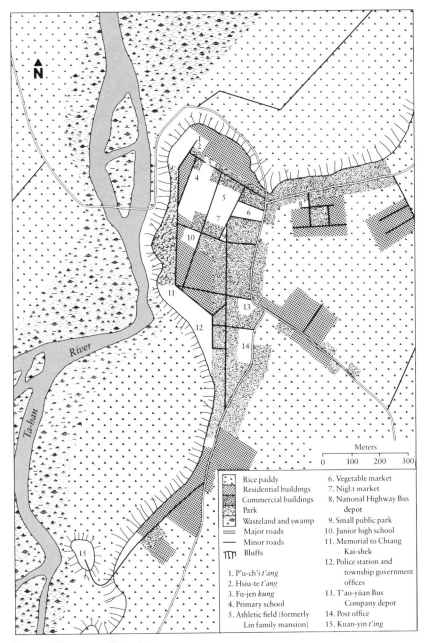

	Rice paddy
	Residential buildings
	Commercial buildings
	Park
	Wasteland and swamp
	Major roads
	Minor roads
⊓⊓	Bluffs

1. P'u-ch'i *t'ang*
2. Hsiu-te *t'ang*
3. Fu-jen *kung*
4. Primary school
5. Athletic field (formerly Lin family mansion)
6. Vegetable market
7. Night market
8. National Highway Bus depot
9. Small public park
10. Junior high school
11. Memorial to Chiang Kai-shek
12. Police station and township government offices
13. T'ao-yüan Bus Company depot
14. Post office
15. Kuan-yin *t'ing*

Meters
0   100   200   300

Map 2. The town of Ta-ch'i

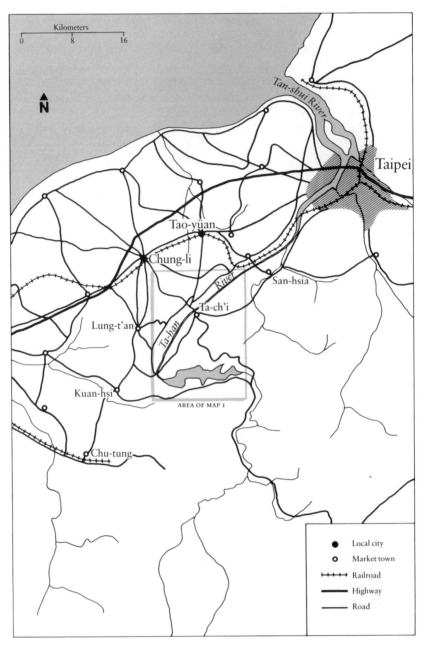

Map 3. Northern Taiwan

planted in tea and fruit orchards, and occasional rice paddies are carved into the hillsides bordering mountain streams. Tea is also cultivated on the plateau to the west and south, but since the construction of the large T'ao-yüan Canal in 1925, much of this formerly water-deficient region has been converted into rice paddies. Secondary forests thrive on the occasional ridges that protrude from the terraces east of the river and on the slopes that drop off steeply between the eroded terrace levels. The flat paddy land on these steps and on the plain to the west is broken by lines of bushes, trees, and, most frequently, bamboo, which serve simultaneously as windbreaks, boundary markers, and sources of building material and fuel. Rice is also grown in the river's bottomland, but there is a wide wilderness of boulders on either side of the river left by the violent seasonal flooding in the days before the Shih-men Dam was constructed.

Settlements tend to be more clustered east of the river than west of it, probably because clustered settlements afforded some protection from aborigine attacks from the hills. In the town itself, closely packed buildings crowd the edge of a steep bluff directly overlooking the river (see Map 2). Although some 15,000 people—mainly merchants and artisans—reside in Ta-ch'i, a casual visitor would probably make a much lower estimate. The picturesque location and turn-of-the-century, Japanese-influenced architecture differentiate Ta-ch'i from other Taiwanese towns of its size.

Ta-ch'i is often referred to by other Taiwanese as a typical, traditional rural market town (*chen*). Its marketing area (including the town itself) had a population of some 60,000 in 1977. Most people are engaged in agriculture (rice, tea, and oranges are major crops), small-scale factories, service industries, and coal mines.

It is said that the scenery around Ta-ch'i reminded the deceased president and deified national hero, Chiang K'ai-shek, of his native province, Chekiang. During his life he was a frequent visitor to his three villas in the area. Chiang's remains are interred a few miles east of town at Tz'u-hu, his favorite villa and the object today of a ceaseless stream of pilgrims who come to pay homage to his memory.

Chiang's death in 1975 was a boon to Ta-ch'i's economy. Formerly a sleepy country town largely bypassed by the rapid economic and social changes occurring in Taiwan's urban centers, Ta-ch'i is now a well-known tourist attraction. Local businessmen have taken advantage of the publicity that accompanies frequent visits by the country's leading figures to promote local products (particularly furniture and dried bean cake). They find a ready market in the busloads of tourist-pilgrims who usually stop in the town during visits to Chiang's mausoleum.

Still, the town preserves a reputation for conservatism and a traditional Chinese character. Indeed, this traditional atmosphere is one of its attractions. Approaching the town from the west, the visitor first notices the ornate silhouettes of two temples near the edge of the bluff upon which the town stands. After crossing the suspension bridge that connects the town to more populated centers, one passes a smaller Buddhist shrine boasting a large statue of the deity Kuan Yin on its roof. From the bridge and the Kuan Yin temple at the base of the bluff, the main road into town ascends a steep hill. The road enters the town proper from the northeast, near the picturesque old merchant establishments that still line the main street.

At the town's center is the marketplace. The Ta-ch'i vegetable, fruit, meat, and poultry market was officially established during the Japanese colonial period, but it must have been in operation unofficially much earlier. Each morning housewives from the town make their purchases for the day at the market, see their friends, and hear all the latest gossip. Most of the residents of the town are members of families that have lived in Ta-ch'i for generations, and people generally know something about the families of anyone they are likely to meet at the daily market. In Ta-ch'i neighbors take an interest in one another's private affairs to a degree that is uncommon in larger cities. Ties of kinship and native place still retain an importance in defining relationships (*kuan-hsi*)—an importance that is diminishing in Taiwan's increasingly individualized and rationalized urban society.

Natives of Ta-ch'i view this traditionalism as a mixed blessing. On the one hand, it is comforting to have a definite place in a large network of kin and neighborly relationships; loneliness and rootlessness do not seem to be common problems. On the other hand, the tight network of personal relationships that provides emotional security also demands that behavior and aspirations remain within the limits set by convention. As in small towns everywhere, one must take care not to excite the disapproval of the community for fear of losing one's good reputation. Thus, the lure of economic opportunity in larger cities is augmented in the minds of many young people by the promise of freedom from the constraints of small-town life.

Many who have sought their fortunes in the city try to have the best of both worlds by maintaining strong ties with their relatives and friends in Ta-ch'i. Consequently, weekends and holidays find Ta-ch'i's normally quiet streets crowded with Ta-ch'i natives returning on visits from Taipei, T'ao-yüan, and Chung-li. While enjoying the economic opportunities and cultural stimulation of city life, these people continue to consider Ta-ch'i their hometown. Meanwhile, Ta-ch'i's teenagers can hardly wait until they, too, can get away from the sleepy country town (and the control of their families) and find jobs or attend school in the city.

Across the street from the vegetable market is the primary school's playground. The land for the primary school and playground was donated by one of Taiwan's wealthiest and most prominent families, known to all as the Lin Pen-yüan lineage. The Lins have an illustrious history dating back to the late Ch'ing dynasty, when they were one of the largest landowning families in Taiwan. A carved stele on the playground commemorates the Lins' gift.

Following the river downstream from Ta-ch'i, one soon comes to a range of hills that slopes steeply down to the east bank. These hills divide Ta-ch'i's marketing system from the systems of San-hsia and Ying-ko to the north. They also separate areas inhabited primarily by Chang-chou people (Ta-ch'i) from ones inhabited by Ch'üan-chou people (San-hsia and Ying-ko). Although both groups are descended from immigrants from adjacent prefectures in Fukien Province and speak the same southern Min language (albeit with slightly different accents), there is a lengthy history of rivalry and occasional violence between them. The days of factional fighting are past, but ethnic contrasts are still important markers of social identity.

When people in Ta-ch'i think of the city, they think of Taipei. In its range of services, entertainments, products, and general urban excitement, Taipei has no rival in Taiwan. Unlike T'ao-yüan and Chung-li, however, Taipei lies outside the range of practical daily commuting, and those who wish to take full advantage of its economic opportunities must make a greater commitment and move there. However, it is still close enough that frequent visits home are possible (see Map 3).

In sum, Ta-ch'i today is a rural market town approximately equidistant from two local cities, T'ao-yüan and Chung-li. These, in turn, are part of a greater-city trading system centering on Taipei. Taipei also serves as the center of a regional-city trading system for northern Taiwan, and as a regional metropolis for the entire island.* Ta-ch'i's position in Taiwan's hierarchy of regional economic systems has greatly influenced the course of its history, and it is to a detailed description of this process that we now turn.

*I employ Skinner's well-known typology of levels of regional economic integration here.

2

Local History in Spatial Context

Frontier Expansion, 1750–1850

At the time of Ta-ch'i's initial settlement by Chinese in the mid-eighteenth century, Taiwan was a frontier periphery of China's Southeast Coast macroregion (Skinner 1977a,b,c; see Map 4). Chinese settlers had been moving to Taiwan from economically depressed areas in the upper-Han and Chang-Ch'üan regions (in southern Fukien and northern Kwangtung) since early in the seventeenth century. The flight of Ming loyalists under Koxinga and, later, the drastic depopulation of the Fukien coast resulting from punitive Manchu policies led to a prolonged period of economic depression in the emigrant regions (Skinner 1977b; 1985). But the regional decline of the Southeast Coast proper stimulated Taiwan's development. Deprived of their lands in coastal Fukien or suffering in the depressed economic conditions there, immigrants saw an opportunity for a new start in Taiwan's fertile frontier.

The earliest urban concentrations in Taiwan were west-coast seaports. These served both as import centers for supplies needed by the pioneers and as collection centers for Taiwan's exports (initially deerskins and rice). The most important port cities were linked directly to ports on the mainland, and the island's own transport infrastructure developed slowly. The inland expansion of Chinese settlement from these ports resulted in a dendritic marketing pattern in which each port monopolized the import/export trade for its hinterland.

Settlement in northern Taiwan lagged some 50 years behind that in the south, but the north had the advantage of a navigable water route in the

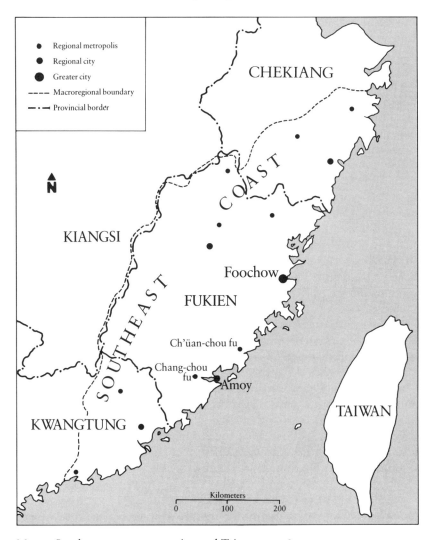

Map 4. Southeast coast macroregion and Taiwan, ca. 1800

Tan-shui River and its tributaries (see Map 3). The town of Tan-shui at the river's mouth was the first important urban center in the region, but was later rivaled by Meng-chia and Ta-tao-ch'eng, upstream ports near present-day Taipei (Feuchtwang 1974a; Baity 1975).

The expansion of Chinese settlement during the eighteenth and nineteenth centuries was organized by a complicated system of land grants and tenancy. In the Ta-ch'i area, the government recognized most of the land as belonging to "cooked" or assimilated aborigines (*shu-fan*). Typically, Chinese landlord/entrepreneurs negotiated with aborigine leaders for rights to large tracts of unreclaimed land, for which they recruited tenants to perform the actual labor of reclamation. In return, these patent-holders paid aborigine leaders fixed annual rents (*fan-ta-tsu*). The Chinese landlord was responsible for investing in tools, food, and shelter for the tenants during the initial period of land development. He also organized labor for irrigation projects and defense against hostile, unassimilated ("raw") aborigines (*sheng-fan*). Tenant/pioneers paid annual rents for both land and water use, while the landlord paid government taxes in addition to aborigine rent (*fan-tsu*). The situation was complicated by the fact that tenancy rights were transferable. Thus, pioneering tenants who actually cleared a tract of land could rent out parts of it to subtenants. The first tenant or "small landlord" (*hsiao-tsu hu*) thus paid "big rent" (*ta-tsu*) to the "large" landlord (*ta-tsu hu*) and collected "small rent" (*hsiao-tsu*) from the subtenant. These arrangements seem to have been adapted to the situation on the Taiwan frontier from similar systems of rent contracts in Fukien.

During the pioneering era, a relative abundance of land and shortage of labor enhanced the bargaining position of tenants. New tracts were being opened, and tenants were in a position to bargain for small-landlord (*hsiao-tsu hu*) rights over the tracts they cleared. By leaving developed areas (either on the mainland or in Taiwan), tenants were thus able to upgrade their status. However, as the productive, easily developed lowland areas filled with settlers, land came into shorter supply and the bargaining position of newcomers deteriorated. But compared to long-settled regions on the mainland, the opportunities afforded to tenants in Taiwan undoubtedly mitigated some of the harsher aspects of class exploitation.*

A combination of factors gave rise to these relations of production: a government policy that was at best ambivalent about the incorporation of chaotic new frontiers, precedent in customary law and contract from the settlers' homelands on the mainland, and the particular circumstances the

---

*Rawski (1972) makes the important point that peasant welfare in China was not a simple function of the peasants' relation to means of production. In the foreign-trade-based economic boom in the Chang-chou region during the sixteenth century, for example, the peasants' lot seems to have improved at a time when the rural economy was becoming commercialized and absentee landlordism was rising. Rawski makes the further point, quite consistent with this argument, that location relative to marketing networks is a key factor in both the development of particular forms of the social organization of production and the effects of these forms on peasant welfare.

settlers faced in seeking new land already occupied by potentially hostile aborigines (Shepherd 1981).

In any case, Ta-ch'i's first land-patent agreement was issued in 1755, though illegal settlement may have begun as early as the 1730s (TYHC 1962: 75). Investment in the opening of new land was risky, but potentially very profitable for patent-holders. "Opening" new land involved both the actual clearing of forest and the construction of paddies and irrigation facilities. In areas like Ta-ch'i that bordered hostile mountain aborigine lands, the landlord's expenses were increased by the need to hire armed guards to defend his tenants.

The pattern of patent-initiated land reclamation in Ta-ch'i was similar to that in other areas in northern Taiwan (Knapp 1976: 51). Once the patent was granted, development was rapid. Other patents were quickly obtained from the Hsiao-li She, a tribe of plains aborigines (TCS: 85, 134; Shepherd 1981), and by the early 1800s most of Ta-ch'i's easily developed bottomland had been put into rice production. However, the mountainous eastern border of the growing community continued to be the province of defiant Atayal headhunters. The unsuitability of hilly land for paddy and the danger of aborigine attack combined to make reclamation of upland areas unprofitable. Consequently, after the initial flush of development, the expansion of Chinese settlement around Ta-ch'i slowed considerably.

Ta-ch'i itself developed first as a river port. A number of other market towns were established along the river between Ta-ch'i (then known as Ta-k'o-k'an) and the downstream town of Meng-chia (part of present-day Taipei), but Ta-ch'i had the advantage of being located at the upstream end of the portion of the river navigable by sanpans. Areas farther south relied on ground transport (mainly porters) to Ta-ch'i. By about 1800 a few shops in Ta-ch'i supplied local settlers with the imported products they needed, and a modest export of rice ensued (TYHC 1962: 35).

In sum, the century beginning in the 1750s was a period of steady agricultural and commercial intensification of an essentially traditional character. After the initial influx of settlers in the mid-1700s, the size of the marketing system centered on Ta-ch'i increased rather slowly, but the intensity of commercial activity within this area increased steadily with the population. By the turn of the eighteenth century, Ta-ch'i was already a small market town where pioneers could get the supplies they needed, and where the area's modest exports were gathered for shipment downstream.

Economic and demographic factors internal to the Southeast Coast macroregion were the primary forces accounting for Ta-ch'i's development and expansion during this period, and reclamation proceeded in the absence of any significant government encouragement. The government sustained a tenuous authority primarily to prevent Taiwan from becoming a base for rebellions against the empire. Despite periodic attempts by the Ch'ing government to gain some measure of control over revenues from a few products such as camphor, there is little evidence that the market networks developed toward what Carol A. Smith (1976, 1:2–68, 1978) terms an "administered" system (see also Crissman 1976).

Given these conditions, the neoclassical (in anthropological parlance, "formalist") assumption that behavior is best viewed as individuals' seeking to "maximize" self-evident material values provides an adequate and parsimonious interpretation of local-level developments: Landlord patent-holders sought to maximize profits, and tenant settlers sought to improve their incomes. However, "maximization" cannot explain the complex institutional framework (including the cultural and political basis of land rights, contracts, and so forth) that formed the contexts within which this maximizing took place, nor can it explain the forms of communal organization that developed in frontier areas. Similarly, the social organization of production cannot be derived directly from the forces of production, but must be viewed as essentially a product of (1) the social distribution of economic privilege in emigrant homelands, and (2) the cultural repertoire of organizational and productive techniques that the Chinese settlers brought with them to Taiwan.

World-System Incorporation, 1850–1920

Taiwan's incorporation into what has become known as the "world system" (e.g., Wallerstein 1974; 1975) marked the period from about 1850 to 1920. A heyday of economic development in Ta-ch'i's marketing system during this period must be viewed in the context of this transformation.

The initial basis of Taiwan's (and Ta-ch'i's) incorporation into the world system was the export of two products—tea and camphor (Davidson 1903: chaps. 23, 24). Beginning about 1850, Taiwan's rich resources and potential for commercial export of tea and camphor attracted considerable foreign interest and consequent concern on the part of the Ch'ing government (Eto 1963; Chan Lien 1973; Gordon 1970, 1972; Davidson 1903). Despite the government's attempts to support Taiwan's commercial ties to mainland ports by requiring foreign merchants to buy Taiwan's exports there, foreign businessmen steadily pressured Ch'ing authorities to allow freer and more direct access to Taiwan's lucrative tea and camphor trade. The partial success of these efforts (especially the Treaty of Tientsin, which, in 1858, opened Taiwan to foreign trade) served to undermine Taiwan's commercial dependence on the mainland (Gordon 1970: 100).

Camphor, manufactured by a technologically simple distillation process from camphor trees once abundant in Taiwan's foothills, had been produced in small quantities since the beginning of Chinese settlement on the island. Early in the eighteenth century, the Ch'ing government declared a monopoly over camphor production, requiring the purchase of licenses. In the Ta-ch'i area, the Hsiao-li She aborigines initially held rights over camphor trees. But as with their land rights, the right to exploit camphor was generally sold to Chinese entrepreneurs. Increasing European and American demand beginning in the 1850s led to a steady increase in camphor production. Atayal response to the new influx of Chinese camphor workers into the foothills near Ta-ch'i was violent, and camphor workers often required the armed protection of hired guards.

Under increasing pressure from foreign merchants and their governments, the Ch'ing administration ended its monopoly over the camphor trade in 1867, and the industry grew more rapidly. The high profits of the ensuing period provided sufficient incentive for Chinese landlords and camphor workers to risk the attacks of aboriginal headhunters and push into border areas that had previously been considered too dangerous.*

Beginning in the 1860s, tea began to rival camphor as the area's most important export. Tea had been produced for local consumption since the beginning of Chinese settlement in Taiwan. But it was not until 1865, when John Dodd, an English entrepreneur, first encouraged the development of tea as an export, that cultivation of the plant began to expand rapidly (Davidson 1903: 371–96; SE: 396–401). The boom in tea production created a demand for new agricultural land and stimulated Chinese penetration of aboriginal territory. Tea grows best in the foothills of northern Taiwan, land also valuable for its camphor trees. The first major tea-producing area was the foothill region surrounding the Taipei Basin. Later the plateaus of present-day T'ao-yüan and Hsin-chu counties proved to be well suited to the crop. In 1868, a landlord-entrepreneur, Huang An-pang, recruited tenants to develop what was the Ta-ch'i vicinity's first important tea-producing area in present-day Yung-fu *li*, northeast of the town.† Aborigine land thus became doubly valuable to Chinese—first for the quick, one-shot profits to be made from camphor, and second for its longer-term value in tea production.

*In 1868, landlord-entrepreneurs made their first attempts to penetrate Nan-tzu-kou and San-min, hilly areas southeast of the town. Their incursions were fiercely resisted by the Atayal, who succeeded in driving the intruders out of the area in 1881 (TYHC 1962: 37).

†TYHC 1962: 37. According to Davidson (1903: 380), these pioneer tea planters, after clearing and burning off the land, planted sweet potatoes to sustain them for the first year. It was not until the second year that tea bushes were planted.

Ta-ch'i was an important entrepôt for tea and camphor export. Both products were carried by porters to merchant middlemen in the town. From Ta-ch'i, boats carried these mountain products downstream to bulking centers at Meng-chia, Hsin-chuang, and Ta-tao-ch'eng.

The thriving trade in tea and camphor led to an increase in the size of Ta-ch'i's marketing hinterland. This expansion occurred on two levels. First, there was an expansion of the area encompassed by the town's standard marketing system. Previously marginal lands were exploited for the new products, attracting camphor workers and tea farmers from other areas of Taiwan and the mainland, all of whom brought their business to the shops and market in Ta-ch'i. This southeastward expansion of Ta-ch'i's standard marketing system continues, although at a decelerating pace, to the present. Second, in the last quarter of the nineteenth century, Ta-ch'i began to develop as an intermediate market for a larger area. Products produced in neighboring marketing systems to the south and west (centered on the market towns of Chu-tung, Kuan-hsi, and Lung-t'an) were transported by porters to Ta-ch'i for shipment upstream.

According to Skinner (1964–65: 214), "Agrarian modernization within a city trading system normally begins with successive waves of commercialization whose advancing rim is always well ahead of the area served by modern transport." This observation is borne out in the development of northern Taiwan, where modern transport during this period was limited to the shipping lines that transported tea and camphor overseas. Ta-ch'i's rapid commercial growth during this period seems to have taken place under the influence of this foreign trade, despite the absence of significant improvement of transport in the town's marketing area itself.

The commercial boom in Ta-ch'i was accompanied by a dramatic change in the local role of the central government. To understand this change, we must shift focus to the wider arena of international affairs during this period of world-system expansion. Until the last quarter of the nineteenth century, the Chinese government had pursued a laissez-faire if not obstructionist policy toward Taiwan's development. The island was an administrative headache, home of rebellious frontiersmen (Lamley 1977b; 1981) and headhunting aborigines. Settlement and development were accomplished by the immigrants in the absence of any significant encouragement from the government. All this changed in 1884, when the Ch'ing government appointed Liu Ming-ch'uan governor of Fukien Province (of which Taiwan then constituted two prefectures) and instructed him to prepare the island's defenses for an anticipated French invasion. In 1885 Taiwan was raised to provincial status. Liu continued as governor until 1891; an energetic and progressive leader, he instituted many changes that laid the groundwork for reforms brought to completion under the Japanese (R. Myers 1972a,b,c; Chu 1963; Speidel 1976).

Liu's influence was felt very directly in Ta-ch'i, for it was there that he established the headquarters of a new Bureau of Pacification and Reclamation (*Fu-k'en-chü*). Ta-ch'i thus became the center of a major effort to subdue hostile Atayal tribesmen and open up the mountains for exploitation of their resources. A member of the locally prominent Lin family, Lin Wei-yüan, was placed in charge of the bureau, and its headquarters were in the Lin compound in Ta-ch'i (for details of Lin's career, see Speidel & Wang 1974).

Liu's program called for both the sinicization of the aborigines (to which end schools were established in Ta-ch'i and other frontier towns) and their pacification by force. The objectives of the sinicization program were related to Liu's economic and political goals for Taiwan (Speidel 1976: 457):

If he could sinicize the aborigines and change them from warrior-hunters into peaceful (and productive) farmers, he then would open the hills to more Chinese settlers. Economically, this would expand agricultural production, increase land tax revenues, and make available more of the mountain timber and camphor. Politically, with a greater Chinese presence in the hills, foreigners would have less pretext to occupy frontier portions of Taiwan. To facilitate these changes, Liu's program consisted not only of educating the aborigines, but also of constructing numerous roads and encouraging Chinese from the mainland to settle in the mountains.

The aborigines put up a stubborn and ultimately successful resistance. Ch'ing troops succeeded in penetrating the mountains near Ta-ch'i as far as Chiao-pan-shan (present-day Fu-hsing village), and set up fortified outposts at Chu-t'ou-chiao, San-chiao-yung, Shui-liu-tung, and Wu-chih-shan (Kumata 1897: 264). However, their efforts met with defeat as often as victory (Liu's nephew was killed in battle against the Atayal), and it remained for the Japanese army to subjugate the aborigines many years later (TYHC 1962: 42; Davidson 1903: 406).

Ta-ch'i's accelerated development during Liu's tenure as Taiwan's governor was part of an economic boom that encompassed much of northern Taiwan. Liu's programs, particularly beginning the construction of a north–south railway and establishing a new capital at Taipei, initiated a process that eventually resulted in a fundamental spatial restructuring of northern Taiwan's economy. Train service first began in 1887 between the deep-water port at Chi-lung and Taipei, eventually reaching as far south as Hsin-chu before Taiwan fell to the Japanese. In addition to making a significant contribution to the economy of northern Taiwan, the railway completed the shift of the axis of Taiwan's linear central-place system from a string of westcoast ports inland, to a line of cities and towns along the railroad (see also R. Myers 1972b). Unfortunately for Ta-ch'i, the route (said to have been planned originally to pass through the town) passed some miles to the west. Consequently, as the railway slowly began to eclipse the river as northern Taiwan's major axis of transport, Ta-ch'i was gradually relegated to a more peripheral position in the region's commerce. However, at first the railroad was not a serious competitor to river transport, and Ta-ch'i continued to prosper and grow.

The newly founded capital at Taipei was located near the old river port of Meng-chia and its more recently founded neighbor, Ta-tao-ch'eng. By 1880 Meng-chia and Ta-tao-ch'eng had a combined population of about 100,000 and had begun to rival older southern ports in commercial importance (Lamley 1977a: 173). Greater Taipei soon became the region's most important center. Its location on the new railroad, its easy access—via the Tan-shui River—to the sea, and its central position in a large, agriculturally productive basin reinforced its rapid rise to commercial as well as administrative prominence.

Ta-ch'i's commercial heyday should thus be seen in the context of this rapid development of the northern Taiwan region with Taipei at its hub. And northern Taiwan's boom was, in turn, a consequence of the region's incorporation into the capitalist world system. This latter circumstance was to prove unfortunate to the Chinese government. In spite of Governor Liu's many accomplishments, his program appears to have been doomed from the outset. On the one hand, Liu was trying to increase the strength of Chinese political authority over Taiwan in order to resist what the Chinese government correctly perceived as the colonial aspirations of foreign powers. On the other hand, he was attempting to increase the island's capability for self-defense by promoting development of an economic infrastructure that would diminish the island's economic dependence on the mainland.

Despite the Ch'ing government's efforts to place itself in a position to benefit from control over the profits of Taiwan's growing foreign trade (and Liu's effort was a remarkably competent one), it lacked the military clout and diplomatic foresight to prevent the island's loss. By the time Liu arrived to resist imperialistic encroachments on the island, it was already exporting significant quantities of tea and camphor, and the trend toward increasing commercial ties to the capitalist world system was seemingly irreversible. The growth of economic ties to the world system was eventually followed by political separation from China when, in 1896, Taiwan was ceded to Japan as a provision of the Treaty of Shimonoseki.

The Japanese takeover was not a major watershed in Ta-ch'i's economic development. Rather, Ta-ch'i's political incorporation into the Japanese Empire was in part a delayed consequence of the island's earlier economic reorientation to the world system. (Of course, a very important contributing factor was Japan's successful transformation from "marginal" to "core" status.) The high tide of commercial growth and expansion in Ta-ch'i, based on the export of camphor and tea, continued through the first two decades of Japanese rule on much the same trajectory as during the waning years of Ch'ing rule.

In the absence of effective central leadership during the transition to Japanese rule, local gentry in Ta-ch'i organized militia units to defend the town from marauding bandits, Ch'ing army deserters, and the invading Japanese army. Despite a spirited resistance, however, they were quickly defeated by the much superior Japanese forces (see Takekoshi 1907: 88, 95; TCS: 318–24; TYHC 1962: 61–62; TKS: 193–213; Lamley 1973: 246, 254). Almost immediately the Japanese picked up where Liu had left off in a lengthy campaign of pacification directed against the aborigines. As a result, the area controlled by the Atayal eroded steadily, although sporadic outbreaks of violence continued well into the 1920s.

Camphor and tea continued to be Ta-ch'i's major exports, and production increased as the Japanese expanded control over previously hostile territory. However, rights to exploit these new territories were generally granted to large Japanese companies. Most of the southeastward expansion of Ta-ch'i's marketing area was controlled by the Mitsui Company. Acting much like any Chinese landlord, the Mitsui Company followed traditional practice and rented out small parcels to tenants who performed the actual labor of clearing the land, constructing paddy fields and irrigation canals, and planting tea orchards. Rights to cut camphor trees were granted to both Chinese and Japanese businessmen, who hired wage laborers to exploit the privilege.

Thus, while development continued to be rapid and the demand for labor remained high, there were fewer opportunities for tenants to become small landlords and for small landlords to become large ones. The fortunes made by local Chinese during the early years of Japanese rule were made in commerce, not land reclamation.

The Japanese administration conducted extensive investigations into Taiwan's land-tenure system,* and instituted a number of reforms in tax collection and rent designed to rationalize revenue collection so that Japan's colonial endeavor could be financially self-sustaining (Barclay

---

*Some of the results of these studies were published in the many volumes of *Taiwan shihō* (Private Law in Taiwan); see R. Myers (1971).

1954). Nonetheless, rural relations of production remained essentially unchanged; although the Japanese reduced the number of levels of rent payments (doing away with the old "large rents"), tenants continued to pay
rent to landlords.

Location within even the limited domain of Ta-ch'i's marketing community figured importantly in the nature of relations of production during this period. Tenancy rates (the ratio of tenant cultivators to owner
cultivators) and rents were highest in the most productive, most intensively cultivated parts of the community. This was a result of the facts
that the most productive areas were generally the first settled; that only
on relatively productive lands could tenants be required to pay high rents
(thus attracting wealthy investors); and that the Japanese did not substan-
tially alter these arrangements. In less productive areas, tenancy rates and
rents were somewhat lower because the land could not support high
rents, and the original settlers had probably been induced to develop the
land only when granted "small landlord" rights over it. In sum, the spatial distribution of forms of relations of production reflected the history
of the region up until that time.

Despite the persistence of essentially traditional landlord-tenant relations at the local level during the Japanese colonial period, the imposition
of colonial rule significantly diminished the power and privileges of traditional elites. From the point of view of localities like Ta-ch'i, the Japanese
effectively monopolized political power and bureaucratic linkages with
other communities. This was accomplished by a variety of means, but
most effective was the institution of a large, rationalized, and pervasive
bureaucracy whose policies were enforced by an efficient and powerful
police force (Eto 1963; Takekoshi 1907; Tsurumi 1967; Chang & Myers
1963; R. Myers & Ching 1964; Chen Ching-chih 1967; Kublin 1973; Barclay 1954). Consequently, although traditional landlord-tenant relations
were preserved in local communities, important economic and bureaucratic mobility pathways, leading mainly out of local systems and up the
hierarchy of central places (Skinner 1964–65; 1976), were truncated. Key
administrative and economic roles integrating local economies into larger
regional systems were filled by Japanese.

Devolution, 1920–1960

The next period in the town's economic history was marked by a
change in Ta-ch'i's position in the regional structure of north Taiwan's
economy, brought on by the introduction of new modes of transport.

This restructuring combined with the world system's economic depression to produce a prolonged period of stagnation in the community.

Wishing to increase the efficiency and profitability of the colony, the Japanese administration initiated improvement of Taiwan's still primitive transportation system (Takekoshi 1907: 253). Of highest priority was completion of the north–south railroad begun under Governor Liu. By 1908 the line was extended to the southern port at Kao-hsiung. The Japanese also began a program of road and highway construction using labor conscripted through the *pao-chia* system.* By the Second World War there was a highway running near the railroad, and the beginnings of a secondary system of roads, one running along the coast and one along the edge of Taiwan's foothills to the east (U.S. 1944: 23). Local roads connecting Ta-ch'i to Lung-t'an and T'ao-yüan were improved during the 1930s to carry truck and bus traffic. A suspension bridge over the Ta-han River in Ta-ch'i was completed in 1934, eliminating the inconvenience of ferrying people and materials across the river.

Push-car railroads were also important in the early years of Japanese rule. A push-car line was completed between Ta-ch'i and T'ao-yüan in 1903 and extended to Chiao-pan-shan (present-day Fu-hsing) in 1910 (TYHC 1966: 56–61). The line was used principally to transport tea from Ta-ch'i's orchards in the foothills to processing and bulking centers near the town, and to transport troops and supplies to the mountains in support of the Japanese pacification drive. The push-car railroads began to decline in the 1930s and 1940s as roads were completed and truck and bus transport became faster and cheaper.

All these developments undermined the preeminence of water transport along the Ta-han River, although the river continued to be an important artery until 1925, when the T'ao-yüan Aqueduct was completed. Designed to irrigate a large, water-deficient plateau west of Ta-ch'i, the aqueduct diverted a large portion of the river's flow from a point several miles upstream from the town. As a consequence, boats were no longer able to navigate the passage from Ta-ch'i to Taipei. The completion of the railroad (bypassing Ta-ch'i to the west) combined with the demise of river transport to end the rise of the town's status in the hierarchy of central places. Ta-ch'i retained its importance both as a local market town and administrative center and as a staging point for further penetration and exploitation of the mountainous headwaters of the Ta-han River, but its potential emergence as a higher-level center (indicated by the extensive

*For more on how the Japanese adapted the traditional Chinese *pao-chia* system to the needs of social control in their colonial policy, see Sangren (1980); Eto (1963); Takekoshi (1907); Chen Ching-chih (1967); U.S. (1944); Barclay (1954).

tea-producing area that had exported through Ta-ch'i before the railroad and canal were built) was thwarted by the change from traditional water transport to modern land transport.

Ta-ch'i's economic growth was further dampened by the world economic depression. The depression brought a rapid decline in demand for tea, which was exported principally to the United States, and for camphor. The camphor industry was further injured by the development of cheaper synthetic substitutes that replaced it in the manufacture of celluloid (Kublin 1973: 327). To a very limited degree, the introduction of new agricultural products—notably sugar and bananas—offset the decline in Ta-ch'i's traditional exports, but these proved to be less profitable in northern Taiwan than in the south, and Ta-ch'i's small sugar factory ceased production after retrocession in 1946.

Although Ta-ch'i's rise in the regional-systems hierarchy came to a halt with the development of modern land transport in Taiwan (the town remained at about the intermediate-market level), Ta-ch'i's marketing community participated fully in Taiwan's steady improvements in agricultural production under the colonial regime. Scholars are divided in their evaluations of Japanese economic policies on Taiwan, supporters of the Republican government generally emphasizing their exploitive aspects (Koo 1973), and critics giving the Japanese much of the credit for Taiwan's subsequent rise to prosperity (various essays in Mancall 1963).

Among the indisputable accomplishments of the Japanese administration were steady increases in agricultural production. These increases were accomplished mainly by intensifying traditional techniques (better irrigation systems and the application of more labor), bringing new land into production, and introducing new plant strains and fertilizers (Barclay 1954: 55; see also Chang & Myers 1963; R. Myers & Ching 1964). The Japanese were able to mobilize the farm population both through the police and *pao-chia* systems and through the many local farmers' associations that they established as instruments of their agricultural development policy. The same administratively intensive techniques were used to introduce improvements in sanitation, public health, and education. As always, the costs were borne by the local population, and the government relied on "administrative efficiency and energy in execution" rather than on capital investments in equipment or technology (Barclay 1954: 171).

In sum, Ta-ch'i's economic stagnation from the 1920s through the early 1950s was the result of a combination of forces emanating from different levels of the regional economic hierarchy. First, the world depression and the exploitation of even cheaper sources of supply led to a decline in demand for Ta-ch'i's exports. Second, the spatial restructuring of north Taiwan's economy, resulting from the introduction of new forms of transportation, effectively relegated Ta-ch'i to a more peripheral position than it had occupied during its heyday.

Renewal, 1960–1978

Two related developments are responsible for renewed economic growth in Ta-ch'i: the highly touted land-reform program of the early 1950s and the subsequent industrialization of Taiwan. Despite the long process of economic transformation just described, it is only with this period that either "modernization-theory" or Marxist notions of development and transformation seem to apply. After Japan's defeat and Taiwan's retrocession to the Chinese Nationalist government—and partly in response to the political success of Communist land reform on the mainland—the KMT initiated land reform in 1949.

The land reform was executed in three stages, beginning with rent reduction and culminating in the "land-to-the-tiller" program that subsidized the compulsory sale of land to tenants. The impact of these reforms was greatest in the most productive areas, where tenancy rates and rents had been highest (M. Yang 1970: 91–93).* Although it is clear that land reform transformed relations of production in Ta-ch'i, the full social and economic significance of the program is difficult to assess (Gallin 1963, 1966: 93–118; Pasternak 1968; Koo 1968; Wei 1973; Chen Cheng 1961; M. Yang 1970). Land reform has not made Ta-ch'i's farmers rich, and farming remains a marginally profitable business on the small, fragmented holdings (M. Yang 1970: 258). But Ta-ch'i's farmers do enjoy a perceptibly higher standard of living than in the past, and their standard is certainly higher than that of peasants in most other parts of China. Former tenants in Ta-ch'i generally bear out the claims of proponents that land reform has endowed farmers with a new sense of self-confidence and communal spirit, and that egalitarian values have to some degree replaced traditional deference to landlords.

---

*Ownership of more than 50 percent of the paddy land and 10 percent of the unirrigated land in Ta-ch'i township was transferred to tenants as part of the land-to-the-tiller program (TYHC 1969: 45). Among farming households, the proportion of owner/cultivators increased from 31 percent in 1921 to 54 percent in 1955; the proportion of part-owner/part-tenant cultivators declined from 18 percent to 11 percent; and the proportion of tenant households declined from 51 percent to 35 percent (TCKK; compare R. Myers 1972c). Considering that today even landless tenants pay a maximum of 37.5 percent of their annual yields in rent (prior to land reform, rents had been as high as 70 percent), these figures support the conclusion that land reform profoundly altered landlord-tenant relations in Ta-ch'i.

Taiwan's land reform could reasonably be interpreted as a transformation to capitalist (or "capitalistic") organization in agricultural production. The relative success of this reform depended on a particularly fortunate convergence of circumstances. These included the colonial legacy of a well-developed transport network; the government's policy of repaying landlords in stocks and bonds, contributing to the island's subsequent industrialization; and the flexibility and ingenuity of some former landlords in adapting essentially traditional forms of cooperation to changing arenas of economic opportunity.

The land reform program's effects on Taiwan's economy cannot be clearly separated from those of the concomitant industrialization. Gallin (1966: 113) summarizes this important connection in the following terms:

Before land reform it was traditional in China for the wealthy to buy land for investment or simply for purposes of security. To these landlords, and especially to many urban people, the land reform program made it evident that it was no longer profitable nor even safe to invest their capital in land. Instead, these people, in addition to their forced participation in industry through being paid in shares of stock for expropriated land, have now in many cases begun to shift their excess capital willingly into industrial, commercial, and small business activities in urban centers and in the smaller market towns.

In short, land reform hastened the transformation of the economic base of Ta-ch'i's elite from landholding to commerce. The fortunate circumstance of concomitant industrialization reduced the impact of what might otherwise have been a devastating blow to the local elite. Former tenants, obvious beneficiaries of the program, enjoy a better material existence today as a result of land reform, but perhaps even more as a consequence of Taiwan's postindustrial prosperity.

Industrial development in northern Taiwan has concentrated in the vicinity of Taipei and in the smaller cities of T'ao-yüan and Chung-li (both located on the north–south railway; see Map 3). Although in recent years a few electronics and textile enterprises have been established in Ta-ch'i's marketing area (mainly west of the town and river, nearer major transport routes), the impact of industrialization has been less in the construction of new plants than in the creation of a labor demand in easily accessible industrial centers elsewhere. Today many rural families augment their incomes by sending members to work in textile, garment, electronics, and other industries in T'ao-yüan, Chung-li, and Taipei. Wages paid at these factories are low by Western standards, but have nonetheless contributed significantly to Taiwan's rising standard of living. Today the government proudly boasts of the second-highest living standard in Asia (Japan, of course, having the highest). The impact of this prosperity is readily apparent. Thirty years ago most rural families lived in mud houses with dirt floors, but today brick houses with concrete floors are common in Ta-ch'i. Motorcycles, refrigerators, and color television sets, unheard-of luxuries half a generation ago, are also becoming commonplace, if not ubiquitous.

Industrialization has undeniably changed people's lives in Ta-ch'i. However, accounting for these changes is another matter. It is insufficient merely to cite the labor requirements of the growing capitalist mode of production and the consequences of this growth on local life (a common penchant in some Marxist treatments), or local responses to new economic opportunities (as in many neoclassically informed analyses). Although these factors are part of the story, it is also necessary to recognize the important mediating role of traditional institutions and the values they embody. These latter factors give specific form to local responses to new wage-earning and profit-making opportunities, and constrain the forms in which capitalism's "requirements" can be achieved locally.

In this regard, the most important institution is the family, and the most important value associated with it is what might be termed "patrilineal continuity." Much apparently "economic" behavior can be understood only when one realizes that Ta-ch'i's families are concerned above all about ensuring the continuation of the patriline. In brief, every married couple must have at least one son, to provide for economic security in old age and for proper worship of the spirit after death. One must have sons, and one's sons must be economically successful and filial regarding their duties to their patrilineal ancestors. In popular as well as Confucian thought, one of the most unfilial acts is to fail to produce sons. Moreover, women depend upon sons as much as men do (M. Wolf 1968; 1972).

That this constellation of values is fundamental to the Chinese worldview and religion is as true in Ta-ch'i today as it was in the past. It is also necessary to understand that in many crucial economic contexts, the "maximizing actor" is not an individual, but a family.* For example, the choice to enter the urban labor market or to continue in school is almost always a family, not an individual, decision.

The attraction of the factories is strongest for the young—especially girls. For youths of modest means and academic achievement, graduation from junior high school is usually followed by recruitment into the labor force. Their families expect them to contribute to the household budget,

---

*Of course, there are many contexts in which individual ends and strategies within the family may be at cross-purposes (see, for example, Margery Wolf's descriptions of women's strategies). But patrilineal continuity is always the foremost value in decisions about the education and employment of family members. (For an analysis of the distinction between line and the family, see A. Wolf & Huang 1980: 57–69.)

and the income from their labor often means the difference between pov-
erty and economic viability (and hence the hope of upward mobility).
This is true for both boys and girls, but the pressure to work is felt more
acutely by girls. Girls can be depended upon to contribute to the incomes
of their natal families only as long as they remain unmarried, and most
girls aspire to adopt traditional domestic roles and marry virilocally
(i.e., "out"). If they are to make any significant economic contribution to
their natal families, they must thus do so while they are still young and
unmarried.

In contrast, families' hopes for continuity and upward mobility center
on the careers of sons. Consequently, boys generally hope to move into
occupations with longer-term possibilities, even at some short-term sacrifice in income. Factory work, in addition to being both tiring and dull,
presents limited opportunities for advancement. For wealthier families,
the alternatives for sons may include higher education, but for most families they consist of acquiring training in skilled occupations like construction, auto repair, bricklaying, baking, and so forth. To these ends, various forms of apprenticeships are contracted between youths (or, rather,
their parents) and friends or relatives already established in small businesses. The apprentice exchanges his labor for the training (and sometimes room and board) that he receives from the owner. Such apprenticeships are modeled on a long tradition in Chinese small industry and
commercial enterprise, but have expanded to include many new kinds of
small-scale manufacturing and service enterprises. Eventually, appren-
tices hope to learn enough and to acquire enough capital—usually by
calling on the pooled resources of family and relatives—to start their own
businesses.

Girls seldom have such ambitions, knowing that their families place a
higher priority on their brothers' careers. Girls contribute their wages to
their families, but are usually allowed to retain some portion to spend on
themselves or to use as a "nest egg" for their marriages. Because girls
usually leave the factories as they marry and have children, Taiwan's industrial labor force is predominantly a very youthful one.

My impressions in this regard are consistent with Janet W. Salaff's
(1981) observations of working daughters in Hong Kong. Salaff argues
that, "disjunctive theories" to the contrary, women's wage labor does not
significantly undermine their subordination to the economic goals of the
"centripetal family." Lydia Kung (1976) arrives at a similar assessment
based on her study of women's participation in factory work in Taiwan. In
short, however much modes of production are being restructured in the
course of Taiwan's industrialization, traditional forms of cooperation,

domination, and social reproduction in domestic groups have been re-markably persistent.* Indeed, even in the People's Republic, where over-throwing "feudal" family relationships has been an explicit goal of the revolution, recent studies suggest that basic values and institutions (e.g., filial piety and patrilineal continuation) have been much more resistant to change than either Marxist theory or communist revolutionaries would have predicted (Croll 1981; Parish & Whyte 1978).

This persistence of traditional values challenges the notion that domi-nant modes of production (capitalist in the case of Taiwan, socialist in the People's Republic) clearly determine the nature of the "articulation" be-tween domestic modes of production and the wider economy (compare Meillassoux 1981; Terray 1972). In fact, Chinese peasants and workers have effectively resisted attempts to obstruct the pursuit of traditional do-mestic values. This seems to indicate that, at least to some degree, it is the wider sphere of economic organization that is constrained by the require-ments of the Chinese form of the "domestic mode of production and re-production" and associated values.

Although many traditional domestic values in Ta-ch'i persist despite rapid industrialization, the movement of youth to employment outside the vicinity has significantly "opened" the community culturally.† Of course, the rising standard of living has resulted in increased demand for consumer goods, and hence in a greater circulation of money and com-modities. Perhaps more significantly, the rising geographic mobility of the labor force and numerous television sets have increased awareness of the cultural amenities and commercial opportunities available in urban centers. Consequently, there has been a great increase in the frequency of trips to the city, for both business and pleasure. In short, Ta-ch'i is be-coming a much more "open" local system than it was under the Japanese.

In this era of profound transformations both in landlord-tenant rela-tions and in the spatial structure of regional and national economies, Ta-ch'i nevertheless retains much of the character of a traditional marketing community. The town's relative conservatism is largely a result of its loca-tion in relation to other urban centers in northern Taiwan. It is near enough to industrial centers for its citizens to participate fully in the de-veloping industrial sector without losing daily (or at least frequent) con-tact with the community. But it is far enough away to be insulated from

---

*This is not to deny some very significant changes, including, for example, the elimina-tion of foot-binding, "little-daughter-in-law" marriages, and "blind" arranged marriages.
†See Eric Wolf (1957) on the influential and useful notion of relative openness and closed-ness of peasant communities, and Skinner (1971) on an application of that notion to changes through time in the nature of local community integration into wider Chinese social and cultural systems.

the more disruptive aspects of urban growth. Similar market towns located on the fringes of urban centers have been overwhelmed by this growth and have become industrial suburbs of cities like Taipei. Towns more distant from the cities feel the loss of their sons and daughters to urban opportunities more acutely, since visits are more costly and inconvenient, and tend to diminish over time.

The same aspects of locale that relegated Ta-ch'i to peripheral status in the 1920s show signs of becoming the basis for its future economic development. Once again it is as a gateway to mountain resources that Ta-ch'i is most likely to prosper. These resources consist of products such as lumber (significant stands of virgin and secondary forests cover the mountains) and hydroelectric power. But the same could be said for many towns bordering the mountains. What makes Ta-ch'i different is the possibility of exploiting the combination of its relative proximity to Taipei, its "unspoiled" scenery, and its traditional atmosphere to develop still further an already growing tourist industry. A recent growth of interest in camping and mountaineering among Taiwan's urban youth indicates that the rising standard of living and consequent leisure will probably continue to increase the demand for recreational opportunities.

The headwaters of the Ta-han River provide some of Taiwan's most strikingly beautiful scenery; waterfalls, peaks, and ancient giant cypress trees combine in scenes that resonate strongly with the Chinese sense of "Chineseness." Tourism in the area, already on the upswing, will surely increase as access restrictions are relaxed (in 1977 special mountain passes were required to visit areas off the single, gravel-paved road that traverses the range).*

Conclusions

This chapter has illustrated the analytical advantages of attending to the spatial organization of economy and the hierarchical embeddedness of local communities in periodizing local social history. I have attempted to show that shifts in the structure of Ta-ch'i's ties to higher-level economic regions were among the most important factors underlying development

---

*There are two ways to interpret the rising value attached to the leisure-time use of the wilderness in Taiwan. On the one hand, the formalist would argue that leisure and wilderness values are highly income-elastic, and that the new interest in hiking and camping in Taiwan is simply a consequence of rising incomes, basic values remaining constant. On the other hand, the substantivist would argue that the value of wilderness has increased relative to other values. Both would be right to some degree: rising standards of living and education probably prepared the way for changing values (no doubt influenced in part by the similar changes in the West), which in turn reflect more than income effects.

within the town's marketing community (see Fig. 1). Thus the shift from traditional frontier expansion to an export-oriented exploitation of camphor and tea, which began in the 1850s, resulted from Taiwan's incorporation into the world economic system. The period of economic stagnation beginning about 1920 (exacerbated, of course, by the world economic depression of the 1930s) was in large part owing to the introduction of modern transport, which restructured northern Taiwan's hierarchy of central places, relegating Ta-ch'i to a more peripheral status. Only with the major historical transition that began in the early 1950s was there a fundamental change in modes of production. In agriculture, this shift saw the most productive land transferred from landlords to owner-cultivators, but certainly greater in its impact on Ta-ch'i's economy was the growth of industrial capitalism. Yet I have emphasized that even these fundamental changes in the organization of production were mediated by the town's position in the spatial structure of northern Taiwan's economy.

The forces from larger arenas of social action that affected Ta-ch'i's economy were variously political, economic, or cultural during different periods. The shifting nature of these external forces and the complexity introduced when the hierarchically embedded position of local communities is taken into account have recommended the eclectic appeals to divergent theoretical stances adopted here. In other words, the analyst must be flexible regarding the direction of causal relations among economy, polity, and values as relevant arenas of social action shift.

Thus I have employed a Marxist lexicon in describing Ta-ch'i's political economy, but have refrained from relying on its claims to universal explanation. My reticence is based on the complexities introduced when abstract, aspatial theoretical categories confront the nested hierarchies of concrete social organization. Failure to take note of these complexities undermines many of the claims of ambitious, universalizing theories. Just as culture, economy, and polity are regionally structured, so are the forces and relations of production. An analysis of landlord-tenant relations in Ta-ch'i, for example, must consider both variation in tenancy rates within the marketing community and the regional context of economic, political, and institutional transformations in higher-level systems that impinge upon these relations (Rawski 1972).

Taking into account the spatially nested structure of social interaction has the further advantage of avoiding inflexible and unilinear historical typologies (as in some "dependency-theory" arguments—e.g., Moulder 1977). Such typologies would be hard-pressed to account for the ups and downs of economic development in a local system like Ta-ch'i.

The idea that case studies serve as "tests" for general theoretical orien-

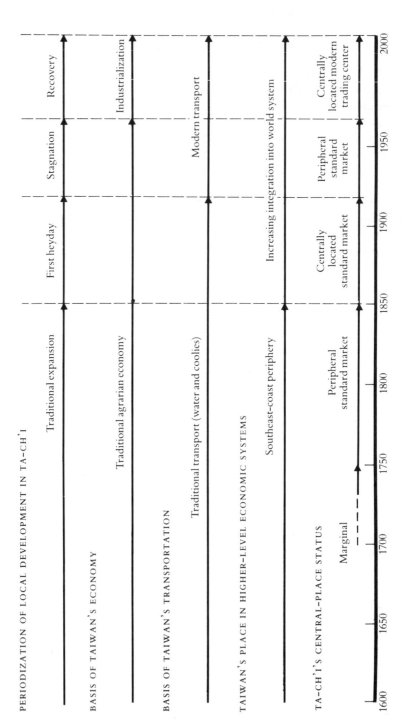

Fig. 1. Time-line summary of economic development in Ta-ch'i

PERIODIZATION OF LOCAL DEVELOPMENT IN TA-CH'I

	1600	1650	1700	1750	1800	1850	1900	1950	2000
			Traditional expansion			First heyday	Stagnation	Recovery	

BASIS OF TAIWAN'S ECONOMY

Traditional agrarian economy — Industrialization

BASIS OF TAIWAN'S TRANSPORTATION

Traditional transport (water and coolies) — Modern transport

TAIWAN'S PLACE IN HIGHER-LEVEL ECONOMIC SYSTEMS

Southeast-coast periphery — Increasing integration into world system

TA-CH'I'S CENTRAL-PLACE STATUS

Marginal — Peripheral standard market — Centrally located standard market — Peripheral standard market — Centrally located modern trading center tations is so much a part of Western academic thought that it is unquestioned. But the embeddedness of local communities in complex higher-order economic, political, and cultural systems logically limits the use of local case studies as tests of general theory. Rather than abandon what I view as the legitimate goals of "positivist" social science, the proper response is to incorporate precisely what frustrates social theory—this spatial and temporal boundedness of the concrete and empirical—into theory itself. A beginning may be made by multiplying analytical categories, of whatever theoretical stripe, by the empirically observed levels of spatial and temporal interaction. This procedure unsettles aspatial assertions regarding the analytical priority of categories like "production," "exchange," and "value," but the gains in descriptive accuracy should outweigh the losses in parsimony.

Part II

The Ritual Construction
of Social Space

Western understanding of Chinese religion and culture is conditioned both by the most accessible Chinese institutions and performances and by our own culturally constructed sociologies that allow us to order the exotic. In the first instance, the ideologized native elite construction of Chinese reality, which first appeared to Westerners in the form of translated editions of Chinese classical texts, has been richly augmented in recent years by sociological and anthropological descriptions based on systematic observation of Chinese life and religion. But this "direct observation" is itself mediated by the questions, assumptions, and methodologies the observer brings to her/his object. In this book I attempt to construct a revisionist portrait of Chinese ritual, religion, and historical consciousness, based in part upon the application of different, but still Western, sociological and anthropological perspectives.

For the most part, this revisionist analysis is developed in Part III; Part II is mainly a description of ritual organization in Ta-ch'i. Chapter 3 summarizes in broad outline current anthropological understanding of Chinese "popular" or local religion. In Chapter 4 I adopt the "ethnographic present" voice of conventional community studies to describe territorial cults in Ta-ch'i's marketing community. My presentation here differs from most other ethnographies primarily in its broader territorial scope: the unit of analysis is the marketing community rather than a village or hamlet. In addition, Chapter 4 describes how territorial cults are linked to wider ritual spheres by means of pilgrimages to pan-island cult centers.

Chapter 5 summarizes the major spatial and temporal features of the ritual construction of social life in Ta-ch'i, and outlines what I term the "intensification" of territorial-cult organization over time. The discussion here employs an "objectivist" historical voice; the diachronic dimension enters the analysis mainly as the "time frame" within which the synchronic ritual structures discussed in Chapter 4 emerge. Chapter 6 deals with the functional connections among ritual, economic, and administrative patterns of interaction in Ta-ch'i's history.

Part II thus constitutes a more or less traditional ethnographic account of social structure. Taken together, Parts I and II present some of the data that I interpret from a more "cultural" vantage point in Part III, but only in a rather loose sense. The argument in Part III requires that additional data be introduced, consisting of iconography, myth, native exegesis, and so forth, rather than "social structure" or behavior. And the selection of descriptive data in Parts I and II anticipates the interpretive framework of Part III.

3

Taiwanese "Folk Religion"

Gods, Ghosts, and Ancestors

In Ta-ch'i three levels of social and economic interaction—the neighborhood, the village, and the multivillage-level ritual community—take explicit ritual form in a nested, three-tiered hierarchy of territorial cults. Neighborhood-cult ritual is generally associated with worship at Place God (T'u Ti Kung) shrines; village ritual is conducted at more elaborate village temples, and honors deities of higher celestial status than T'u Ti Kung; and multivillage ritual centers on the worship of the red-faced deity-general Kuan Kung. Significantly, in Ta-ch'i the perimeter of participation in multivillage community ritual coincides very nearly with the boundaries of the marketing community.

Despite differences in the magnitude of ritual festivities, the characteristics associated with focal deities, and many details of ritual organization, all of these cults explicitly refer to an essentially unified set of cosmological assumptions. The most salient of these assumptions is that cosmic order is administered in much the same way the mundane world is administered. Many observers of Chinese religion have noted that the Chinese pantheon very much resembles the Chinese bureaucracy of imperial times (see especially A. Wolf 1974a). Just as lower-level bureaucrats governed local administrative districts and higher-level officials more encompassing ones, so lesser deities administer small communities and more exalted gods larger ones. From the Stove God who supervises (or spies on) the affairs of a single household to the Jade Emperor who reigns over the cosmos, the hierarchical structure of imperial bureaucracy appears to be replicated in the Chinese pantheon.

The logic of this administered cosmos explains in part why Ta-ch'i natives participate in several territorial cults. The cosmic hierarchy, like the mundane, is a "nested" one; everyone is simultaneously a member of neighborhood-, village-, and multivillage-level communities. It also explains why people living in different locales worship different constellations of deities, the degree of overlap depending on relative position in the structure of cosmic administration.

Aspects of territorial-cult ideology, then, explicitly parallel aspects of past administrative hierarchy, a fact most often explained as a projection of social categories into the supernatural. Arthur P. Wolf (1974a) has made this argument most convincingly: the three most important categories of supernatural beings in Chinese culture—gods, ghosts, and ancestors—are modeled directly on the three most important categories of people in peasants' experience—officials, strangers, and kin. Wolf demonstrates that many characteristics attributed to each category of supernatural being correspond to those of their earthly counterparts. For example, gods, like officials, are powerful and susceptible to bribery, live in palaces, and require lavish entertainments marked by conspicuous consumption. Since officials in imperial times were the most powerful people in peasant experience—holders of apparently arbitrary, capricious, and unlimited authority—it makes a great deal of sense that gods should be modeled after them. However, as I argue at length in Part III, the reasons that Chinese cosmological notions take the forms they do are more complex than this theory suggests. For instance, why is it that past rather than present officialdom constitutes the model of celestial bureaucracy? Nonetheless, in some contexts there are striking correspondences between an image of past imperial bureaucracy and the Chinese pantheon.

Given this set of correspondences, much of Chinese ritual activity can be viewed in terms of various forms of exchange between people and categories of spirits. To put it rather crudely, one propitiates dangerous ghosts, provides for the material and spiritual needs of deceased kin, and bribes powerful gods (Ahern 1981a). But Chinese ritual life is more than a summation of exchanges between individuals (or households) and imaginary spirits, conducted as "need" arises. On the contrary, Chinese ritual is complexly structured in social space and time, in line with an encompassing set of cosmological assumptions. Again, the nature of these assumptions is addressed in more detail in Part III, but at this point we must at least note the connection between the annual cosmic cycle and the ritual calendar.

The Annual Cycle of Rituals

Chinese notions of time, cosmic order, and legitimate authority are complexly articulated in the ritual calendar.* Three foci of the Chinese ritual year are *shang-yüan*, *chung-yüan*, and *hsia-yüan*, which occur on the fifteenth day of the first lunar month, the seventh lunar month, and the tenth lunar month, respectively. Both domestic and communal rituals and sacrifices are performed on each of these dates, but in Ta-ch'i, relatively more emphasis is placed on the first two.†

Shang-yüan is a part of Chinese New Year's celebrations. The essential theme of Chinese New Year beliefs is that household gods (e.g., the Stove God) return to heaven to report the state of household affairs directly to the Emperor of Heaven (T'ien Kung). While the household gods are absent, the order they represent is in danger. In theory, whether or not this order will be restored is in some question, and many of the rituals of the New Year's season are conducted in an attempt to ensure that chaos (yin) will not overpower order (yang).

Summarizing an important message of the complex of New Year's rituals, Feuchtwang (1974b: 115) argues that

in reestablishing its relation with heaven, the household's own hierarchical order is asserted. Only the male head of the household may address heaven. His wife may worship the ancestors. Children of the household, and, on another day, employees of a firm, are given bonuses by parents and bosses. The hierarchical order of worshipped beings is apparent at New Year's as at no other time because at this time all the spirits and deities of domestic worship are addressed in turn and the rule of privileged access to food must be applied. On the one hand, in the worship of ancestors, the continuity of the household as a patrilineal descent group is re-created. On the other hand, its continuity on earth as base unit of a cosmic empire is guaranteed in the worship of heaven and the return of the gods.

Ancestors are worshiped at both New Year's and *chung-yüan*, but the emphasis at New Year's is on the inward-directed ancestral spirits of individual households, whereas during the seventh lunar month it is on an outward-directed worship of ancestors who correspond to larger collectivities (e.g., lineages; see Feuchtwang 1974b). Similarly, all the gods are worshiped at New Year's, but the emphasis is on heaven on the one hand and on the god associated most directly with the lowest-level unit of so-

*Feuchtwang (1974b, especially 111–16) provides the best analysis of how this articulation is achieved in popular Taiwanese rituals.

†Whereas in Feuchtwang's Mountain Street, *hsia-yüan* coincides with the celebration of the territorial-cult deity's "birthday" celebration, in Ta-ch'i, the major village-level territorial-cult celebrations all occur between *shang-yüan* and *chung-yüan*.

cial order—the Stove God—on the other. (Heaven, as I argue in Part III, is more abstract, less personalized, and less connected to specific social institutions than other divinities.) Social collectivities (e.g., neighborhoods, villages) are, at most, minor themes during the New Year's season. Thus it is not surprising that despite the importance of New Year's in the Chinese ritual calendar, the most important public rituals occur at other times. In Ta-ch'i, the most important communal rituals are associated with *chung-yüan* and with the birthdays of territorial-cult deities.

The emphasis at *chung-yüan* is on the worship of ghosts. Gods are also worshiped, but they are gods who either protect the community from ghosts or save ghosts from purgatory. During the seventh month, the gates of purgatory are said to open, allowing the spirits trapped there to roam the yang world of the living. One of the major rationales commonly offered in explanation of *chung-yüan* rituals is that the community must be protected from these dangerous ghosts.

Ritual separation of insiders (community, ancestors) from outsiders (ghosts, strangers, the outside world) is also apparent in the communal rituals associated with territorial-cult gods' birthdays, but with less emphasis on the salvation of lost spirits in purgatory than in the *chung-yüan* ceremonies. Territorial-cult gods are said to protect communities. The most frequently cited evidence of their power is the assistance they are said to have rendered in intervening to defend the community against outside threats (e.g., floods, epidemics, the depredations of aborigine headhunters, or the insidious plots of Chinese gangs from rival ethnic factions).

Feuchtwang (1974a: 116) contrasts New Year's and *chung-yüan* rituals as follows:

In New Year ritual the unit is the household and its ancestors, and it is in a subordinate position to the main deity worshipped, who is the supreme deity or group of deities. Between the supreme deity and the small base unit are on the one hand the mass of gods, and on the other an individual savior god and a household god. In seventh-month ritual the unit is a neighborhood and its constituents are the ancestors. This territorial unit is in complementary opposition with other such units and with masses of kui. Between them, between the territorial group and the mass of kui, are single guardian gods and individual savior gods. At New Year's a continuity is reestablished that involves hierarchical relation [of household and patriline to cosmic order], whereas in the seventh month a discontinuity [between insiders and outsiders] is reestablished that involves a symmetrical relation of opposition.

Many of the implications of Feuchtwang's suggestions are developed in Part III, where particular attention is devoted to complexities associated with the fact that the Chinese social world consists of more than the three levels Feuchtwang discusses (household, community, and heaven). Territorial-cult festivals are among the main occasions in which these complexities are produced and displayed, and it is to the organization of these that we now turn.

Territorial-Cult Organization

THE LU-CHU

Territorial cults combine at least two characteristics. The first is, broadly speaking, cultural: a territorial cult coalesces around worship of a deity who is conceived as having jurisdiction over a certain spatial territory. The second is sociological: territorial cults are concretely constituted in communal rituals. It is at these rituals that community members congregate and act as a corporate body. Thus, although territorial-cult shrines and temples stand as permanent symbols of ritual community, a shrine or temple does not itself constitute a territorial cult; rituals do.

Several essential features characterize territorial-cult festivals *(pai-pai)* at all levels. Households bring sacrifices to the shrine or temple, and these are later taken home and shared with friends, relatives, or neighbors. The stated purposes of the ceremonies and sacrifices are to honor the gods and to request that peace and prosperity be granted to the community. There is great variation in elaboration of ceremonies, entertainments, and sacrifices, depending on the size and level of the cult, whether the holiday is in honor of the temple's main god or a subsidiary deity, the wealth of the community, and the degree of community solidarity. The basic forms of *pai-pai* are quite consistent, however.

Responsibility for *pai-pai* at all levels—neighborhood, village, and multivillage community—rests with the *lu-chu*. The *lu-chu* (literally, "host of the incense burner") is the holder of an office that is filled each year by a respected household head. Every communally celebrated ritual has its *lu-chu*, and one of the concluding activities in any *pai-pai* is to cast divination blocks to determine the deity's choice to become the following year's *lu-chu*.* Only men who are respected household heads are considered for the honor of serving as *lu-chu*. By convention the office should

*Divination blocks made of wood are used to communicate with gods or spirits. Two blocks are used, each having a flat surface and a convex surface. After asking the deity a question, the questioner casts the blocks on the ground. If the blocks land with a flat surface and a convex surface face-side up, the deity's response is positive, and if both blocks are flat, it is negative. Two convex surfaces mean that the god finds the request humorous or inappropriate—that is, "try again."

rotate; no one who has recently served as *lu-chu* for a particular ritual is likely to hold the same office again for a number of years.

The office of *lu-chu* brings honor and prestige to its holder, commensurate with the level and importance of the communal ritual involved. At the neighborhood level, practically all male household heads may serve as *lu-chu*. At the marketing-community level, wealthy heads of important families serve. The zenith of prestige in Ta-ch'i is to serve as *lu-chu* for a *chiao* for the P'u-ch'i *t'ang*, the center of the township's most encompassing territorial cult. The *chiao* is an elaborate ritual celebration of communal renewal that occurs periodically (in Ta-ch'i, every 20 to 50 years) when a temple is built or restored (see Liu 1967, 1974; Saso 1972; Jordan 1976; Pang 1977). The *lu-chu* for a *chiao* must be one of the community's most respected leaders, a man of both experience and means, since the proper management of the *chiao* is believed to profoundly affect the future fortunes of all in the community.

Besides bringing prestige and honor to its holder, the office involves considerable responsibility, time, work, and risk. The *lu-chu* for a rural neighborhood ritual is responsible for hiring an opera troupe and Taoist priest, and for supervising the collection of contributions to pay for the celebration. He may be aided by an assistant (*fu-lu-chu*) and various helpers (*shou-shih*). Often the local *li-chang* (head of the lowest-level administrative unit, the *li*) takes a hand in ensuring that the arrangements proceed smoothly. The *lu-chu* must provide a strict account of all income and expenditures, and he may be held personally responsible for any cost overruns. His budget is usually posted on the shrine, along with the sums contributed by parishioners.

Arrangements for communal rituals tend to follow precedent closely. As a matter of convenience, the same opera troupes and priests are hired in successive years, through the same middlemen. Thus the *lu-chu* of a neighborhood ritual does not spend too much time in his duties. However, the time and effort involved increase significantly for higher-level communal rituals. For a village-level ritual, the *lu-chu* may be assisted by the temple's manager and other village leaders. He must arrange to invite and transport deity images from neighboring temples and obtain local-government permission to conduct festivities. More elaborate (and expensive) operas and Taoist rituals must be arranged. Precedent is still his guide, but the village-level *lu-chu* finds that the increased scale and complexity of the celebration demand a much greater expenditure of time and effort than did his tenure as a neighborhood-level *lu-chu*.

The *lu-chu* for the P'u-ch-i *t'ang*'s *chiao* must contribute the most in labor and managerial expertise. The Taoist ceremonies required in the performance of a *chiao* are much more elaborate, lengthy, and expensive than for annual celebrations. Since they occur so infrequently, precedent is a less practical and reliable guide to their arrangement. It is impossible for one man to supervise personally all the preparations for a ritual of such scope and importance. To prepare adequately for a multivillage-level *chiao*, an elaborate organization for the delegation of authority is necessary.

Nonetheless, the *lu-chu* remains personally responsible for the ritual's success or failure. Any shortcomings reflect upon him and his family. Moreover, the *lu-chu* for an important *chiao* is thought to be taking a considerable risk in accepting the job. Should any of the gods or ghosts worshiped in the course of the *chiao* be displeased, or should any of the ritual manipulations be bungled, bad luck or disaster may befall the *lu-chu* and his family and relatives. Many in Ta-ch'i attribute the decline of the once-prominent family of the *lu-chu* for an important *chiao* held some 25 years ago to the fact that the *chiao* was not performed properly. Conversely, the office holds great prestige, and a successful *chiao* brings good fortune to the community, and especially to the *lu-chu* and his family.

At each level of communal ritual there are relatively more and less important occasions. Infrequently held *chiao* are more important than annual sacrifices, and some annual sacrifices receive more attention than others. Some occasions call for the hiring of operas and priests, while others are celebrated modestly. Household heads generally serve as *lu-chu* for neighborhood rituals or for less important village-level celebrations (sometimes several times) before they take on the greater responsibilities of the more important village or multivillage festivals. Another way men prepare for *lu-chu* leadership roles is by assisting their fathers, uncles, and brothers.

The *lu-chu* institution is thus an important mechanism for diffusing leadership among male household heads at each level of territorial-cult hierarchy. It effectively socializes and educates the *lu-chu* in the content and organization of territorial cults. Moreover, many of the organizational techniques employed in mobilizing cult activities are also used in a wide variety of Chinese business and voluntary organizations (Sangren 1984b). The training acquired during service as *lu-chu* is thus of a very general order, preparing men for leadership roles in many other areas as well.

Note that this kind of leadership is essentially "representative," in the sense that the *lu-chu*'s power derives from that of the community he represents, not from higher authority. This argument is developed more fully in Part III with reference to the contrasting trajectories of power embodied in the notions of *ling* (efficacy) and virtue. Note also that the *lu-chu*'s power and authority are not hierarchically authoritarian. For these reasons, arguments that emphasize the presumed inability of Chinese culture to imagine nonauthoritarian patterns of leadership and social relations seem to me overstated (e.g., Solomon 1971; Pye 1968; Silin 1976).

TEMPLE COMMITTEES

The Japanese administration, in its effort to rationalize and control Chinese institutions, imposed a system of managerial organization on village- and higher-level temples. It seems probable that in so doing, it essentially codified what in many cases had been preexisting organizations (R. Myers 1972b: 436–37). In the case of Ta-ch'i's temples, I was unable to establish with any certainty the status of temple committees and formal leadership prior to the Japanese colonial era. My general impression is that the Japanese rationalizing impulse caused forms of organization that had previously existed only at the higher levels to descend in the hierarchy of territorial cults.

Today, for example, the rotating *lu-chu* is generally the only form of cult leadership associated with neighborhood shrines. Prior to the Japanese era, I suspect that many village-level temples also lacked permanent committees or managers. But even during the Ch'ing dynasty, large temples required permanent supervision by respected community leaders, so that committees were established and managers appointed to this end. In short, although the organization of territorial-cult leadership in Ta-ch'i today reflects the impact of Japanese and Republican policies, it would be a mistake to dismiss such organizational forms as "externally imposed" and hence alien to local culture. Rather than attempting to distinguish elements of local culture from elements imposed from outside, it is more appropriate to acknowledge that all Chinese local institutions develop in complex relation with externally generated forces, including government.*

The basic form of temple leadership (for village- and higher-level cults) consists of a manager (*kuan-li-jen*) and a governing committee (*wei-yüan-hui*). Within this general framework, there is considerable variation. At the Fu-jen *kung* (the village-level temple located in the town of Ta-ch'i itself), for example, the officially registered manager (a member of the county legislature) plays only a small role in temple affairs. For the most part, the temple is run informally by prominent representatives of the

---

*Ch'en Jui-t'ang (1971) provides the most complete account of the organization and legal status of temples during the late Ch'ing, Japanese, and Republican periods.

various surname groups, who also serve on the temple's governing committee (*kuan-li wei-yüan-hui*). Periodic reconstruction of the temple is overseen by the similarly constituted reconstruction committee (*hsiu-chien wei-yüan-hui*). Particular rituals are organized by the *lu-chu* and his assistants. The temple's governing committee meets irregularly (only a few times a year), when there is specific business that requires a consensus.

Other village-level temples in Ta-ch'i's marketing area are similarly organized, although temple-committee organization tends to be more formal at the larger temples than at smaller ones. *Li-chang* and township and county representatives (*chen-min tai-piao* and *hsien i-yüan*) often serve on temple committees. Their prestige is thought to reflect positively on the temple. In recent years, however, participation of county representatives and other officials above the *li-chang* level has declined, probably in response to the national government's ambivalence toward local ritual activity.

The P'u-ch'i *t'ang*'s committee organization is the most elaborate in Ta-ch'i township. The governing committee (*kuan-li wei-yüan-hui*) is composed of 20 of Ta-ch'i township's 21 *li-chang* (the only unrepresented *li* is Ch'iao-ai, an enclave of ethnically distinct mainland immigrants near the northwest border of the township); representatives from each of Ta-ch'i's seventeen ritual clubs (*she-t'uan*); and eight members selected from among the parishioners (*hsin-t'u*) at large. The governing committee meets about twice a year, leaving routine matters to an executive committee (*ch'ang-wu wei-yüan-hui*). The members of the executive committee are chosen by the governing committee from among its own members, and are headed by the temple chairman (*chü-jen wei-yüan*). There is also a small steering committee (*chih-hsing wei-yüan-hui*) of five members. An administrative secretary (*tsung-wu*) is hired to oversee daily administrative affairs at the temple (e.g., that proper records of contributions are maintained, that the temple grounds are in good order, and that other temple employees are fulfilling their responsibilities).

All but the smallest village temples hire a custodian (*miao-kung*), often an elderly man retired from some other occupation, to watch over the temple grounds, keep the area clean, and accept contributions (*hsiang-yu ch'ien*) from worshipers. Larger temples may also hire janitors and attendants to sell spirit money and incense.

When a temple is being constructed or rebuilt, a special committee (*hsiu-chien wei-yüan-hui*) is formed to oversee the work of collecting funds for construction and hire contractors to do the job. The building of a new temple or refurbishing of an old one also requires the formation of a special committee (*chiao-chü*) to plan and carry out the dedication ceremonies (*chiao*). The larger and more important the temple, the more important it is to have competent and respected men in active leadership roles. Conversely, if a temple is to maintain its popularity, it is very important that it retain the commitment of capable and respected leaders. For example, a decline in popularity of Ta-ch'i's Fu-jen *kung* relative to the P'u-ch'i *t'ang* can be attributed in part to the defection of the town's most capable leaders to the P'u-ch'i *t'ang*. Temple cults may thus wax and wane in tandem with the social fortunes of their leaders and of the constituencies they represent.

View of Ta-ch'i's business district

Right: Territorial-cult sacrifice at the Kuan-yin *t'ing.* *Above:* Ta-ch'i's P'u-ch'i *t'ang* (Kuan Kung temple).

Three examples of
simple T'u Ti Kung
(Place God) shrines.
The one at the upper left
is sited at the margin of
a rice field.

Procession in honor of Kuan Kung, part of the annual festival for Ta-ch'i's multi-village territorial cult centered on the P'u-ch'i *t'ang*

Two guardian generals in the Kuan
Kung procession

Above: Sacrificial pig (*chu-kung*)
at annual village-level territorial-
cult celebration. *Above right:*
Medicine salesman at village festival. *Below right:* The burning of
Ta Shih Yeh (the demonic transformation of Kuan Yin) after the
pu-tu (hungry ghosts) ritual

Crossing the fire (*kuo-huo*) to return deity image to village temple

Taoist priests aiding the deceased's soul to cross the bridge between the yang and yin worlds

View of Ta-ch'i facing east. The Ta-han River is in the foreground, the foothills of Taiwan's central mountain range in the background.

4

Territorial Cults and Pilgrimages

Neighborhood Cults

The smallest communal rituals, associated with what I term neighbor-hood cults, generally focus on worship of the Place God, T'u Ti Kung. Rural hamlets and urban neighborhoods in Ta-ch'i are ritually defined, territorially discrete units under the authority of their respective Place Gods. The boundaries of these "administrative units" in the cosmic bu-reaucracy correspond to other patterns of social interaction and commit-ment. One T'u Ti Kung parish in Ta-ch'i, for example, is coextensive with the former living quarters of the town's once large population of stevedores. In rural areas, the spatial definition of ritual-community boundaries generally coincides with microecological systems, insofar as they are socially appropriated. For example, T'u Ti Kung domains may coincide with irrigation networks, the watersheds of small streams, and so forth. In short, all of the technological and environmental forces that pattern social interaction in the historical development of people's rela-tions to the land also impinge upon people's cultural construction of the landscape.

However, it would be a mistake to see this cultural construction of space as merely a superstructural reflection of ecologically, technologi-cally, or economically determined patterns of interaction. Deterministic arguments most nearly approach sufficiency at the historical founding of a communal ritual focused on a Place God shrine. Clearly, the group that convenes at such a moment must have some social significance beyond that defined by the as yet nonexistent T'u Ti Kung domain. But once such a ritual community is institutionalized, it takes on an existence of its own. As in the case of the neighborhood of stevedores in Ta-ch'i, the primordial "determinants" of ritually institutionalized community may be forgotten or disappear, yet the community and its ritual persist.

Moreover, even at the moment of its creation, the ritually defined parish is more than a mere reflection of the patterns of interaction that define its boundaries. The very impulse to institutionalize community in ritual presupposes a conceptual model of space, social relations, and cosmos that in a deterministic explanation would be viewed as epiphenomenal "reflections" of forces (economic, technological, or environmental) external to culture.

Consider the typical historical sequence of events leading to the establishment of neighborhood-cult ritual. The decision to build a T'u Ti Kung shrine may be undertaken either individually or collectively, and there are many T'u Ti Kung shrines, especially in remote locales, that do not function as foci for communal rituals. Should population in the vicinity increase, however, a second, always collective decision to convene annual communal rituals may follow. In such cases, then, cultural superstructure temporally precedes social infrastructure in the typical developmental sequence of rural neighborhood cults; in other words, cosmology antedates social structure. Of course, the historically and spatially bounded nature of such cases precludes assigning ultimate causalities in the wider context of Chinese civilization and history, but such cases do undermine the straightforward sociocentric determinisms of synchronic functional analyses.

T'u Ti Kung shrines in Ta-ch'i vary from tiny nooks constructed of conveniently shaped stones to ornate temples with gaudily colored, mosaic roofs. Households bring sacrifices to T'u Ti Kung on all important ritual occasions, but he is singled out for special worship on his official birthdays—namely, the second day of the second lunar month and the fifteenth day of the eighth lunar month. On the first of these dates, household sacrifices, most often brought by housewives or elderly grandfathers and grandmothers, are placed individually before T'u Ti Kung's image. Religiously conscientious households may also bring sacrifices to the neighborhood shrine on the first and fifteenth days of every lunar month.

P'ING-AN-HSI

There is a great deal of variation in the ardor and frequency of T'u Ti Kung worship, but participation is greatest in the annual *p'ing-an-hsi* ("festival of peace and harmony") that takes place at all neighborhood shrines sometime during the eighth lunar month. The *p'ing-an-hsi* is the *pai-pai* that gives concrete expression to the neighborhood. The gods—and especially T'u Ti Kung—are petitioned to grant the neighborhood another year of peace and prosperity, and are asked to enjoy the sacrifices and entertainments provided by the community.

The limits of participation in the *p'ing-an-hsi* are territorially defined in terms of T'u Ti Kung's administrative domain. Ideally, every household in this domain contributes to the expenses of hiring Taoist priests and opera troupes, and brings an offering to the communal sacrifice. In urban Ta-ch'i, the unit of *p'ing-an-hsi* participation may be termed a "street" (*chieh*) or described in terms of secular administration as part of a *li* (administrative village) or *lin* (administrative neighborhood). In rural areas, terms such as "corner" (*chiao*) or "hamlet" (*chuang*) may be used. I use the term "neighborhood" for both rural and urban *p'ing-an-hsi* communities.

In rural areas, sacrifices for *p'ing-an-hsi* are generally arranged together on a long table set up either before the T'u Ti Kung shrine or in the village-temple courtyard. Each household is represented by a similar offering, and all offerings are brought to the shrine at a preappointed time (usually midmorning). The dedication ceremony is performed by a Taoist priest hired for the occasion. His job is to perform the prescribed ritual that notifies the gods of the identities of the sacrificers. In most cases, these ceremonies are abbreviated versions of *chiao* designed to stem entropy and restore order. The ritual itself is opaque and of little interest to its beneficiaries. The priest also petitions the gods to grant the neighborhood another year of peace and prosperity. The culmination of the ceremony, as in *pai-pai* at all levels, is the burning of the celestial petition (*chu-wen*), sealing this communication with the gods (see also Schipper 1974). A cacophony of firecrackers announces the receipt of the sacrifice and petition, ending the formal ritual.

After the ritual, households begin to carry home their offerings, which are consumed at feasts in the afternoon and evening. Those with sufficient leisure (especially elderly people and small children) spend the rest of the afternoon and evening enjoying the opera performance and socializing in a relaxed way with friends and neighbors.* The eighth month usually comes well before the second rice harvest, and farmers often have more free time to participate in the festivities than during other periods in the agricultural cycle.

Communal spirit is less evident at *p'ing-an-hsi* held in urban neighborhoods. Households bring sacrifices to T'u Ti Kung throughout the day and evening, but there is less a sense of ritual climax than in rural *p'ing-an-*

---

*As Ward (1979) points out, the opera performance is itself a ritual with complex symbolic resonances.

hsi. The same Taoist ceremonies are performed, but attendance is lower. The relative wealth of the town makes it easier to raise funds through the contributions assessed on each household, so opera performances are often quite spectacular. The modest enthusiasm of Ta-ch'i's urbanites for *p'ing-an-hsi* is hardly surprising, given the relatively lower significance of neighborhood ties in nonritual contexts and the ready availability of competing entertainments. Nonetheless, there is no sign that commitment to neighborhood ritual is declining, even in urban Ta-ch'i.

As already noted, some *p'ing-an-hsi* are held in village-temple court-yards rather than in front of T'u Ti Kung shrines. This apparent anomaly raises an interesting point regarding the nested structure of territorial cults: some village-cult territories encompass only one neighborhood cult. In such cases, the village temple serves as the center for both neighborhood-level ritual and village-level ritual. However, the distinctions between the two are conceptually clear. The term *p'ing-an-hsi* is reserved for neighborhood ritual focusing on the worship of T'u Ti Kung, whereas village ritual focuses on the worship of the village temple's main god, who is always of higher status than T'u Ti Kung. A separate shrine housing T'u Ti Kung is often built near the village temple, even though the temple itself usually has a T'u Ti Kung image. Moreover, village sacrifices in Ta-ch'i are marked by the slaughter of specially raised pigs (Ahern 1981a); I never observed pig sacrifices at *p'ing-an-hsi*.

Even in village-cult domains that include more than one neighborhood cult, the neighborhood in which the village temple is located often holds its *p'ing-an-hsi* in the temple courtyard. The role of the village temple is thus structurally analogous to that of higher-level capitals in imperial China; just as a prefectural capital served simultaneously as the capital of one of its constituent counties, the village temple may serve as the ritual center for both the village and one of its neighborhoods.

As one would expect, there is considerable variation in the details of *p'ing-an-hsi* organization and practice. Some of the variation can be attributed to such factors as population density and centrality. Other differences reflect aspects of local history and social organization. A few examples suggest the range of variation.

In 1976, at the Chen-nan *kung* T'u Ti Kung shrine (Maps 5 and 6, No. 2) in the town of Ta-ch'i, approximately 100 households contributed enough money to hold two days of opera performances (on the twelfth and thirteenth of the eighth lunar month). A *lu-chu*, assistant, and ten helpers were in charge of inviting priests to conduct the ceremonies, hiring the opera troupe, and soliciting funds for the event from all the families in the neighborhood. Turtle cakes (*kuei*) of two types were displayed, with signs indicating their weights and their donors' names. Images of three higher-order deities—Kuan Kung from the P'u-ch'i *t'ang*, K'ai Chang Sheng Wang from the Fu-jen *kung* (the ascendant multi-village- and village-level deities), and Kuan Yin from the Kuan-yin *t'ing*—were invited to the opera and placed prominently on the shrine's altar. Several other T'u Ti Kung from neighboring shrines were also invited, but were represented by packets of ash from their censers rather than by images.

The Chen-nan *kung* is one of the most elaborate T'u Ti Kung shrines in Ta-ch'i. Its domain includes the residences of many of the town's wealthiest families. This wealth accounts for the shrine and the two days of opera. However, in other respects the organization of the *p'ing-an-hsi* is quite representative of urban neighborhoods. Parishioners come at their convenience to offer sacrifices. In contrast to some rural *p'ing-an-hsi*, the parish does not gather for the actual dedication ceremony conducted by a Taoist priest.

In comparison, the *p'ing-an-hsi* celebrated in rural Nan-tzu-kou (Map 5, No. 21) conveys a stronger impression of community solidarity. Nan-tzu-kou is located in a valley surrounded by mountains, about 20 minutes by bus plus half-an-hour's walk from Ta-ch'i. The area was first settled some 75 years ago by eight families who were tenants of the Japanese Mitsui Company. Most of the 55 families living in the hamlet in 1976 were descendants of these original settlers. There are two T'u Ti Kung shrines in the valley, one at the upstream end (*shui-t'ou*) and one at the downstream end (*shui-wei*). The *p'ing-an-hsi* is held at a point midway between the two. Images from the two shrines are placed at a temporary altar, along with privately owned images of Kuan Yin and two or three other gods. Images of K'ai Chang Sheng Wang and Kuan Kung are borrowed from the village temple in Pai-chi. In addition, other T'u Ti Kung are represented by packets of incense ash.

Nan-tzu-kou's households are divided into three groups (*tsu*) that rotate responsibility for the *p'ing-an-hsi*. Every three years a *tsu* must provide a *lu-chu*, his assistant, and fourteen helpers. These officers collect funds, hire the opera troupe and priest, and make other arrangements. The *tsu* are said to correspond to Nan-tzu-kou's three administrative neighborhoods (*lin*), but it is unclear which came first, the administrative boundaries or the *tsu* domains.

The people of Nan-tzu-kou are careful and proud to point out what they consider to be a custom unique to their *p'ing-an-hsi*. In Nan-tzu-kou, any family blessed with a male child is expected to contribute a special cake (*hsin-ting-kao*) to each of the other 54 families in the hamlet. These

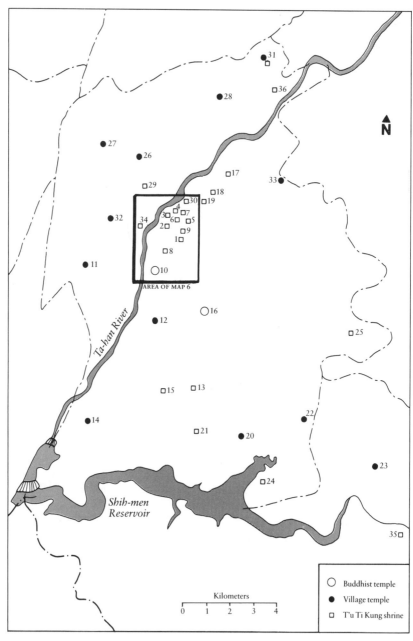

Map 5. Locations of the *p'ing-an-hsi* ceremonies, 1976. (For the schedules for 1976 and 1977, see Table 2.)

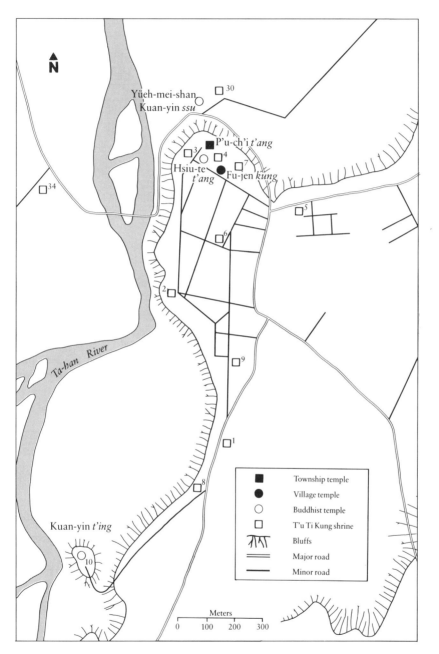

Map 6. Sites of temples and shrines in the town of Ta-ch'i

cakes are presented at a *p'ing-an-hsi* sometime before the boy is twelve (usually when he is between three and five). They are displayed prominently at the end of the long table of sacrifices nearest the deity altar. Although the presentation of *hsin-ting-kao* does not appear to be part of *p'ing-an-hsi* celebrations elsewhere in Ta-ch'i, identical cakes are distributed in some lineage corporations and deity cults. Nan-tzu-kou residents may have borrowed the custom to demonstrate the diffuse, enduring solidarity of their community, with implicit reference to such corporations.

Community solidarity is also evident in the fact that the entire hamlet is present during the Taoist dedication ceremonies and burning of the *chu-wen*. Only at the ceremonies' conclusion do households begin to remove their offerings (including any *hsin-ting-kao* coming to them) and return home.

Money is collected each year for the following year's celebration. Each household contributes an equal amount; assessments are not made according to wealth or male population, as in some other Ta-ch'i neighborhoods. In sum, by a variety of means, Nan-tzu-kou organizes its *p'ing-an-hsi* in such a fashion as to display a greater degree of communal solidarity than is evident in Ta-ch'i's urban neighborhoods.

Comparison of the deities "invited" to *p'ing-an-hsi* at the Chen-nan *kung* and in Nan-tzu-kou raises the question of the logic underlying such invitations. In urban *p'ing-an-hsi*, the most commonly invited images are Kuan Kung from the P'u-ch'i *t'ang*, K'ai Chang Sheng Wang from the Fu-jen *kung*, and Kuan Yin from the Kuan-yin *t'ing*. The same three images (or their duplicates) are also usually invited to *p'ing-an-hsi* in rural areas nearest the town, especially east of the river. West of the river, the image of K'ai Chang Sheng Wang from the Jen-ho *kung* in P'u-ting (considered older and, hence, of higher status than the Fu-jen *kung*'s K'ai Chang Sheng Wang) is also a frequent guest. In remote areas like Nan-tzu-kou, gods from the local village temple are usually invited, but gods from more distant temples in Ta-ch'i, even though directly ascendant in hierarchical logic, may be neglected. Neighboring T'u Ti Kung, represented either by images or by incense-ash packets, are almost always represented. To generalize rather broadly, it seems that at least the immediately ascendant village-cult deity must be invited. Gods from higher-level cults (e.g., the multivillage-level deity Kuan Kung) are usually invited only to neighborhoods in or near the town itself.

A third example of variation in *p'ing-an-hsi* organization comes from Ta-ch'i's Kuan-yin *t'ing* (Maps 5 and 6, No. 10). The temple is at once a Buddhist shrine, and hence outside the logic of territorial-cult hierarchy, and a center of a *p'ing-an-hsi* community. As Buddhist shrine, the Kuan-yin *t'ing* has no clearly defined parish. People from all over Ta-ch'i township—indeed, even pilgrims from an area including large parts of T'ao-yüan and Hsin-chu counties—worship at the temple. Nonetheless, it also serves as the focus for a territorial cult, although some Chinese would see a contradiction in this, given the temple's Buddhist orientation (Sangren 1983). Every year 300 to 400 households celebrate a *p'ing-an-hsi* at the Kuan-yin *t'ing*, making it the center of the largest *p'ing-an-hsi* domain in the township. The domain includes most of I-te *li* (an administratively defined village, really a part of urban Ta-ch'i). The *li* is divided into six territories that rotate responsibility for the festival. A *lu-chu*, assistant, and ten helpers are chosen from the area whose turn it is to sponsor the celebration. In addition to the normal duties associated with organizing the *pai-pai*, each of these officials must provide a special sacrifice in the form of a pagoda-shaped tower of cakes (*kao-t'a*). After bringing their sacrifices to the Kuan-yin *t'ing*, most households also place them before one of the several T'u Ti Kung shrines in the *p'ing-an-hsi* domain.

The population of the Kuan-yin *t'ing*'s *p'ing-an-hsi* domain is larger than that of some villages. One of the reasons the cult employs what is elsewhere a neighborhood ritual (*p'ing-an-hsi*) may be that much of the domain is populated by Hakkas. Although these Hakkas speak Hokkien, they are identified as different by Ta-ch'i's Chang-chou majority. I suspect that the use of Kuan Yin as a territorial-cult focus appeals to this ethnic minority because they can thereby deny ready incorporation into higher-level cults focused on deities identified with Chang-chou people. As a bodhisattva (a category of Buddhist divinity) generally thought of as female, Kuan Yin cannot be viewed as bureaucratically subordinate to such celestial officials as Kuan Kung or K'ai Chang Sheng Wang. But by the same token, because Kuan Yin is a bodhisattva, it would be inappropriate to offer her the slaughtered pigs that mark most village-level sacrifices. Thus the cult ritual form remains that of the neighborhood, even though its size warrants village-level status and its domain includes several T'u Ti Kung shrines.

CH'IU-KUEI

The *p'ing-an-hsi* is commonly (but not invariably) accompanied by a practice referred to as *ch'iu-kuei*. Literally, the term means to request or demand a turtle, the "turtle" being a cake made of sweet glutinous rice in the form of a turtle. Each year these cakes are brought to the village temple or T'u Ti Kung shrine (usually on the day preceding or following the *p'ing-an-hsi*), where they are displayed throughout the day. Each cake is the fulfillment of a promise made by its donor to replace a similar cake taken from the temple the previous year. However, whereas most sacrifices remain the property of their donors after the gods have enjoyed their spiritual "essences," the material aspect of these turtle cakes is transferred to the god. Anyone may request and take one of the cakes, provided he or she promises to reciprocate with a larger one the following year. The amount of increase ("interest") is divined with divination blocks. The temple keeps a careful record of these transactions between worshipers and gods, and a list of defaulters is posted at each year's festivities. Consequently, the number of defaulters is low.

The motive for requesting turtles is the belief that, by eating them, one gains the supernatural assistance of the god in one's business endeavors. I heard stories of several successful businessmen, long since moved to Taipei or T'ao-yüan, who conscientiously return each year to *ch'iu-kuei* at rural T'u Ti Kung shrines and village temples near their old homes.

A less frequent variant of this custom involves the requesting of oranges. Small sums of money may also be borrowed (and repaid the following year with interest, of course) in the belief that, when invested, such money is bound to reap a large return.

The *ch'iu-kuei* custom does not in itself constitute a neighborhood communal ritual, but its frequent close association with *p'ing-an-hsi* gives it a decidedly communal flavor. Cakes are donated and requested on behalf of individual households, but they are displayed together in front of the shrine rather than individually throughout the day, as in the case of ordinary, bimonthly sacrifices. Moreover, the fact that cakes are consumed not by their donors, but by neighbors, suggests that household welfare, mediated by the territorial-cult deity, is embedded in that of the community. The underlying ethic symbolized in this set of reciprocal exchanges mediated by the god seems to be consistent with Skinner's (1976) analysis of local-system mobility strategies in traditional China: one relies on the resources of one's native community with the hope of turning a profit in the world outside. This success, however, is not an end in itself; real value is generated only when debts are repaid with interest and the aggregate well-being of one's native place is increased.

An air of competitive display surrounds *ch'iu-kuei* festivities. Donors' names and the weights of the "turtles" are conspicuously posted on each. At a ceremony in Fan-tzu-liao (Map 5, No. 11), the donor of the largest turtle (actually a consortium of ten households) also provided funds for an opera.

How does one interpret the potlatch-like redistributive consequences of such customs, and the metaphors of profit-making investment, contract, and interest that accompany them? This question draws attention to what may be an important ritual expression of a fundamental distinction in Chinese thought between the ethics of social exchanges with insiders and outsiders. In brief, the *ch'iu-kuei* custom marks rather clearly the boundary between village or neighborhood community—where, in Sahlins's (1965) terms, "balanced reciprocity" is the primary value embodied in social relations—and the wider "external" world, where "negative reciprocity" or the attempt "to get the better" of outsiders is the objective of exchange.

In this regard, the connection between contracts negotiated with supernatural entities and fertility or increase in this Taiwanese custom is usefully contrasted with the structure of contracts between Colombian plantation workers and the devil. Michael Taussig (1980) argues that Colombian peasants believe it possible to strike a bargain with the devil and thereby increase their productivity and wages. The money earned as the result of such contracts, however, can only be spent on luxuries. "To invest this money to produce more money—that is, to use it as capital—is to invite ruin. If one buys or rents some land, the land will not produce. If one buys a piglet to fatten for market, the animal will sicken and die" (Taussig 1980: 94). Taussig argues that capitalism is viewed by South American peasants as the negation of reciprocity, which is the most important communal value of traditional culture. In the culture of peasant communities, fertility and increase depend on reciprocity. In contrast, the "fetishism" of commodities in capitalist culture radically separates and mystifies the connection between social relations and the locus of productive value. In the minds of South American peasants, still grounded in an ethic of reciprocity in their village cultures, capitalism amounts to the negation of reciprocity because it attributes value to things, not social relationships. A contract with the devil is thus viewed as an antisocial negation of reciprocity: "Rather than an exchange that reinforces and perpetuates a set of perennial reciprocal exchanges . . . the devil contract is the exchange that ends all exchange—the contract with money which absolves the social contract and the soul of man" (Taussig 1980: 118).

The *ch'iu-kuei* custom obviously puts a much more positive light on contracts with the supernatural. T'u Ti Kung is not the negation of communal relations but their embodiment, and the benefits provided by the contract are precisely the magical fertility of investment. Yet this investment must be reciprocally returned with interest to the community if the cycle of prosperity is to remain unbroken.

Taiwanese notions of the associations among value, fertility, and social relations might thus be seen to lie midway between those of Taussig's informants and modern capitalism. Capitalist notions of the productive power of money through investment do not seem to have the antisocial meanings for Taiwanese that they do for some South American peasants, but the domain in which this kind of fertility seems to apply is defined as external to community. Within the boundaries defined by the territorial cult, reciprocal values should come first.

These observations help to illuminate the "preadaptive" aspects of Chinese "ethnoeconomics" (Gates 1983). One of the transformations that seems to accompany the transition to industrial capitalism is the progressive narrowing of the circle within which Sahlins's "balanced reciprocity" reigns. In other words, some of the basic economic concepts that capitalist culture attributes to economic relations in general can be fully formed in noncapitalist societies, but they are assigned only a restricted relevance therein. Thus the case in Taiwan is less one in which different commodities are restricted to separate "spheres of exchange" (e.g., Bohannon 1955) than one in which different principles of economic integration (Polanyi 1957) pertain to different kinds of social relations.

In sum, very different values obtain between those defined as members of one's community and those defined as outsiders. However, the line that divides the two categories is not a rigid one. The nested hierarchical structure of territorial cults themselves is one manifestation of the contextual relativity of the contrast between insiders and outsiders. For example, neighbors may engage in buying and selling property and commodities with a view to maximizing their respective advantages, but they certainly do not do so in any transactions having to do with a communal ritual. Part III explores the structural logic of insider/outsider iconography in more detail. What I wish to suggest here is that the very significant contrast between the balanced reciprocity (one might even say, concern for the common social welfare) due insiders and the negative reciprocity (exploitation?) due outsiders is a pervasive characteristic of Chinese culture. Moreover, manipulating and defining the social divide at which this distinction ought to apply in particular contexts constitutes a very important political skill.

For example, much is made of Chinese concern with *kuan-hsi*, a term usually glossed as "connections" or "personal relations." Indeed, anyone who has dealt with Chinese bureaucracies can testify to the very different results obtained when one can claim even the most distant relationship with relevant officials. It is important to note, however, that the notion of relationship implied in *kuan-hsi* is that of common membership in a "community," however improbably defined, rather than that of an ego-focused network of relationships. When the alternative to common membership in a community is negative reciprocity, it is easy to understand Chinese talent and enthusiasm for institutions such as native-place associations (*t'ung-hsiang-hui*). By the same token, it is nearly impossible for Taiwanese businessmen to enter into contractual relations until some definition of common insider status has been constructed. Ta-ch'i natives who engage in businesses in Taipei, for example, conduct as much of their business as possible with other Ta-ch'i natives.*

Village Cults

TI-FANG SHEN

T'u Ti Kung's association with territory is quite clear in the deity's name, which means "Earth God" or "Place God." But when we move up the hierarchy of territorial cults to the village level, the question of what constitutes a territorial-cult deity becomes more complicated. Although it is true that Taiwanese often indicate the territorial nature of village- and multivillage-level gods by referring to them as "locality gods" (*ti-fang shen*), it is not always obvious which gods should be included in this category. The Place God, the Stove God, and City Gods (Ch'eng Huang Yeh) for Ch'ing administrative capitals down to county seats were considered posted bureaucrats in both official and local pantheons. Others, like K'ai Chang Sheng Wang and Kuan Kung, who were considered members of the Jade Emperor's court in the Ch'ing imperial cult, are treated in Ta-ch'i much as T'u Ti Kung and the City God—that is, as supernatural governors of their districts. In Taiwan, many of these "supernatural governors" are associated with particular ethnic groups and are believed to act as patrons of their constituencies in the celestial bureaucracy. K'ai Chang Sheng Wang, for example, is a patron of Taiwan's Chang-chou people, and he is the most popular village-level territorial-cult deity in Ta-ch'i's marketing community. Gods with clear ethnic connections are usually found in communities dominated by a single ethnic faction.†

Not all deity cults are territorially discrete, however. Many Buddhist temples, for example, do not serve as centers for territorially defined communal rituals. Other deities are worshiped individually, as "specialists" in handling specific kinds of problems, and these may also lack discretely defined domains of influence; among these gods, probably the

---

*One of the main activities of the Taipei branch of Ta-ch'i elementary school's alumni association is publishing a list of business addresses of members.

†But see Wang (1974) and Baity (1975) for cases in which the deities' ethnic associations have diminished as communities became more heterogeneous.

most popular are female deities like Ma Tsu, Kuan Yin, and the Eternal Mother (Sangren 1983). In short, not all gods are officials, and not all temples are centers of territorial cults.* Nonetheless, the structural fit between celestial bureaucracy and the hierarchy of local social identities does mean that most territorial cults focus on worship of bureaucratically conceived deities.

This fit is far from perfect, however. For example, the San-ts'eng village temple's main deity is Ma Tsu, and the communal rituals performed in her honor are essentially identical to those performed in honor of the male bureaucrats who reside in most of the other village temples in Ta-ch'i's marketing community. Ma Tsu was incorporated into the Jade Emperor's court and endowed with the title "Queen of Heaven" in official religion, but her gender makes her a somewhat anomalous supernatural governor of a village community, even though she is treated as such in San-ts'eng's communal rituals.

Even more anomalous is the celebration of *p'ing-an-hsi*, including meat sacrifices, at the Kuan-yin *t'ing* Buddhist temple. The elemental "kings" of heaven, earth, and water (San Kuan Ta Ti) are also popular territorial-cult deities, despite the fact that, as personified spirits of nature rather than deified historical personages, they diverge somewhat from the most bureaucratically rational model of administered cosmos. But as Arthur Wolf (1974a) has pointed out, even when territorial-cult deities are not mythically endowed with offices in the celestial bureaucracy, they tend to be treated as supernatural governors in territorial-cult rituals. In other contexts these same deities may show little resemblance to celestial bureaucrats.

Of the fourteen village-level temples listed in Table 1 (and shown on Map 7), six are devoted to K'ai Chang Sheng Wang, three to San Chieh Kung (another name for the three "kings"), and one each to Yüan Shuai, Wu Ku Hsien Ti ("god of the five grains"), Ch'ing Shui Tsu Shih (a patron of Ch'üan-chou people), Ma Tsu, and Kuan Yin (the Chinese transformation of the Indic Avalokiteśvara: Sangren 1983; Dudbridge 1978). Of these, K'ai Chang Sheng Wang is clearly viewed as a celestial official, but only the female deities Ma Tsu and Kuan Yin defy incorporation into an essentially bureaucratic model. Although I cannot marshal any convincing historical evidence, I suspect that in the long run there is a tendency for territorial cults to replace such irreconcilably nonbureaucratic (especially female) deities with bureaucratic ones (or, at least, for deities

---

*See Baity (1975) for a useful taxonomy of temples and cults. I do not adopt Baity's terminology here because the analysis of meaning and symbol that I develop in Part III suggests a context-dependent meaning for temples and deities that fits Baity's schema only roughly.

TABLE I
Village-Level Temples in Ta-ch'i's Ritual Sphere

Location	Name of temple	Main deity
Ta-ch'i	Fu-jen *kung*	K'ai Chang Sheng Wang
P'u-ting	Jen-ho *kung*	K'ai Chang Sheng Wang
Fan-tzu-liao	Jui-yüan *kung*	K'ai Chang Sheng Wang
Pai-chi	Fu-hsing *kung*	K'ai Chang Sheng Wang
Fu-hsing	Fu-hsing *kung*	K'ai Chang Sheng Wang
San-min	Tung-hsing *kung*	K'ai Chang Sheng Wang
San-ts'eng	Fu-an *kung*	Ma Tsu
Nei-chia	Jen-an *kung*	Yüan Shuai
Yüan-shu-lin	San-yüan *kung*	San Chieh Kung
Nan-hsing	Yung-ch'ang *kung*	Wu Ku Hsien Ti
Ch'i-chou	Fu-shan *yen*	Ch'ing Shui Tsu Shih
Yung-fu	Hsiang-yün *ssu*	Kuan Yin
Kung-kuan	Yung-an *kung*	San Chieh Kung
Chung-hsin	Fu-te *kung*	San Chieh Kung

N O T E : The Nan-ya *kung* at A-mu-p'ing was inundated with the completion of the Shih-men Dam. Its former parish is now served by the temples at Pai-chi, San-min, and Fu-hsing. Some of the people whose land was flooded were given land in Shu-lin Hsin-t'sun, Kuan-yin township, on the T'ao-yüan county coast. Some of the old Nan-ya images and incense burners were installed in a new Fu-hsing *kung* there.

that become foci for territorial cults to become incorporated into the bureaucratic idiom), unless there is some socially compelling reason not to do so.

Native informants sometimes distinguish territorial-cult temples from Buddhist ones by referring to the former as *miao* and the latter as *ssu*. But as in the case of focal deities, the names of temples do not provide a clear-cut or reliable guide to the social parameters of their cults. Note in Table 1 that most temple names end with *kung* ("palace"), the type of official residence appropriate to a celestial official. In practice, *kung* generally denotes a territorial-cult temple.

The final character in P'u-ch'i *t'ang*, Ta-ch'i's multivillage-level cult center, means "hall," or "meeting place." Halls for ancestor worship may also be termed *t'ang*. I was told that in the case of the P'u-ch'i *t'ang*, the term refers to the fact that the temple is privately owned. In fact, the god was originally the property of a wealthy merchant family. Later, a deity-cult association (*shen-ming-hui*) was organized, and the god's popularity increased to the point where the temple is now the center for multivillage-level ritual.

Although the term *ssu* denotes a Buddhist temple, the Hsiang-yün *ssu* in Yung-fu is essentially a territorial, village-level temple. Pigs are sacrificed there, and in most respects the temple resembles those in other vil-

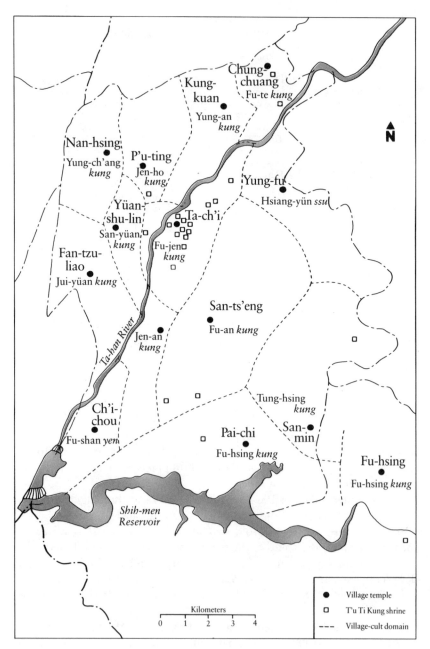

Map 7. Village temples in Ta-ch'i's ritual sphere

lages. The use of the word *ssu* in this case seems to be a remnant of the past, when Buddhist monks lived in the temple. Over a period of years, the temple has come to play a more important role in territorial ritual. At the same time, the worship of territorial gods (Ch'ing Shui Tsu Shih and K'ai Chang Sheng Wang) has increased in importance, while the worship of the temple's main deity, Kuan Yin, has declined.*

In addition to a village temple's main god, images of other gods are also worshiped. These are usually placed in a subordinate position at the main altar or at separate side or rear altars. Each temple has at least two side altars, one to either side of the main altar. Larger temples may have additional altars located in alcoves along the sides of the temple, on upper floors, or to the rear of the main altar. The deities most commonly placed on these additional altars are Kuan Yin, T'u Ti Kung, and Ma Tsu. Although in general all sacrifices to gods are thought to be received by the entire pantheon, the sacrifices offered on any particular day usually single out one deity for special attention. Thus, deities other than the main god in the temple may be subjects of separate sacrifices, which are usually less elaborate than those performed on the main deity's birthday.

PIG SACRIFICES

As in the case of the neighborhood cults, in the last analysis it is the form of communal ritual action rather than the personality of the deity worshiped that defines a village community. Aside from *chiao* held every 20 or more years, the most important communal rituals performed at village-level temples are (1) annual sacrifices made on the occasion of the main god's birthday, and (2) *p'u-tu* sacrifices on behalf of the spirits in purgatory, which are held during the seventh lunar month. These rituals, more costly and elaborate than *p'ing-an-hsi*, set the village temple apart from the T'u Ti Kung shrine. In particular, specially raised pigs are sacrificed on the village god's birthday; T'u Ti Kung is not generally so honored. Most of the village temples in Ta-ch'i have modeled the organization of these communal rituals on those held at the Fu-jen *kung*. Con-

---

*Worship at the Hsiang-yün *ssu* is complicated by Yung-fu village's ethnic heterogeneity. Yung-fu borders San-hsia township, a marketing community dominated by Ch'üan-chou people, and residents of the village hail from both Chang-chou and Ch'üan-chou. People of Ch'üan-chou background maintain ritual ties with San-hsia and Ching-mei, inviting images of Ch'ing Shui Tsu Shih and other deities from temples in these towns to festivals in Yung-fu. Until recently Yung-fu's Chang-chou people participated in the pig-sacrifice rotation at Ta-ch'i's Fu-jen *kung*, but now they bring pigs to the Hsiang-yun *ssu*. This "ungrammatical" use of a Buddhist deity like Kuan Yin has certain advantages as a territorial-cult focus for ethnically heterogeneous communities like Yung-fu, as we will see.

sequently, it is useful to examine ritual practice at the Fu-jen *kung* in some detail.

K'ai Chang Sheng Wang's birthday is celebrated on the eleventh day of the second lunar month at the Fu-jen *kung*. Although each god in the Chinese pantheon has a conventionally established birthday, a communal sacrifice may be scheduled at any time during the month in which its birthday falls (preferably earlier than the conventional date).

At some time early in the cult's history in Ta-ch'i, a system of rotating responsibility for the annual sacrifices to K'ai Chang Sheng Wang was established. The cult originally encompassed the entire marketing community, but as villages established independent cults, the Fu-jen *kung* devolved to a village-level cult for the town of Ta-ch'i. The population of Ta-ch'i's marketing community was divided into ten groups based on surname. An effort was made to divide the population into roughly equal groups by assigning a single surname to some positions in the rotation and several surnames to other groups. Thus the Lis are group 1, the Chiangs group 2, the Lins group 3, the Chiens group 4, the Huangs group 6, the Lus group 7, and the Ch'ens group 9. Groups 5 and 8 each encompass two surnames, the Changs and Liaos and the Wangs and Yus, respectively. Group 10 incorporates all other surnames.

Once every ten years, each group must take responsibility for the *pai-pai* held in K'ai Chang Sheng Wang's honor. Group leaders are responsible for collecting funds, hiring entertainers and religious specialists, and arranging sacrifices. In effect, some of the *lu-chu*'s charisma is shared by all the household heads in the group; each household is responsible for displaying a sacrificial pig before the temple on the morning of the eleventh day of the second lunar month. A formal competition is held among each group's household heads to see who can raise the largest pig for the sacrifice. Prizes and prestige accrue to the winners (see also Ahern 1981b).

The atmosphere of competitive generosity and conspicuous consumption that surrounds village-level *pai-pai* is reminiscent of the potlatches of North America's Northwest Coast. Three levels of status competition converge in pig sacrifices: first, each household head is concerned to demonstrate his generosity and community spirit by raising as large a pig as he can afford and by entertaining a large group of friends and relatives with a lavish banquet; second, each surname group strives to demonstrate its solidarity in competition with other groups; and third, the community as a whole expresses its pride relative to other communities by participating enthusiastically in the sacrifices and celebration.

Ta-ch'i townspeople freely admit that rural folk show greater enthusiasm for pig competitions. Some rural villages manage to muster many more pigs than the Fu-jen *kung* does. After all, say townspeople, it is much easier to raise a pig in the country than in town. Nonetheless, this superior performance by rural villagers in sacrificial displays is cause for some discomfort; a statement about prestige and hierarchical relations is intended and understood, and it is a statement that inverts what townspeople consider proper relations between town and hinterland.

Early on the morning of the *pai-pai*, each family arranges to have its specially raised pig (Ahern 1981b) ritually killed and prepared for presentation to the god. In Ta-ch'i, this sacrifice is usually performed by an experienced specialist after the pig (*chu-kung*) itself is worshiped. The prizewinners among the dozens of pigs brought before the temple are elaborately decorated, much like the floats in a Fourth of July parade in the United States. The largest pig is placed before the temple's main doors, directly opposite the deity altar; runners-up are put on either side. The hierarchical yin/yang order of the cosmos embodied in the ordering of deities on the temple altar is mirrored in the ordering of the pigs (representing their owners) directly opposite. In other words, cosmic order is conceptually recreated in an iconic model of local social structure.

After all the pigs are assembled, the formal ceremonies conducted by Taoist priests on behalf of the community can begin. Although these ceremonies are essential—indeed, they constitute the raison-d'être of the sacrifice—they are left to the Taoist specialists and attract little interest on the part of spectators. The ceremony is usually an abbreviated version of those performed at *chiao*, and involve a ritual purging of entropic yin influences and the restoration of yang order on behalf of the community.*

In practice, the complex meanings associated with the rituals performed by Taoist specialists are lost on most of the sponsors, who are, for the most part, satisfied that they have fulfilled their obligation to the local god by hiring Taoist specialists and by providing a sufficiently festive celebration. One aspect of the Taoist ritual is clear to all participants, however: the ritual burning of the official document (like a "petition" to an official or the emperor) that lists in detail all the contributors and requests peace and prosperity on their behalf (Schipper 1974).

After the dedication, the pigs are taken home and prepared for the evening's feast. Each of the households that sacrificed a pig invites neighbors and friends to a catered banquet. All who attend are obligated to make this feast a very festive occasion, and each host strives to outdo others in demonstrating his generosity. A popular man of means may require dozens of tables, each seating ten guests, to satisfy his social obligations.

---

*As Feuchtwang (1974b) points out, these rituals parallel at the community level the renewal of the household that characterizes many New Year's rituals.

80 The Ritual Construction of Social Space

A CONFUCIAN RITUAL

Although Taoist rituals are held at all of Ta-ch'i's village-level temples, on at least two occasions in the recent past a distinctly more Confucian type of ceremony was held at the Fu-jen *kung* (see also Thompson 1981). In 1976, experts in Confucian ceremony from Taipei were invited to take charge of the annual *pai-pai* in honor of K'ai Chang Sheng Wang. The ceremony they directed (termed *san-hsien-li*) is considerably more sober and dignified in tone than the more popular Taoist rituals. A similar ritual performed at the Confucian temple in Taipei is a major tourist attraction. The *san-hsien-li* is modeled on the rites of the official religion of imperial times (Feuchtwang 1974b). A professional master of ceremonies (*chu-chi-che*) leads representatives of the surname group responsible for the sacrifice and other community leaders (including the mayor) through a series of obeisances to the gods. As in Taoist ceremonies, a formal dedication (*chu-wen*) is read informing the celestial powers of the origin of the sacrifices and of the community's request that it be blessed with peace and prosperity during the following year.

The choice of Taoist or Confucian ritual is left to the surname group in charge of the sacrifice for that year. Not all groups choose the Confucian ritual, some preferring the more familiar and colorful (and probably less expensive) Taoist one. The second year I witnessed the ritual, the Confucian form was retained, but on a reduced scale. No outside experts were called in to conduct the ceremony, and the number of participants and the length of the ceremony were reduced. It was explained to me that perhaps, since the surname group was a small one, it could not raise enough money for a ceremony as elaborate as that of the preceding year.

I was quite interested to know how Ta-ch'i came to have a Confucian ceremony generally associated with official temples at higher-level centers. Two explanations were suggested by people in Ta-ch'i. First, Ta-ch'i is quite proud of its tradition as a center for Confucian learning, having produced several *sheng-yüan* (locally called *hsiu-ts'ai*) degree-holders and one of Taiwan's few *chü-jen* scholars during the late Ch'ing dynasty. The use of Confucian ceremony in the temple thus draws attention to this proud tradition of scholarship. It is also a means of authenticating Ta-ch'i's historical and cultural superiority over both the new urban centers in northern Taiwan that have eclipsed Ta-ch'i in economic importance and the village temples in Ta-ch'i's ritual sphere that have set up autonomous village-level cults. Second, Confucian ritual is more palatable to the central government. By sponsoring Confucian rituals in the context of what is otherwise a communal festival identical to the festivals conducted elsewhere, citizens of Ta-ch'i hope to avoid restrictive government action (see also Ahern 1981b; Jordan 1976).

It is tempting to speculate that the use of Confucian ritual in Ta-ch'i constitutes a rural variant of what Feuchtwang (1974a: 300) views as an emerging Republican transformation of imperial state religion. According to Feuchtwang, a synthesis of traditional local and official religious styles (termed *ju-tao-chiao*) has developed around several popular temples in Taipei. In any case, it seems clear that the use of Confucian ritual forms is somehow connected to the changing nature of relations between state and local religion in Taiwan. It also pertains to the aspirations of Ta-ch'i's leaders to reconcile their roles as community leaders with their desires to identify with China's great tradition and with Taiwan's emerging national elite culture.

P'U-TU

Most village temples hold a communal festival during the seventh lunar month (*chung-yüan*). This festival is traditionally defined as one of three important calendrical events (*shang-yüan*, *chung-yüan*, and *hsia-yüan*, associated with heaven, earth, and man). In Ta-ch'i, as in the town of Mountain Street studied by Feuchtwang (1974b), *shang-yüan* and *hsia-yüan* are, for the most part, domestic affairs, while *chung-yüan* is a communal celebration.

The seventh lunar month and *chung-yüan* are concerned primarily with the spirits of the underworld. It is believed that during the seventh month the gates of the yin underworld open and the spirits there roam freely in the yang world of the living. Hence, the most important communal rituals associated with *chung-yüan* are the ceremonies (*p'u-tu*) performed on behalf of these yin spirits.

The term *p'u-tu* means "universal salvation." The ceremony is inspired by the Buddhist goal of universal deliverance from the world of suffering and rebirth, but in Taiwan the emphasis is on freeing souls believed trapped in purgatory (e.g., deGroot 1885; Liu 1967; Saso 1972; Overmyer 1980). *P'u-tu* ceremonies are held on various occasions at Buddhist temples, and they form part of the ritual of any *chiao* dedication. *P'u-tu* ceremonies are also held at Ta-ch'i's central market, the night market, the Kuan-yin *t'ing*, the Hsiu-te *t'ang*, and the Feng-ling *ta-mu-kung* mass-grave in Wei-liao. However, it is the *p'u-tu* performed yearly at village-level temples that I describe here.

Informants agree that *p'u-tu* ceremonies are at once an act of mercy toward yin spirits (with the object of gaining their early release from purgatory) and an act of propitiation (because such spirits are potentially dangerous during the month they are allowed to roam the yang world, sacrificial "bribes" to prevent them from exercising any malevolent influence in the community are offered).

As in the case of pig sacrifices, the Fu-jen kung's p'u-tu ceremony is the standard by which other village temples measure their own. Each year a lu-chu is chosen on a rotating basis from one of the five li that constitute the Fu-jen kung's domain. In addition to the usual responsibilities of his office (e.g., collecting funds, hiring opera troupes and religious specialists, and making general arrangements), the lu-chu is expected to provide a long table of special treats for the lonely ghosts (ku-hun). The ceremonies and beliefs associated with p'u-tu ritual are symbolically complex; the following will only touch on its salient features (see Baity 1975 and Liu 1967 for further details).

I was told that in the past p'u-tu ceremonies at large, centrally located temples could last as long as seven days (see also Doolittle 1865, 2: 98). Before retrocession, chung-yüan ceremonies (including p'u-tu) at the Fu-jen kung are reported to have been more elaborate than today. On the evening of the ninth day of the seventh lunar month, there was a festive placing of "water lamps" (fang-shui-teng) in the river to invite wandering ghosts to the p'u-tu. On the following day, there was a ceremony "dedicating the lamp pole" (chien teng-kao)—another message inviting ghosts to come to the banquet. The taller the lamp pole erected, the greater the distance from which hungry ghosts would see it. Therefore, it was not considered wise to make the pole too high, lest too many ghosts arrive for the quantity of sacrifices the community could afford to offer. The p'u-tu ceremony itself was held on the eleventh day of the seventh lunar month.

The ceremonies of placing water lamps in the river and raising the lamp pole are no longer practiced at the annual p'u-tu at the Fu-jen kung, and the three days of festivities have been condensed to one, but I did observe these customs at a p'u-tu performed as part of a chiao. P'u-tu at smaller village-level temples are more modest. The only essential element is the offering of sacrifices to the "good brothers" (hao-hsiung-ti), the standard euphemism for ghosts.

One of the reasons for the attenuation of p'u-tu festivities is the disfavor with which they have been viewed by government authorities. Before the Japanese colonial administration ended the practice, p'u-tu offerings were given to the poor once the gods and then the ghosts had enjoyed their "essence." Apparently, the end of the ritual was marked by a mad scramble over the food. The Japanese government prohibited this custom, but a vestige persists in the current practice of allowing children to scramble for some of the sweets included in the offerings.

The Republican administration has further curtailed the festivities by insisting that they do not exceed a single day's duration. Moreover, in the past there was a loosely coordinated rotation of *p'u-tu* dates in which villages held their festivals in sequence rather than on the same day. In an effort to limit what the government views as the economic "waste" associated with religious festivals, it insists that all villages hold sacrifices on the same day.*

Multivillage Ritual

Multivillage-level ritual in Ta-ch'i centers on the P'u-ch'i *t'ang* and worship of its main deity, Kuan Kung. The temple's role as the most encompassing territorial cult in Ta-ch'i evolved gradually during the past 60 years. During this period it eclipsed the neighboring Fu-jen *kung*, formerly the center of township-wide pig sacrifices (see Map 6). Today the only major ritual uniting the entire marketing community is the annual celebration of Kuan Kung's birthday and the procession in his honor on the twenty-fourth day of the sixth lunar month.

The history of the P'u-ch'i *t'ang*'s rise in popularity and its present organization reveals much about social life in Ta-ch'i. Whereas the Fu-jen *kung*'s early leadership consisted mainly of Ta-ch'i's landed gentry (the name most intimately associated with the temple during the Ch'ing was that of a *chü-jen* degree-holder who lived in a rural part of the marketing community), from its inception the P'u-ch'i *t'ang* has been associated with Ta-ch'i's urban merchants. The eclipse of the former by the latter temple parallels a decline in the importance of landholding as the primary source of power and prestige in Ta-ch'i.

The temple's image of Kuan Kung was first worshiped at the domestic altar of one of Ta-ch'i's merchant households. According to a history of the temple published in conjunction with a recent *chiao*, the god's popularity spread quickly. A deity-cult corporation (*shen-ming-hui*) was founded in his name and provided a ferry service across the river before the bridge was built in 1925. By 1907, the corporation had acquired enough funds to build a temple.

Kuan Kung is popular among Chinese merchants everywhere. He is

---

*Ahern (1981b) observes that from the point of view of participants, religious festivals are hardly wasteful, since their raison-d'être is precisely to ensure peace and productivity for the community.

believed to embody the virtues of the businessman. He is also a popular patron for various types of sworn brotherhoods (chieh-pai-hui) and voluntary associations. Since the cult was established in Ta-ch'i, seventeen she-t'uan ("ritual societies") have been formed to honor Kuan Kung at the P'u-ch'i t'ang's annual procession. Because of the circumstances of their founding, the she-t'uan embody and perpetuate important events in Ta-ch'i's past. Thus it is worth discussing them at greater length.

The majority of the she-t'uan are headquartered in the town; a smaller number represent rural villages on the route of the annual procession. Urban she-t'uan are occupationally defined; wage laborers, carpenters, contractors, merchants, and wealthy entrepreneurs are each represented by a she-t'uan. The expressed purpose of the she-t'uan is to add to the festivity of the annual Kuan Kung procession. These ritual societies provide bands of musicians, floats, jugglers, lion and dragon dancers, and other entertainment to enliven the parade. They are also responsible for carrying the sedan chairs housing the temple-deity images. At the conclusion of the parade, teams representing each she-t'uan run barefoot across hot coals (kuo-huo) while carrying the images of the gods in sedan chairs. Evil influences are thus prevented from entering the temple with the returning images.

During the procession, she-t'uan members are conceived as the gods' soldiers; their role, much like that of local militia or braves (yung), is to help the gods protect the community from malevolent influences. Thus they share in diluted form some of the god's magical power (ling), a fact thought to account for the failure of the fire to burn their feet.

In the past, the larger she-t'uan sponsored three days of operas at several locations in Ta-ch'i. A spirit of competition prevailed among the various groups, each vying to outdo the spectacle provided by the others. Operas performed by the children of she-t'uan members (tzu-ti-hsi) were once popular, but are no longer performed in Ta-ch'i, and the general level of festivities is said to have declined in recent years.*

Despite the claim that the Kuan Kung procession is not what it once was, it remains a very festive occasion, certainly without rival in Ta-ch'i's marketing community. The various she-t'uan, temple gods, and hired entertainers parade through the town itself and through parts of San-ts'eng and Nei-chia villages and surrounding rural neighborhoods before re-

---

*Another abandoned practice is the custom of repaying Kuan Kung for granting a wish by marching in the parade as one of his servants. The Japanese administration abolished the related practice of carrying penitential canques and donning opera-style makeup on the grounds that the wearing of disguises would encourage thievery. Arthur Wolf informs me that these customs persisted in nearby San-hsia in 1958.

turning to the temple in the late afternoon. Peddlers selling everything from clothing to Chinese medicine set up temporary stands and compete with Ta-ch'i's own merchants for the business attracted by the spectacle.

On the twenty-third day of the sixth lunar month, the evening before the procession, there is a ceremony in the P'u-ch'i *t'ang* attended by the mayor, township and county representatives, the *lu-chu*, and temple officers. These dignitaries represent the community in thanking Kuan Kung for his protection and in entreating him to continue to ensure the community's peace and prosperity.

Each *she-t'uan* holds its own private feast, either after the procession on the twenty-fourth or on the following day. Each group also goes to the P'u-ch'i *t'ang*, where the god selects a *lu-chu* for the next year's festivities by divination (through the casting of "moon blocks"). The *lu-chu* and his assistants are given images of Kuan Kung to place on their domestic altars during the tenure of their offices.

She-t'uan functions are not confined to participation in the Kuan Kung procession. Club members assist at the funerals of fellow members, and the *she-t'uan* as a group sends a formal representative and contribution. More informally, membership in a *she-t'uan* is valued for the social relationships (*kuan-hsi*) it creates. Active men are often members of more than one *she-t'uan*.

In their occupationally based membership criteria, some of Ta-ch'i's *she-t'uan* resemble traditional Chinese guilds and merchant associations (Golas 1977; DeGlopper 1977; Morse 1909). Upon closer scrutiny, however, this similarity masks important differences. Golas (1977: 559) prefers "to reserve the term 'guild' for those associations where economic goals play a major role and to define a Ch'ing guild as 'an urban fraternal association whose members usually engaged in a single economic activity; often, but not necessarily, shared a common geographical origin that was not the city in which the guild was located; and joined together under the protection of one or more patron deities to promote their common economic and other interests.'" Ta-ch'i's *she-t'uan* lack the sojourner, compatriot character of guilds in such (mainly Ch'üan-chou) cities as Lu-kang and Meng-chia; moreover, they do not exert any perceptible economic power. Nonetheless, guilds might have developed from *she-t'uan* had Ta-ch'i continued to grow in a traditional instead of a modernizing environment.

If the *she-t'uan* are not guilds, what explains their attraction for their members? Part of the answer is apparent in the fact that informants were unanimous in asserting that the groups' raison-d'être is to enhance the spectacle surrounding Kuan Kung's procession. But to understand what they mean by this, it is necessary to know something more about the history of each *she-t'uan*. For example, pride of place at the end of the procession goes to the oldest *she-t'uan*—that representing the laborers—who carry the temple's main image of Kuan Kung. This *she-t'uan* (the T'ung-jen *she*) was originally formed some 50 years ago by workers on the T'ao-yüan Aqueduct. The work involved the use of dangerous explosives, and the association was formed to solicit Kuan Kung's protection. Because Ta-ch'i's work groups gained a reputation for skill and bravery, they were hired for similar large-scale engineering projects throughout Taiwan. Work on these projects paid relatively well, and the T'ung-jen *she* contributed generously to the P'u-ch'i *t'ang*. This history figures significantly in Ta-ch'i's sense of collective identity, not only for the members of the *she-t'uan*, but for the rest of the townspeople as well.

Each *she-t'uan* possesses a similar tradition, and symbols of these traditions are displayed prominently during the Kuan Kung procession. One of the most prominent of these symbols is a float-sized replica of a carpenter's chalk-line carried by the carpenter's *she-t'uan*. One of Ta-ch'i's craft specializations is the manufacture of traditional-style furniture, and this specialization is a source of pride to all.

Given these associations, the Kuan Kung procession constitutes a representation of meaningful social constituencies that combine to form an encompassing entity in the spectacle of the procession. At the same time, the procession is an iconic representation of significant aspects of the past, which are also important in the town's construction of itself as a unique social entity. As we will see, this simultaneous assertion of differentiation within encompassing identity parallels a similar process that occurs at a higher level in pilgrimage rituals.

Today the association between *she-t'uan* and occupation is weaker than in the past. Sons tend to join their fathers' *she-t'uan* without regard to their own occupations, and the enthusiasm of the younger generation for *she-t'uan* activities is waning. Moreover, the geographic and occupational mobility of modern Taiwanese society has undercut whatever tendencies the *she-t'uan* might have had toward assuming the characteristics of guilds. As a result, they remain essentially social clubs of limited scope. Apparently they persist in the absence of any significant economic function because of their symbolic utility in contributing to the reproduction of local identity.

Pilgrimage

Nearly 25 years ago, Milton Singer (1961: 295–96) argued that anthropologists specializing in complex agrarian civilizations ought to pay more attention to "the concrete media of song, dance, play, sculpture, painting, religious story, and rite that connect the rituals and beliefs of the villagers with those of the townsmen and urbanite, one region with another, and the educated with the uneducated." As the proliferating interest in popular culture not only among anthropologists but also among other social scientists attests, Singer's challenge has by no means been ignored.* Largely as a result of the works of Victor and Edith Turner, religious pilgrimage is the concrete medium of nonlocal cultural performance that has received the most attention to date.

In Taiwan pilgrimages play an important role in linking local territorial-cult communities to much larger ritual systems. This section describes the social organization of pilgrimages in Taiwan, focusing on their local-level organization in Ta-ch'i. Chapter 6 discusses the role of pilgrimages in the functional integration of regions, and Chapter 10 develops an interpretation of the culturally integrating consequences of pilgrimages.

MA TSU PILGRIMAGES IN TA-CH'I AND TAIWAN

Taiwan's most extensive pilgrimage network centers on the worship of the female deity Ma Tsu. Every spring millions of Taiwanese pilgrims visit the old port city Pei-kang.[†] The object of their visit is the Ch'iao-t'ien *kung* temple, widely acknowledged to be the highest-status center of the Ma Tsu cult in Taiwan. Ma Tsu, a female deity popular throughout southeastern China, is especially revered in Taiwan as a patron saint and protectress of seafarers.

Ma Tsu is believed to have been a young woman who lived on Mei-chou Island, Fukien Province, in the tenth century. She is credited with miraculous sea-rescues of her father and brother, and after her death, she became an important cult figure in southeast China.[‡] By the end of the nineteenth century, Fukienese merchants had carried the Ma Tsu cult to much of maritime and riverine China, and as far as coastal Korea and Japan.

During the seventeenth century, when immigrants from Chang-chou and Ch'üan-chou began to arrive in Taiwan in significant numbers, temples to Ma Tsu were among the first constructed in the newly estab-

---

*The notion of "popular culture" itself is far from unproblematic, implying as it does an entity separate from elite culture (for a summary of some of the issues, see Sangren 1984a).

†Suzuki (1978) estimated that 400,000–700,000 pilgrims visited Pei-kang in the early 1930s; Thompson (1973) put the number of pilgrims in the early 1970s at over 1,000,000 annually. Pei-kang temple officials with whom I spoke in 1984 claimed that more than 3,000,000 pilgrims visit every spring.

‡For more discussion of the history of the Ma Tsu cult, see Sangren (1983); Watson (1985); Thompson (1973); Li Hsien-chang (1979); Saso (1968).

lished west-coast ports. According to temple traditions, fire (*hsiang-huo*) from temple incense burners and deity images (*fen-shen*) consecrated at mainland cult centers (especially Mei-chou) were installed in the new temples. Periodically groups of pilgrims visited the older home temples to rejuvenate the spiritual power (*ling*) of their branch images by passing them through the smoke of the home temple's incense fire (Suzuki 1978; DeGlopper 1977; Schipper 1977: 652–53).

In part because of the obvious political obstacles to free travel between Taiwan and the Chinese mainland, Taiwan's pilgrimage network is but a truncated portion of the much more extensive system of the past (probably encompassing the entire maritime domain of Fukien merchant influence). Today Taiwan's oldest Ma Tsu temples, especially the Ch'iao-t'ien *kung*, have assumed cult-center status.

The great majority of pilgrims arrive in groups (*chin-hsiang-t'uan*, "incense offering societies") by chartered bus. Organized by local-temple and religious associations in rural villages, country towns, and urban neighborhoods, these pilgrimage groups continue the tradition of ritual rejuvenation by passing branch images through the smoke of Ch'iao-t'ien *kung*'s incense burner.

During the height of the pilgrimage season (beginning several weeks before Ma Tsu's "birthday" on the twenty-third day of the third lunar month), a carnival atmosphere prevails in Pei-kang. Groups from every part of the island converge on the streets leading to the temple, competing with each other in performances in honor of the goddess. As spectators fill the streets, each pilgrimage troupe proudly parades its image, ensconced in an elaborate sedan chair and accompanied by entranced shamans, colorful dance groups, bands of musicians, and the continuous cacophony of firecrackers, omnipresent signifiers of the sacred in Chinese ritual. Taiwanese society, much given to what may seem to Western eyes to be excessive ritual display,* produces nothing to rival the spectacle in Pei-kang.

In Ta-ch'i, Ma Tsu is frequently included among the handful of important deities represented on domestic altars, and her image is usually included in village-level territorial-cult temples (sometimes as a focal deity, but most often at a subsidiary side altar). The images from local territorial-cult temples are the objects of organized pilgrimages.

Pilgrimage groups (*chin-hsiang t'uan*) from the Ta-ch'i area are generally organized at the village territorial-cult level. Indeed, accounts by such early observers as Arthur Smith (1899: 102–4) and R. F. Johnston

---

*Chinese government administrators during the Ch'ing also noted the islanders' fondness for lavish religious spectacle (R. Myers 1972b: 440).

(1913: 149) indicate that pilgrimages throughout China were probably most commonly organized at the village level (see also Baker 1925; Pratt 1928; Day 1940).

A *lu-chu* is selected each year to preside over the festivities associated with the Ma Tsu pilgrimage and accompanying ritual at the local temple. Ma Tsu herself is said to select the *lu-chu* from among eligible male heads of households, making her choice known through the casting of lots. By implicit agreement, however, an attempt is made to ensure that the office rotates among all those who are eligible, and in particular that there is a fair alternation among the different surnames and neighborhoods in the villages. The *lu-chu* is often assisted in his organizational responsibilities by the administrative village head (*li-chang*).

In addition to the *lu-chu*'s usual responsibilities (collecting funds from participants, hiring opera troupes and Taoist priests for ceremonies in the local temple, and so forth), the *lu-chu* for the Ma Tsu *pai-pai* must be sure that a bus is chartered and hotel reservations secured. In more affluent, generally more urbanized areas, a permanent, property-owning association set up specifically for the worship of the deity (*shen-ming-hui*) may use the annual return from its holdings to finance a pilgrimage for its shareholders.*

Each of the fourteen village-level cults in Ta-ch'i's marketing community organizes a pilgrimage to the cult center in Pei-kang (often stopping also at Ma Tsu temples in Hsin-kang and Lu-kang) sometime between the lunar New Year and the twenty-third of the third lunar month, which is Ma Tsu's birthday. The pilgrimage is scheduled to end a day or two before the village temple's annual sacrifice to its main deity. There is an important economy involved in this scheduling, because both Ma Tsu and the village-cult deity can benefit from the same ritual performances and sacrifices.†

Buses are reserved well in advance of the pilgrimage, the demand during the peak pilgrimage season being quite high. Indeed, many excursion companies in Taiwan depend on pilgrimages for a large portion of their business. In Ta-ch'i's marketing community, the number of buses required for any village's pilgrimage in 1977 varied from two to seventeen, each bus accommodating about 50 pilgrims.

---

*For a discussion of the form and functions of deity associations, see Sun Sen-yen (1969). For an argument comparing *shen-ming-hui* with lineage corporations (*chi-ssu-kung-yeh*), see Sangren (1984b).

†Victor Turner (1974: 215) suggests that Mexican pilgrimage centers may try to coordinate visiting groups, since there is a clear tendency for groups from distant parishes to alternate with those from nearby ones. But the evidence from Ta-ch'i suggests that the scheduling of pilgrimages occurs within local marketing communities and results in a geographically random sequence of arrivals at pilgrimage centers.

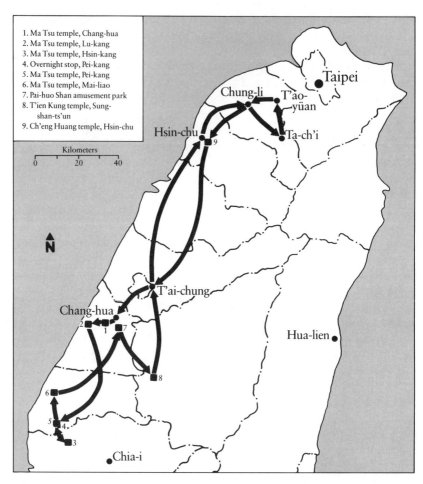

1. Ma Tsu temple, Chang-hua
2. Ma Tsu temple, Lu-kang
3. Ma Tsu temple, Hsin-kang
4. Overnight stop, Pei-kang
5. Ma Tsu temple, Pei-kang
6. Ma Tsu temple, Mai-liao
7. Pai-huo Shan amusement park
8. T'ien Kung temple, Sung-
     shan-ts'un
9. Ch'eng Huang temple, Hsin-chu

Map 8. Route of Ch'i-chou Ma Tsu pilgrimage, 1977

The routes taken on the Ma Tsu pilgrimage vary (see Map 8). All visit Pei-kang, the ultimate destination of the journey, and the nearby temple at Hsin-kang. Stops at Lu-kang and Chang-hua temples are desirable but not essential. Pilgrims generally spend a night in Pei-kang at hotels reserved in advance.

The only major religious ceremony of the trip is conducted at the Pei-kang temple. While the pilgrims offer incense to Ma Tsu, a Taoist priest reads a memorial listing the participants' names and the village they represent. The memorial is then burned and thereby communicated directly to the deity. Subsequently, the branch image of the deity is first passed over the temple's main censer, restoring its efficacy, and then passed hand-to-hand along a line of the pilgrims and onto the bus. A bundle of flags bearing the name of Pei-kang's Ma Tsu is also passed over the temple's censer.* When the pilgrims return home, these flags are distributed to participating households, who display them on their domestic altars. A box of burning charcoal lit from the censer may also be carried home by the pilgrims. This fire is sustained until the village temple's own festival a day or two later, when villagers use it to light charcoal or spirit money in fire-walking ceremonies (*kuo-huo*). It is also used to light incense sticks later placed in censers at domestic altars.

PILGRIMAGES AND TAIWANESE IDENTITY

The ritual community embodied in burning incense connects domestic altars directly to the Pei-kang Ma Tsu temple. Although pilgrimages are organized on a village-level territorial-cult basis, higher levels in the territorial-cult hierarchy are bypassed. Even more important, the ideology of Ma Tsu pilgrimage stresses an unmediated and direct relationship between Taiwan's households and the deity. Her imperial title Queen of Heaven (T'ien Hou) notwithstanding, Ma Tsu is no celestial bureaucrat, and she may be approached directly by even the most humble pilgrim.

But this concern for individuals does not deny Ma Tsu an important role in Taiwan's social structure. More than any other religious symbol, Ma Tsu has come to stand for a level of cultural identity based on the shared historical experience of Taiwan's settlers. Moreover, although this experience unites Taiwanese of diverse ethnic groups and localities (e.g., Hakkas, Chang-chou, and Ch'üan-chou people), it differentiates them from the more recent immigrants who followed Chiang K'ai-shek to Taiwan after the defeat of the Nationalists on the Chinese mainland.

The potential of Ma Tsu pilgrimages to constitute a Taiwanese identity that excludes mainlanders has been cause for considerable ambivalence in the government's view of the cult. Recently, however, high government officials have visited famous Ma Tsu temples with increasing frequency. In making gifts of honorific plaques to temples, today's officials carry on a long Chinese tradition; the plaques are often hung in the temples near those donated by former emperors and high imperial officials. By granting the Ma Tsu cult official recognition in this way, the state legitimates the cult's central myths. And by acquiescing in this recognition, the cult

---

*By custom, pilgrims to Hua-shan had their flags stamped at the Temple of the Golden Heavenly Palace (Geil 1926: 281).

implicitly acknowledges its place in a larger ritual hierarchy, in which the state transcends local identities.

This process can be seen more clearly in the government's relationship to two famous Ma Tsu temples near Tainan (at Ma-tsu-kung and T'u-ch'eng). Advocates for both temples claim that their temple is the legitimate heir of an official Ma Tsu temple destroyed by a flood. The original temple is said to have been established by Koxinga at the point where he first landed his army before he defeated the Dutch in the seventeenth century. Visits to these temples by government officials emphasize Koxinga's image as a Chinese patriot. Indeed, Koxinga is explicitly seen as a model for the present government's defense of Chinese culture against attacks on it by the government on the mainland (in Koxinga's case, the Manchus, and in the Nationalists' case, the Communists). In short, the government seems to be attempting, in classic fashion, to co-opt the popular Ma Tsu cult to its own ideological purposes. Although the details of the rivalry between the two temples are too complex to rehearse here, each side's concern to gain a propaganda advantage has probably aided the government's attempts to influence cult ideology.

In its efforts to construct a more inclusive state cult, the government has gone beyond attempting to influence the meanings of local cults and has borrowed some local techniques for its explicitly secular, nationalistic ritual. For example, Nationalist heroes like Sun Yat-sen and Chiang K'ai-shek are honored in what are essentially pilgrimages. Schools, government bureaus, and even private companies organize trips to the impressive shrines dedicated to Sun and Chiang. Moreover, Chiang's temporary mausoleum near Ta-ch'i, has become the object of a large-scale pilgrimage, as noted in Part I. The attempt, of course, is to make Chiang the focus of a cult that will encompass both mainlanders and Taiwanese. It remains to be seen how successful these attempts will be.

In any case, despite government efforts to inject a more nationalistic interpretation into the cult, for most participants the Ma Tsu pilgrimage remains primarily a matter of Taiwanese ethnic, not Chinese national, identity.

5

Ritual Action

This chapter outlines the spatial and temporal parameters of ritual organization in Ta-ch'i. It begins with a synchronic description of ritual during the period of my fieldwork and then discusses ritual intensification through time. These details provide a comparative base for the evaluation in Chapter 6 of functional connections through time among ritual, economic, and administrative patterns of interaction.

Territorial Cults and Vertical Integration

Territorial cults at any particular level in Ta-ch'i are conceptually discrete. Residence is the criterion defining where one should worship. For example, if a household moves to the territory of a new T'u Ti Kung, it then participates in the *p'ing-an-hsi* of its new neighborhood rather than that of its old one.

(DeGlopper 1974 describes neighborhood-ritual organization in Lu-kang as lacking clearly defined boundaries. But there each neighborhood worships a different god, whereas in Ta-ch'i most cults worship T'u Ti Kung. It may be that the people of Lu-kang are attracted to visit several different temples by the individual characteristics of the gods centered there. In any case, DeGlopper bases his conclusion on the fact that charms [*fu*] from several neighborhood temples are pasted together over the

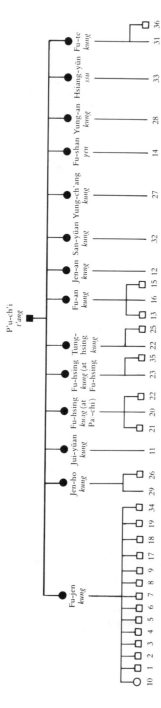

Fig. 2. The ritual structure of territorial cults in Ta-ch'i. The locations for the *p'ing-an-hsi* ceremonies of the 36 neighborhoods are shown on Map 5. Where squares are omitted at the neighborhood level, the *p'ing-an-hsi* is held at the village temple. The festival is held in sequential rotation among temples at the same level.

doorways of many Lu-kang households. Probably a more reliable indicator would be a mapping of households assessed for contributions to annual neighborhood rituals. The key issue here seems to be the context-relative meaning of religious symbols [discussed in Part III]. Although outsiders might worship at a territorial shrine, the shrine's deity would be addressed not in its function as celestial bureaucrat, but for some other power attributed to it. In other words, a distinction must be drawn between the group for which participation is an obligation and those people for whom it is a matter of personal religious devotion. The distribution of *fu* on Lu-kang's doorways may define the limits of the latter group rather than the former.)

Much the same can be said of village and township cults. For example, the P'u-ch'i *t'ang*'s domain includes all of Ta-ch'i township (with the exception of the mainlander neighborhood of Ch'iao-ai), plus the parts of Fu-hsing township inhabited by Han Chinese. Any resident of this domain should, in theory, contribute to the temple's annual celebration.*

As in the case of administrative systems (Skinner 1977a), the span of control in ritual systems (the number of lower-level units encompassed by a higher-level one) is greater in centrally located areas than in peripheral ones. For example, the Fu-jen *kung*'s village-level domain includes twelve neighborhood-level *p'ing-an-hsi*, whereas most rural village domains encompass only one or two (see Fig. 2).

Territorial cults are defined by the existence of communal sacrifices; a temple housing a celestial bureaucrat does not in itself constitute a territorial cult. As previously noted, there are many T'u Ti Kung shrines that do not host *p'ing-an-hsi*, and in the case of Wei-liao hamlet's Feng-ling *ta-mu-kung*, a territorially discrete ritual community coalesces around the worship not of a god, but of a mass-grave spirit.[†] But for the most part the logic of bureaucratic hierarchy is replicated in the hierarchy of territorial cults. Exceptions like T'u Ti Kung shrines without associated festivals and festivals without T'u Ti Kung shrines appear to be historically transitional, temporary anomalies that are likely to be transformed to conform to the logic of nested hierarchy.

Hierarchy implies vertical, superior-subordinate relations. Through the metaphor of imperial bureaucracy, hierarchy also incorporates the notion of encompassment or nestedness; higher levels encompass several

* To say that territorial cults are discrete is not to say that they cannot expand. The P'u-ch'i *t'ang*'s domain continues to expand with Han Chinese penetration of mountain areas formerly inhabited only by aborigines.

† Some territorial cults lack a temple altogether. Such a cult usually rotates an image of its deity among those household heads who serve as *lu-chu*. Members of several of Ta-ch'i's village-level cults told me that such organizations (*shen-ming-hui;* see Sangren 1984b) provide the base and funds for the later founding of a temple. See also Baity (1975).

units of the next lower level. In the terms of the bureaucratic metaphor, relations between lower-level solidarities (e.g., neighborhoods defined through worship of a Place God) are mediated vertically through their common subordination to a higher-level one (common participation in a village-level territorial cult with a focal deity of higher bureaucratic status). This formal structure implies a kind of equality among units at the same level, but in fact suggests nothing about their mutual relations; all formal relations among hierarchical equals are mediated through the higher structural levels. For example, when neighboring *p'ing-an-hsi* domains are included within the domain of the same village cult, a degree of ritual solidarity is expressed. But this expression is in terms of the vertical relations of nested hierarchy; that is, it is mediated through common participation in the next-higher communal ritual.

At first glance, the nested hierarchy of territorial cults seems to parallel an image of administrative hierarchy. However, there are some respects in which the bureaucratic metaphor fails to capture the pattern of local social relations. More specifically, relations among neighborhoods are not all mediated through the village, and relations among villagers are not all mediated through the market town. This lack of fit is expressed for the most part in informal aspects of ritual organization, rather than in formal cult iconography and ideology.

Rotation and Horizontal Integration

Horizontal relations among functional equivalents in a nested hierarchy are expressed in at least two ways. First, as already noted, same-level deities from neighboring territorial cults are sometimes invited to *pai-pai*. Similarly, friends and relatives from neighboring communities are invited to enjoy the entertainment associated with the *pai-pai* and to feast on the sacrifices (after the gods have consumed the essence of the offerings). Second, to facilitate the exchange of feasts and entertainment among these status equals (neighborhoods and their respective T'u Ti Kung), the dates of their respective *pai-pai* are scheduled so as to avoid conflict. In other words, coordinating schedules constitutes a form of higher-level community integration.

My best informants on the subject of *p'ing-an-hsi* scheduling were the middlemen or brokers (*pan-chang*) who arrange the hiring of opera troupes. Ta-ch'i's brokers help *lu-chu* in many neighborhoods to find and hire opera troupes.* Informants agree that operas should be scheduled on

*In 1977, an opera troupe typically charged about NT$ 7,000 (about U.S.$ 200) for a one-day performance. The broker received a 10 percent commission. Brokers solicit busi-

TABLE 2
P'ing-an-hsi Schedules, 1976–77
(by numbered locations shown on Map 5)

Lunar date	Observed in 1976	Brokers' projected schedules for 1977			
		Troupe A	Troupe B	Troupe C	Troupe D
8/9	23				
8/10	23, 14	11			
8/11	13	12		14	8
8/12	2, 12	12		15	1
8/13	1, 2, 17, 18	1		5	1
8/14	3, 4, 19, 26 28, 29			5	
8/15	5, 16		22	16	2
8/16	6, 7, 10		22		6
8/17	8		22		
8/18	9, 22	23	19		9
8/19	22	23			
8/20	24	25			
8/21	20				
8/22	21				

different dates in neighboring parishes. To schedule operas on the same day in adjacent neighborhoods would deprive people of the opportunity to enjoy both. Even more important, opportunities for the reciprocal exchange of feast invitations would be lost, and third parties would have to choose among conflicting obligations. Still, people feel that the *p'ing-an-hsi* ought to be held as near as possible to the fifteenth day of the eighth lunar month (T'u Ti Kung's official birthday). Consequently, in a township with as many *p'ing-an-hsi* domains as Ta-ch'i, some scheduling conflicts are unavoidable, although they rarely occur between adjacent neighborhoods.

This tendency to coordinate the *p'ing-an-hsi* may result as much from the availability of opera troupes as from the desire to avoid scheduling conflicts. In 1976, I observed 23 of the 36 *p'ing-an-hsi* held in Ta-ch'i township.* Of these 23, all but two or three were performed by one of four opera troupes (see Table 2). The limited supply of opera troupes

---

ness by approaching the new *lu-chu* and offering to arrange an opera for the following year. Some *lu-chu* prefer to save money by hiring a troupe themselves, but most are glad to let the broker arrange things. Although the brokers are natives of the Ta-ch'i area, most of the opera entertainers are Hakkas from neighboring Chung-li township. (The operas are, nonetheless, performed in Hokkien, not Hakka dialect. The opera profession in northern Taiwan has become a local specialty of Chung-li.) The broker and the *lu-chu* negotiate a fee and time for the performance. The standard fee may be doubled if the performance is scheduled on T'u Ti Kung's official birthday, when demand for operas is highest.

*There may have been a few *p'ing-an-hsi* that I overlooked altogether, but the total probably did not exceed 40.

TABLE 3
Village Ritual Schedules
(Lunar dates)

| | 1976 | | Hungry-ghosts festival (pre-1949 dates) |
| | Pig sacrifice | Ma Tsu worship | |
Temple			
Fu-jen *kung*	2/11	2/10[a]	7/11
Jen-ho *kung*	1/14	1/14[a]	7/8
Jui-yüan *kung*	1/13	1/13[a]	7/14
Fu-hsing *kung* (at Pai-chi)	2/5	2/3, 2/4[a]	?
Fu-hsing *kung* (at Fu-hsing)	2/8	2/9	7/15
Tung-hsing *kung*	2/15	2/15	?
Fu-an *kung*	3/23	2/8, 3/23[a]	?
Jen-an *kung*	3/2	3/1[a]	7/13
San-yüan *kung*	1/15	1/15[a]	?
Yung-ch'ang *kung*	1/16	1/15	7/13
Fu-shan *yen*	1/16	1/5[a]	?
Hsiang-yün *ssu*	2/11	1/9	?
Yung-an *kung*	1/14	1/14	?
Fu-te *kung*	1/8	?	?

[a] Temple was visited by three Ma Tsu images.

would thus prevent scheduling of all *p'ing-an-hsi* on the same date, even if people desired to do so. Much the same is true of Taoist priests, who are also essential for a successful *p'ing-an-hsi*. Nonetheless, I am convinced that the most important factor accounting for the rotating pattern is, as informants claim, the desire to exchange with neighbors.

The term applied to this rather loose temporal coordination—*lun-liu,* to "take turns in rotation"—is also applied to rotating responsibility among surname groups and neighborhoods in hosting *pai-pai,* and to the selection of *lu-chu.* Moreover, a similar rotating schedule instituted for similar reasons once organized village-level *p'u-tu* sacrifices in Ta-ch'i's marketing community.* Since retrocession, however, as a means of discouraging what it views as economically wasteful religious practices, the government has required that all *p'u-tu* be held on the fifteenth day of the seventh lunar month. Despite this restriction, some village temples have managed to obtain special dispensations, and some indication of the former structure of rotation persists (see Table 3, col. 3).

The horizontally integrating possibilities of rotation are exploited

---

*A similarly coordinated schedule linked settlements in the marketing community of Mountain Street (Feuchtwang 1974b: 113). However, in Mountain Street *p'u-tu* were held at T'u Ti Kung temples, apparently the foci of communal ritual activity below the level of the market-town temple.

more effectively in the series of village-level festivals honoring Ma Tsu. In contrast to the village-level pig sacrifices, which highlight the internal solidarity of the village and its differentiation from the outside world, Ma Tsu worship introduces a countervailing assertion of the village's integration into wider social and cultural communities.

This horizontal dimension of integration is evident in cult ideology. In contrast to the ideology of territorial cults, the relationship between devotee and deity is not mediated through a hierarchy of lesser deified officials. Elsewhere (Sangren 1983) I have argued that female deities are particularly appropriate symbols for this kind of horizontal integration, and indeed, many important pilgrimage cults in China center on the worship of female deities. But in addition to the relative absence of hierarchy in the cult's ideology, a more concrete manifestation of horizontal integration is embodied in its local temporal organization.

Ma Tsu is worshiped at all of Ta-ch'i's village-level temples, either as a main god (in San-ts'eng), or at a side altar, or as an invited guest. As Table 3 (columns 1 and 2) indicates, communal worship of Ma Tsu is generally scheduled on the same day, the day before, or the day after the festival in honor of the village-temple's main god. In most cases, the images worshiped include one or more borrowed from "home" temples that pilgrims have visited in the days immediately preceding the village *pai-pai.* Three Ma Tsu images borrowed from Pei-kang, Hsin-kang, and Chang-hua are brought back by pilgrims from Ch'i-chou village's Fu-shan *yen* every year on the fifth day of the first lunar month. Ch'i-chou celebrates its pig sacrifices for Ch'ing Shui Tsu Shih, the village-temple's main god, on the sixth. After the Ch'i-chou *pai-pai,* the images are placed in Ta-ch'i's Fu-jen *kung.* From the Fu-jen *kung,* the images are lent to seven additional village temples, participating in the annual festivals at each of them. After San-ts'eng village's *pai-pai* at the Fu-an *kung* on the twenty-third of the third lunar month—the last of the nine villages included in the rotation—the images are returned to their temples in the south. While visiting each village, the images are accompanied by the village-temple's gods on a tour of the temple's domain (*yu-ching*).

Practical considerations play an important role in the organization and coordination of Ma Tsu and territorial-cult god worship. At the Fu-jen *kung,* for example, a sacrifice and procession in honor of Ma Tsu is held on the day preceding the pig sacrifices for K'ai Chang Sheng Wang. Worshiping the deities on adjacent days facilitates arrangements for operas, ritual specialists, and government permission. On the day of the festival, the tenth of the second lunar month, the Ma Tsu images, accompanied by the temple gods, are carried in procession through the five *li* that make up the temple's domain.

Before the procession, which begins about nine in the morning, many households not scheduled to sacrifice pigs bring less elaborate offerings to the temple. Others who live along the procession route set up offerings on tables in front of their homes. The deity images are carried in sedan chairs. First is the temple's T'u Ti Kung, followed by K'ai Chang Sheng Wang, the temple's own Ma Tsu image, and finally, the three visiting Ma Tsu images. Before reentering the temple, the images must be carried through a fire of spirit money to ensure that no evil influences accompany them into the temple.

Different *lu-chu* preside over the Ma Tsu and K'ai Chang Sheng Wang festivities. Nonetheless, the scheduling of the two celebrations on adjacent days creates a close association between them in the minds of most people. What seems most significant in the juxtaposition is that a balance between the particularizing emphasis of the village-level territorial cult and the intergrating emphasis of Ma Tsu worship is thereby made explicit.

In sum, both at the level of pan-island pilgrimages and at the level of the cycle of village festivals within a single marketing community, the organization of Ma Tsu worship provides horizontal linkages in the otherwise vertically conceived structure of Taiwan's territorial cults. In motivating Ta-ch'i's villagers to visit distant cult centers, Ma Tsu pilgrimages tie local communities into a wider social network, and within Ta-ch'i's marketing community, Ma Tsu worship constitutes a ritual transcendence of bounded communities. In sharing the three images of Ma Tsu borrowed from distant cult centers, Ta-ch'i's participating village cults ritually assert their common membership in a community that encompasses all of them.

Thus the cycle of Ma Tsu festivals replicates the ritual community defined by Ta-ch'i's P'u-ch'i *tang*. Conceptually, however, the P'u-ch'i *tang*, like other territorial-cult temples, delineates an undifferentiated territory. The celestial bureaucrat's (in this case, Kuan Kung's) efficacy is directed toward protecting the community from harmful outside forces; internal differentiation must be expressed through lower-ranking celestial "officials." At each hierarchical level, relationship to outsiders is expressed in essentially insider/outsider terms. In contrast, the common identity expressed in the cycle of Ma Tsu rotation is concerned less with delineating the boundaries of communities than with connecting them.

This conceptual emphasis is manifest in some of the effects of the institution. For example, informants agreed that one of the advantages of the system of Ma Tsu image rotation is that village festivals must then be coordinated temporally. Since each village must await its turn in the rotation, it is possible for people to enjoy festivities in all of them. This scheduling thus facilitates reciprocity in feasting and other forms of entertainment. More practically, the loosely coordinated schedules mean that villages do not compete with each other for the services of opera troupes and religious specialists. Of course, although the Ma Tsu rotation provides the structure, these same benefits apply to the associated festivals for the village cults' main gods. Although not all of Ta-ch'i's villages participate in the rotation of the three Ma Tsu images, all schedule their pig sacrifices and Ma Tsu worship between the lunar New Year and the climax of Ma Tsu worship at the pilgrimage centers at the end of the third lunar month.

In sum, sequential rotation seems to serve very nicely to express egalitarian and reciprocal values in otherwise hierarchically organized Chinese social institutions. In addition to coordinating events among same-level territorial cults, rotation distributes authority in an essentially egalitarian fashion among household heads who serve as *lu-chu*. Even more generally, rotation constitutes an ingenious solution to the problem of assigning administrative responsibility among status equals. The technique is common in assigning rotating chairmanships in lineage corporations, limited partnerships, and many other forms of voluntary associations. Even at the level of domestic economy, it is common to find brothers' wives rotating responsibility for cooking for extended families, and brothers themselves taking turns representing their household on the boards of various corporations in which they hold shares.

If I am correct regarding the potential role of temporal structure in crosscutting hierarchical lines of organization, an important implication is that Chinese culture may be less "authoritarian" than sometimes supposed. Even where formal religious iconography seems to reinforce authoritarian hierarchies, the existence of crosscutting structures of interaction should not be overlooked.

Intensification of Ritual Structures

Part I summarized what might be termed the process of economic intensification.* This section outlines what in Ta-ch'i has been a concomitant process of ritual intensification. Despite obvious parallels in economic and ritual intensification processes, there is an important difference. Economic interaction, as defined in Skinner's (1964–65) arguments, emerges out of the sum of individual (or household) maximizing decisions. No one sets out to organize a standard marketing system; it grows naturally from the rational decisions of peasants and merchants to maxi-

---

*Skinner's (1964–65) seminal articles on marketing provide a formal model of the intensification process. See also Crissman's (1976) case study.

mize self-evident material values. Ritually defined communities, in contrast, are more formally institutionalized. Participants are more aware of the dimensions of ritual communities than they are of patterns of economic exchange networks.

It would be misleading to overstate this difference, however. Ritual organization does grow historically in ways unanticipated by participants, and markets can be consciously manipulated by local factions and government. But the very activity of ritual that periodically brings the community together as a group endows it with more concreteness in actors' experiences than the less-defined group that, for example, converges at a local marketplace. The following review of the pattern of ritual intensification in Ta-ch'i should give these generalizations more substance.

According to elderly informants who pioneered some of Ta-ch'i's remoter districts, soon after such areas are first settled, the pioneers—or a geomancer (ti-li-shih) hired by them—search for a good location for the inevitable T'u Ti Kung shrine. However, even after such a shrine is built, an isolated cluster of settlers may lack sufficient resources to hold its own p'ing-an-hsi. A threshold of between 30 and 40 household seems to be the smallest group sufficient to sustain a neighborhood cult. At the other end of the spectrum, the largest neighborhood cults encompass between 200 and 300 households. Consequently, in sparsely populated locales it is common to find several T'u Ti Kung shrines in the domain of a single p'ing-an-hsi. In such cases, the p'ing-an-hsi is held either at one of the T'u Ti Kung shrines or at the village temple. If it is held at one of the neighborhood's T'u Ti Kung shrines, all of the neighborhood's residents are likely to contribute to the shrine's improvement.

Thus the construction of T'u Ti Kung shrines and the subsequent institution of communal sacrifices follow closely the settlement of new land. From the very outset, Chinese settlers incorporate land into the nested hierarchy of the cosmos. That which is unincorporated is not only "undeveloped"; it is not part of the domain of heaven (t'ien-hsia). And being outside the domain of celestial hierarchy, foreigners and aborigines, like the unordered masses of ghosts in hell, are termed kuei.

A similar intensification process is apparent in the history of differentiation and upgrading of what were once essentially neighborhood-level cults to village-level ones. With time, some neighborhood shrines come to rival village temples in architectural elaboration, and if population and prosperity increase sufficiently, a higher-status deity may well be installed, so that the former T'u Ti Kung shrine becomes a village temple. In at least two cases in Ta-ch'i (the village temples in Fu-hsing and Chung-chuang), this seems to have happened. In the meantime, other T'u Ti Kung shrines may become the foci for new *p'ing-an-hsi* rituals.

The institution of pig sacrifices at village temples is intensification of another sort—namely, conspicuous consumption. Elderly villagers in Ta-ch'i's marketing area remember when pigs were carried from distant rural villages all the way to the Fu-jen *kung* on the eleventh day of the second lunar month. Some 45 years ago, larger village-level temples (including those at Nei-chia, San-ts'eng, and Nan-hsing) began to break away. The temple in Kung-kuan (Map 7) was the most recent to initiate independent pig sacrifices, in about 1972. This intensification of village-level ritual in Ta-ch'i is related to population growth (some 100 percent between 1955 and 1975) and prosperity. Villages can now support the kind of display that would formerly have been possible only in the market town. Villagers themselves say that they resented the arrogance of the townsmen who controlled the festivities at the Fu-jen *kung*. Besides, since villages have temples, why bother hauling pigs all the way to Ta-ch'i? For whatever reasons, the cycle now appears complete; today all village-level temples conduct their own pig sacrifices.

I was able to discover little reliable information regarding the history of pig sacrifices in Taiwan. According to Ta-ch'i informants, 50 or 60 years ago most households offered only chickens as sacrifices, but with increasing prosperity, people could afford pigs. The Japanese government may have set things going by encouraging pig-raising contests. In any case, there has been an escalation in the displays of conspicuous consumption associated with village-level *pai-pai* during the past 40 or 50 years. This escalation is consistent with what Skinner (1964–65) sees as a characteristic concomitant of economic intensification—to wit, a diminution of the communal importance of the standard marketing community and a (partly compensatory) increase in the salience of the village as a unit of social identity.

This shift in social focus from marketing community to village would also explain the villagers outperforming townsmen in the size and quantity of sacrifices. An additional contributing factor in Ta-ch'i's case has been the changing basis of the township's economy. Today, Ta-ch'i's wealthier families are more involved in business ventures outside the marketing community than during the Japanese colonial era. The elite of the town are increasingly a class of entrepreneurs rather than landlords.* This change is reflected in the eclipse of Ta-ch'i's Fu-jen *kung* by the P'u-ch'i *t'ang*, a temple whose main god, Kuan Kung, is traditionally associated with merchant associations. As a result, the Fu-jen *kung*, once the ritual focus

---

*Wang Shih-ch'ing (1974) notes a similar change in the character of elites in Shu-lin.

of the entire marketing community, has devolved to a status hierarchically equivalent to that of other village cults. The ritual preeminence of the town over its hinterland, however, is preserved in the concomitant rise in the importance of the P'u-ch'i *t'ang*.

The process by which cults are upgraded in the historical growth of communities sometimes results in what might be termed a convergence of levels—as, for example, when the domain of a village cult is congruent with that of a *p'ing-an-hsi*. Cases where village- and neighborhood-cult domains are coextensive represent a particular phase in this process, in which the three-tiered hierarchy of territorial cults in Ta-ch'i collapses to two. But the potential for intensification and expansion to three remains clear in the maintenance of a distinction between the neighborhood-level *p'ing-an-hsi* and the village-level *pai-pai,* even though both may be held on the same site and include the same participants. All that is necessary to make the three-tiered structure explicit is that a new *p'ing-an-hsi* be initiated within the village-cult domain.

For example, formerly the only *p'ing-an-hsi* held in the domain of the Fu-hsing village temple was conducted at the temple itself. However, in 1974 or thereabouts the people of Lo-fu hamlet enlarged their T'u Ti Kung shrine and began to celebrate a *p'ing-an-hsi* of their own instead of participating in the one held at the village temple. Nonetheless, they continue to participate wholeheartedly in the village temple's annual *pai-pai* for its main god, K'ai Chang Sheng Wang. Thus, in ritually affirming independence at the neighborhood level, Lo-fu's inhabitants do not deny solidarity with Fu-hsing at the village level.

In sum, the process of ritual intensification in Ta-ch'i has involved a progressive "filling in" of the ritual landscape. The shape of this filling in is preordained by the hierarchical structure of territorial-cult ideology. Broadly speaking, the process resembles market-system intensification, and this resemblance in turn raises the question of the nature of the relationship between the two. It is to such functional/historical questions that we now turn.

6

Local Ritual, Economic, and Administrative Systems

Territorial cults divide the world into much smaller units than did imperial administration. In Ta–ch'i, neighborhood T'u Ti Kung shrines can serve as centers for communal rituals for as few as 30 households, and several nested levels of ritual community organization generally intervene between a neighborhood cult and the county-level City God temple (the lowest level recognized in rites of the state cult; Feuchtwang 1977).

The absence of administrative apparatus below the county level has generally been viewed as permitting or even requiring local, somehow spontaneous forms of social organization to fill the breach. Certainly in Ta–ch'i's case, territorial cults carry nested territorial hierarchy down to the level of relevant local experience. Territorial-cult ideology during the Ch'ing dynasty was both a metonymic extension of similarly structured administrative hierarchy and a metaphoric expression of the nested hierarchical structure of the cosmos.

What exactly is the nature of the "natural" systems that structure local social life? Are they to be characterized primarily in economic, ritual, or political terms? Skinner gives clear precedence to economy, but I have argued against straightforward determinisms in the historical interactions among patterns of economic, ritual, and administrative organization. Sorting out the dimensions of interaction among ritual, economy, and administration in Ta–ch'i's historical development raises a number of specific questions. For example, before the completion of the north–south railroad, which bypassed Ta–ch'i and precipitated the town's subsequent economic stagnation, Ta-ch'i clearly stood at the apex of a marketing system that included all of its present administrative district. In the past 50 years, rapid development in Chung-li and T'ao-yüan has eclipsed that in Ta-ch'i. What effects have these changes had on ritual relations within and among Ta-ch'i's constituent neighborhood and village communities? How have administrative boundaries reinforced or diminished patterns of economic and ritual interaction?

Skinner (1964–65, 1977c) makes a strong case for preserving a distinction between the hierarchy of economic central places and the hierarchy of administrative capitals, and it is in the same spirit that I approach these questions, preserving clear distinctions among administrative, ritual, and economic patterns of local social interaction. That these distinctions have clear empirical correspondents should become clear in the subsequent discussion.

Administrative Districts, Marketing Systems, and Territorial Cults

It is at the township level that ritual, administrative, and marketing system boundaries correspond most closely. Ta-ch'i township, Ta-ch'i's marketing system, and the conceptual domain of Kuan Kung, although not perfectly isomorphic, include approximately the same territory (see Map 9).

The convergence between administrative district and standard marketing community emerged after numerous short-lived reshufflings of district boundaries at all levels during the early years of Japanese administration, and reshufflings since retrocession have retained the near identity of township and marketing community in Ta-ch'i. Under the late Ch'ing system, the town of Ta-ch'i was lumped with Ying-ko and San-hsia in Hai-shan pao, even though there was little social intercourse between Ta-ch'i's Chang-chou inhabitants and the Ch'üan-chou people of the latter two towns. Moreover, villages west of the Ta-han River that were economically and ritually tied to Ta-ch'i were administratively assigned to T'ao-chien pao. Thus Japanese-era reorganization of administrative district boundaries resulted in a much closer correspondence between local, "natural" systems (the standard marketing community) and administrative units. The convergence between marketing-community and administrative boundaries is striking not only in Ta-ch'i, but in most neighboring townships as well (Knapp 1971; 1976).

Skinner's argument for the social and cultural importance of the standard marketing community in China is well supported in Ta-ch'i (see also

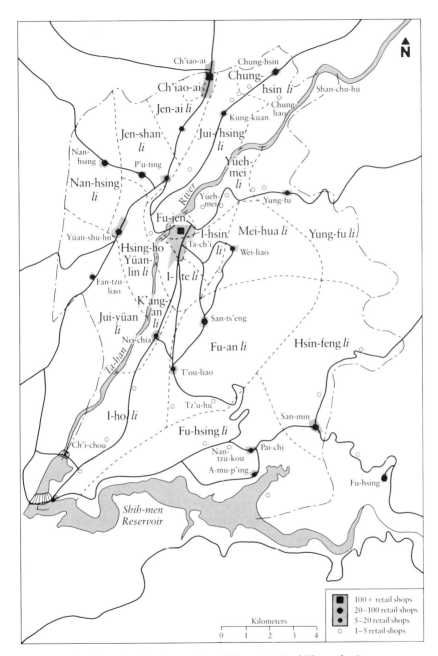

Map 9. Administrative districts and retail shops in Ta-ch'i's marketing area, 1977

Knapp 1971). However, as I have repeatedly noted, the causal priority of economic factors is less than clear. In Ta-ch'i's case, the parameters of the standard marketing community seem to have emerged as much from the historical pattern of patent-initiated settlement and subsequent competition among rival ethnic factions as from economic strategizing per se. The granting of government patents to develop large tracts of land resulted in the territorial clustering of ethnic groups on the island. A landlord generally recruited tenants from his own ethnic group. Once settlement was initiated, it tended to radiate outward from a core area. Knapp (1971; 1976) shows that these former patents correspond closely to present-day township districts and marketing communities.

Feuding among Taiwan's ethnic factions over land and water rights from about 1782 through 1862 (Lamley 1981: 304) increased the tendency of ethnic groups to sort themselves out spatially for purposes of self-defense. The famous Lins of Pan-ch'iao, for example, moved their residence to Ta-ch'i during this period, finding a safer haven there among Chang-chou compatriots (Speidel & Wang 1974).

These historical circumstances resulted in a close correspondence between ethnic group, town, and marketing communities that defies the assignment of clear-cut causal priorities. Much the same is true of the historical convergence of ritual and economic patterns of interaction; again, the prominence of ethnic competition in northern Taiwan's settlement played an important role. Many multivillage-level territorial-cult deities achieved popularity for the aid they rendered in fights with rival factions. As I argue at length in Part III, this symbolic differentiation from outsiders plays an important role in the social construction of the magical power of these deities. The historical and mythical events that authenticate this power are the miracles these gods are said to have performed in defeating outsiders. Hence the convergence between standard marketing community and ritual domain in Ta-ch'i, and in many other townships in northern Taiwan, derives almost directly from the settlers' penchant for differentiating very sharply between insiders and outsiders along ethnic lines. This penchant is certainly as much cultural as economic.

The era of open ethnic conflict is long past, and in many parts of Taiwan—especially ethnically heterogeneous, urban areas (Baity 1975)—the close associations among ethnicity, marketing community, and ritual organization have blurred. But in Ta-ch'i and neighboring communities these associations persist, albeit with somewhat diminished importance. This persistence is partly a result of the relative stability of the community since the late 1800s. Comparatively few outsiders have moved into the area, and net migration is clearly outward and up the central-place hierarchy. Thus at the marketing-community level, ritual, economic, and administrative boundaries continue to converge.

Insofar as Skinner's argument asserts a functional connection rather than a causal determinacy between economic and ritual patterns of interaction, the continued convergence of these patterns in spatial terms in Ta-ch'i supports his views. Moreover, the functional connections linking administrative networks and township-level ritual organization encompass more than a mere convergence of boundaries. In some respects, the two systems interpenetrate, and this interpenetration revitalizes their historical connection. For example, funds for the P'u-ch'i *t'ang*'s annual procession are collected with the cooperation of administrative-village heads (*li-chang*). The *li-chang* frequently makes use of another government institution, the public primary school, to facilitate this task. Children carry the request for contributions home to their parents and bring the money to school. This saves the *li-chang* the trouble of visiting each household personally.* The use of these collection techniques reinforces the Chinese tendency to describe the territorial limits of ritually defined communities in administrative terms, even where the territories thus defined are not strictly isomorphic.

In contrast to the near identity of ritual, administrative, and economic boundaries at the township/marketing-community level, the domains of neighborhood- and village-level territorial cults only infrequently correspond to administrative *li* and *lin*. Ta-ch'i township encompasses 21 *li* but only 12 village cults. The largest village cult, the Fu-jen *kung,* encompasses five *li* and part of a sixth. Most village-cult domains encompass territories roughly equivalent to one *li,* but *li* and domain boundaries are not closely articulated. Nonetheless, some measure of alignment is apparent if one focuses on centers rather than on territorial boundaries. Most official neighborhood- and village-level business is transacted at police posts, and most rural police posts are located near (often next door to) village temples.

There are 490 administrative *lin* in Ta-ch'i township—more than ten times the number of neighborhood-level cults. However, some neighborhood cults (as in the case of Nan-tzu-kou described in Chap. 4) may define their boundaries in terms of constituent *lin*. It is also common to base *lu-chu* rotations on *lin* boundaries (e.g., by stipulating that the *lu-chu* for each year's festival come from one of several *lin* in rotation). Thus it would be incorrect to assert the absence of any functional relationship.

---

*In 1976, most households contributed about NT$ 20 (about U.S.$ .50) for the annual Kuan Kung procession, but businessmen were expected to be more generous (at least NT$ 100).

Ethnicity, Ritual, and Community on the Borders

Several villages in Ta-ch'i township are only ambiguously tied to the town in economic and ritual terms. The complexity of relations among economic, administrative, and ritual dimensions of interaction is placed in sharpest relief when we examine these villages on Ta-ch'i's borders.

Chung-chuang village, although administratively a part of Ta-ch'i township, is inhabited by Ch'üan-chou people, rather than the Chang-chou faction that dominates elsewhere in the township. This ethnic identity is evident in the strong ritual ties Chung-chuang's inhabitants maintain with the Ch'üan-chou towns of Ying-ko and San-hsia. Chung-chuang's village temple maintains close ritual relations with San-hsia's Ch'ing Shui Tsu Shih temple, and in most respects the people of Chung-chuang belong to the ritual domain of San-hsia rather than Ta-ch'i. Moreover, since the nearest market town is Ch'üan-chou–dominated Ying-ko, few inhabitants shop in Ta-ch'i. But despite Chung-chuang's ritual and economic ties to other centers, villagers do contribute to Ta-ch'i's P'u-ch'i *t'ang* procession.

Chung-liao hamlet is part of Chung-chuang village; however, unlike the rest of Chung-chuang village, it sacrifices pigs on K'ai Chang Sheng Wang's birthday. As we have seen, K'ai Chang Sheng Wang is the focus of several village-level territorial cults in Ta-ch'i, and the largest of the pigs sacrificed in Chung-liao are sometimes sent to Ta-ch'i's Fu-jen *kung,* where they are displayed with other champions as part of the temple's village-level *pai-pai*. However, Chung-liao's participation in Fu-jen *kung* sacrifices is anomalous for two reasons. First, the village is outside the contiguous territorial domain that encompasses the rest of the participants in the sacrifices. As just noted, Chung-liao hamlet is part of the village-cult domain of Chung-chuang. All the people of Chung-chuang participate in the multivillage cult of Ch'ing Shui Tsu Shih centered on the town of San-hsia, but only Chung-liao hamlet also participates in the sacrifices at the Fu-jen *kung*. The normally discrete structure of territorial-cult hierarchy is violated by a lower-level cult's simultaneous encompassment within two different cults at a single higher level.

Second, the reasons that Chung-liao's inhabitants cite for sacrificing pigs at the Fu-jen *kung* differ from everyone else's. Chung-liao is a single-surname hamlet—the only one in Ta-ch'i's marketing community. Almost all its inhabitants are patrilineally related Ch'ens. The patron deity of Ta-ch'i's village-level territorial cult, K'ai Chang Sheng Wang, is said to have been surnamed Ch'en during his earthly incarnation. The Ch'ens of Chung-liao thus say that they worship K'ai Chang Sheng Wang because he must have been their ancestor. Others in Ta-ch'i view K'ai Chang Sheng Wang as their patron in the historical competition with Ch'üan-chou rivals; indeed, this partisan patronage accounts for the deity's popularity in Chang-chou–dominated territorial cults. For the Chung-liao Ch'ens, however, emphasis on this aspect of K'ai Chang Sheng Wang's identity would obviously diminish the deity's appeal.

Why do the Ch'ens participate in the Fu-jen *kung*'s sacrifices? In my view, one must look to the historical circumstances that have thrust the Chung-liao Ch'ens into relations with Ta-ch'i's Chang-chou majority, in spite of what must initially have been very strong disinclinations. Since about 1920, the village of Chung-chuang (including Chung-liao hamlet) has been under Ta-ch'i's administrative jurisdiction. Consequently, villagers' direct contacts with township-level authorities have taken place, for the most part, in Ta-ch'i. Probably more important, in the 1920s and 1930s, village children traveled to Ta-ch'i to attend primary school (since then Chung-chuang has built its own primary school), and today junior-high-school children continue to make the daily journey. As we have seen, contributions for the Kuan Kung procession are solicited through the schools. Consequently, Chung-chuang, despite its Ch'üan-chou heritage, is included in the P'u-ch'i *t'ang*'s domain.

In sum, some 60 years of imposed administrative identity have probably mitigated, to some degree, the ethnic and ritual distinctions that divide Chung-chuang village from the rest of the township. Still, only Chung-liao hamlet participates in the pig sacrifices at the Fu-jen *kung*—the rest of Chung-chuang village's ritual ties to Ta-ch'i are limited to contributing to the P'u-ch'i *tang*'s annual procession. I take this to indicate that administrative boundaries have led indirectly to some degree of realignment of patterns of ritually institutionalized solidarity, although this realignment has not erased prior ethnic and ritual divisions. To demonstrate ritual solidarity with a group whose focal symbol, K'ai Chang Sheng Wang, has rallied the enemies of one's own ethnic group, the expedient of converting the god to an ancestor seems to have been a necessary added ingredient. In the Ch'üan-chou village of Chung-chuang, this expedient was available only to the Ch'ens of Chung-liao hamlet.

In another border village, Yung-fu, population is about equally divided between Chang-chou and Ch'üan-chou people. These ethnic divisions coincide with the village's position bordering Ta-ch'i's and San-hsia's marketing systems; although the village is administratively a part of Ta-ch'i township, roughly half of the villagers' trips to town are in the direction of San-hsia. Yung-fu's population is ethnically mixed not only because the village lies on the border between Ch'üan-chou–dominated San-hsia and Chang-chou–dominated Ta-ch'i, but also because of the relatively late historical settlement of this hilly hinterland. As we have seen, patent-initiated settlement in northern Taiwan typically moved outward from the core areas that later became market towns. By the time the Yung-fu area was settled in the 1870s, the era of violent interethnic conflict was waning. Hence there was less danger involved in residing in close proximity to neighbors of other ethnic groups.

These historical circumstances shaped the development of ritual in Yung-fu. The village temple's main god is Kuan Yin, an unusual choice for a village-level territorial cult. In other respects the temple is a typical village cult. Annual pig sacrifices are held there, and in contrast to "purer" Buddhist temples, the Yung-fu temple has a clearly bounded parish. This choice of community ritual focus, although somewhat unconventional, well suits Yung-fu's situation. Deities who emphasize the internal solidarity of the village or marketing community but differentiate it from outsiders are appropriate foci for territorial cults in ethnically homogeneous communities that are located in a wider ethnically heterogeneous environment. But given the ethnic heterogeneity of Yung-fu's population, the choice of an ethnic patron deity would be divisive. In such cases, Kuan Yin, a female divinity whose symbolism emphasizes inclusive rather than differentiating values (Sangren 1983), provides a suitable substitute for the standard celestial bureaucrat.

Because Kuan Yin is a bodhisattva, however, it is inappropriate to offer her sacrificed pigs. In other words, although Kuan Yin can serve as focal deity in a village-level temple, her position and meaning in the Chinese pantheon prevent her total transformation into a celestial bureaucrat. Therefore the pigs brought to the Hsiang-yün *ssu* are not offered directly to Kuan Yin, but are offered to other deities included as secondary images in the temple. The choice of these secondary deities follows ethnic lines. Chang-chou families offer their pigs to K'ai Chang Sheng Wang (some households also participate in sacrifices at the Fu-jen *kung*), whereas Ch'üan-chou families worship Ch'ing Shui Tsu Shih and Hung Kung (maintaining ties to temples in San-hsia and Ching-mei, ritual centers of adjacent Ch'üan-chou marketing communities). In sum, the Hsiang-yün *ssu* functions in many ways as a village-cult center, even though its main deity is no celestial bureaucrat. The conceptual disadvantage associated with a female deity's acting as the focus of a territorial cult (a role usually associated with a male celestial bureaucrat) is outweighed by the advantage of Kuan Yin's ethnically undiscriminating potential.

Like Yung-fu, the village of Nan-hsing borders two marketing systems—that of Hakka-dominated Chung-li to the west and Chang-chou–dominated Ta-ch'i to the east. Also like Yung-fu, Nan-hsing's population is ethnically divided, in this case between Hakka and Chang-chou factions. Not surprisingly, the village temple's main god, Wu Ku Hsien Ti, has no particular ethnic connotations. Moreover, villagers of each of the major ethnic groups maintain ritual relations with Ta-ch'i and Chung-li, respectively.

The practices of these two ethnically divided border villages suggest that, in such cases, ethnic loyalty may be at least as important as economic and administrative considerations in patterning community identities. Villagers in both Nan-hsing and Yung-fu told me that they preferred to market in the town dominated by their own ethnic group. For some villagers, this might mean a marginally longer bus ride, but this disadvantage is outweighed by the security of being a member of a majority ethnic group in the somewhat more distant town.

Most of the people in Ta-ch'i's other villages are of Chang-chou origin. Among these village cults, Ch'i-chou's is something of an anomaly. Ch'i-chou's village temple is dedicated to Ch'ing Shui Tsu Shih, a patron of Ch'üan-chou people, even though most of Ch'i-chou's population originated in Chang-chou. This situation is recognized as an anomaly by Ch'i-chou people, but no one can offer a satisfying explanation for it. One story has it that the image of Ch'ing Shui Tsu Shih now in the temple was originally the property of the village's single Ch'üan-chou family. The god developed a reputation for efficacy (*ling*) by protecting villagers from aborigine attacks and floods. Other families began worshiping the god, and his popularity increased to the point where his worship became, in effect, a village cult.

This explanation is essentially identical to the stories in local historical tradition that authenticate the efficacy of virtually all territorial-cult deities. In view of the history of ethnic warfare in northern Taiwan, it thus sheds little light on why Ch'i-chou's Chang-chou majority came to worship a symbol of their Ch'üan-chou rivals. The explanation may lie in part in the recent origin of Ch'i-chou's village cult. Ch'i-chou is the smallest village-cult community in Ta-ch'i, and is not listed in the register of cults or temples compiled in the 1930s by the township administration (JD). Communal sacrifices were probably formally instituted only about 20 years ago, so that the past importance of ethnic difference had diminished by the time Ch'i-chou achieved village-cult status. Moreover, the major ethnic distinction in Ch'i-chou is between Hokkien speakers and the Hakkas who live just across the river to the southwest, not between Ch'üan-chou and Chang-chou people. In other words, despite Ch'ing

Shui Tsu Shih's widespread association with Ch'üan-chou ethnicity, this association is not relevant in Ch'i-chou.

In this regard, Baity (1975: 49) notes, of the cult of the Taipei City God and Tan-shui's Ch'ing Shui Tsu Shih:

> The popularity of these deities does not seem to result from their particularistic origins. . . . Instead these gods have emerged as a result of their demonstrated efficacy in defending all of the inhabitants of their new locales against a common external threat. In so doing they have become transformed from narrow particularistic gods into universalistic symbols of their new communities.

By the same token, Wang Shih-ch'ing (1974), from his study of Shu-lin, believes that ethnic patron deities tend to take on the characteristics of universal community gods in ethnically heterogeneous communities. But in Ta-ch'i and nearby marketing communities, where the population within the marketing systems is relatively homogeneous, ethnic gods retain their particularistic associations even in ethnically heterogeneous villages. Thus I suspect that the conversions from particularistic to universalistic associations that Wang and Baity document may be limited to cases where the generalizations regarding ethnic heterogeneity are made at the level of the standard marketing community or higher.

In sum, historical complexities in patterns of administrative and economic interaction find ritual expression in ethnically heterogeneous border villages. But even within the core of Ta-ch'i's marketing community, there is considerable variation in patterns of ritual integration.

Ritual Ties Within the Marketing Community

Although conceptually discrete, the boundaries of ritual community in Ta-ch'i encompass considerable variation in the "density" of ritual orientation to the town—that is, the commitment and participation of residents of various locales in the town's religious activities and traditions. For the most part, this density is defined in terms of degree of participation in P'u-ch'i t'ang rituals. A review of spatial variations in ritual participation provides another perspective on the complex relations among patterns of historical settlement, ethnicity, economic relations, and administrative boundaries in the development of ritual relations.

Within the limits already documented, the worship of Kuan Kung at the P'u-ch'i t'ang bridges the gaps among Chang-chou, Ch'üan-chou, and Hakka ethnic groups. By virtue of their common migration from China's Southeast Coast, all these groups are "Taiwanese"(T'ai-wan jen). Unassimilated Chinese mainlander and aborigine residents of Ta-ch'i's marketing community do not normally participate (except as spectators), nor are they invited to do so.

For many Taiwanese, participation is limited to the small contributions they make to the Kuan Kung procession. The procession itself visits only villages east of the river and near the town. Representatives on the temple committee from west of the river complain that, since they contribute, the procession should visit their villages, too. A recent communication from Ta-ch'i speaks of a plan to extend the procession in the future. But even if this suggestion were implemented, the size of the marketing community would preclude the procession from visiting many of the remoter villages and hamlets. A practical effect of this limitation is that enthusiasm for the Kuan Kung procession varies a great deal; understandably, communities visited by the procession feel a greater commitment to support it than others do.

There are several other markers of ritual connection between the town of Ta-ch'i and its ritual domain. One indicator of ritual identification with Ta-ch'i is the adoption of the Fu-jen *kung*'s system of rotation among ten-surname groups for pig sacrifices at the village temple. Villages that formerly sacrificed pigs at the Fu-jen *kung* have usually retained this organization at their own village festivals. In some cases, the groupings of surnames have been slightly modified to create groups that are roughly equal in population and wealth. Villages that do not use the ten-surname rotation system either split off from the Fu-jen *kung* very early or never participated in its rotation.

Villages that participate in Ta-ch'i's Ma Tsu rotation may also be said to identify more closely with Ta-ch'i than those that do not. Of the temples that do not participate, two (those in Nan-hsing and Kung-kuan) borrow Ma Tsu images on their own pilgrimages; one (the Chung-chuang temple) participates in another rotation (centered on the town of Ying-ko); and three (in Pai-chi, San-min, and Fu-hsing) share images in a satellite rotation. In addition, the village temple in Yung-fu did not invite the three images during the period of my fieldwork (the temple was undergoing reconstruction at the time), although I was told that it would normally participate. In each of these cases, the village temple is relatively distant from Ta-ch'i. Yung-fu and Nan-hsing are located in ethnically mixed border areas, and Chung-chuang, although administratively part of Ta-ch'i township, is a Ch'üan-chou village with primary ritual, cultural, and economic ties to Ying-ko.

The temples in Pai-chi, San-min, and Fu-hsing are branches of a temple that was covered by water after the construction of the Shih-men Reservoir about 30 years ago. The villages maintain close ritual ties to Ta-ch'i in most respects, but in the early 1970s, they began their own Ma Tsu

TABLE 4
Villages' Ritual Ties with Ta-ch'i

Temple	Ma Tsu rotation	Contributes to Kuan Kung parade	Ten-surname rotation	Ethnic group[a]	Outside ties
Fu-jen *kung*[b]	X	X	X	C	
Jen-ho *kung*	X	X	X	C	
Jui-yüan *kung*	X	X	X	C	
Fu-hsing *kung* (in Pai-chi)		X	X[c]	C	
Fu-hsing *kung* (in Fu-hsing)		X	X[c]	C	
Tung-hsing *kung*		X	X[c]	C	
Fu-an *kung*	X	X	X[c]	C	
Jen-an *kung*	X	X	X[c]	C	
San-yüan *kung*	X	X	X	C	
Yung-ch'ang *kung*		X		C, H	X
Fu-shan *yen*	X	X		C	
Hsiang-yün *ssu*		X	X	C, Ch	X
Yung-an *kung*		X	X	C	
Fu-te *kung*		X		Ch	X

[a]C is Chang-chou, H is Hakka, Ch is Ch'üan-chou.
[b]On the route of the Kuan Kung parade.
[c]Surnames have been regrouped to create groups of roughly equal sizes.

rotation. Images are borrowed from Hsin-kang and Pei-kang and are carried back to San-min each year. The same two images are then circulated to village temples at Fu-hsing and Pai-chi.

The innermost circle in ritual terms consists of village temples actually visited by Kuan Kung during the annual procession. These various indicators of ritual orientation toward Ta-ch'i are summarized in Table 4.

Other indicators of ritual connection include the invitations extended to gods of neighboring temples to attend operas and sacrifices. Those most frequently invited to village-level *pai-pai* include the Pu-ch'i *tang*'s Kuan Kung, the Kuan-yin *t'ing*'s Kuan Yin, the Fu-jen *kung*'s K'ai Chang Sheng Wang (for villages east of the river), and the Jen-ho *kung*'s K'ai Chang Sheng Wang (for villages west of the river). In addition, villages normally invite the gods from temples in contiguous villages to their celebrations.

In sum, variations in the nature and strength of ritual orientation to Ta-ch'i are correlated with differences in ethnicity, patterns of historical settlement, and distance from the town (hence, broadly, density of economic interaction). For villages west of the river, proximity to larger cities has diminished Ta-ch'i's attractiveness as a market center. The fact that people in these villages can travel to T'ao-yüan or Chung-li nearly as quickly and inexpensively as to Ta-ch'i has also contributed to a weakening of their ritual ties to the town. In short, villages bordering other marketing communities are more divided in their ritual loyalties than villages nearer Ta-ch'i. But in Ta-ch'i, the border villages are also the most ethnically heterogeneous ones. My impression is that ethnic ties have outweighed purely economic factors in the historical development of ritual relations in these border areas, although both forces are reflected in the patterns of ritual relationship that persist today.

Historical settlement patterns are reflected in enduring ritual ties in a number of other ways. The area west of the Ta-han River was settled early, but until the T'ao-yüan Aqueduct was built during the Japanese regime, the land was poorly irrigated and sparsely populated. The river was also a greater obstacle to travel than it is today, making the west bank effectively more peripheral than distance on a map would indicate. Villages on the east bank near Ta-ch'i (including Nei-chia and, later, San-ts'eng) were better watered, more accessible, and more prosperous. This area had, and has maintained, the closest ritual ties with the town. The last areas to be settled by Han Chinese are in the southeastern part of the township and in Fu-hsing township. Settlement in these areas was sponsored by wealthy Ta-ch'i landlords or by Japanese companies, the actual settlers coming mainly from Ta-ch'i, Nei-chia, and San-ts'eng. The Nan-ya *kung* in A-mu-p'ing (which was inundated with the completion of the Shih-men Dam) was built by the same consortium of Ta-ch'i landlords who ran the Fu-jen *kung*. Temples in Pai-chi, San-min, and Fu-hsing (*fen-hsiang* successors to the Nan-ya *kung*) are all branch "descendants" of Ta-ch'i's Fu-jen *kung* and maintain close ritual ties to the town.

Distance from town also affects the development and maintenance of ritual ties. For example, the Hakka settlers who reside near the Kuan-yin *t'ing* have been essentially assimilated by the surrounding Chang-chou majority. They speak Hokkien, participate fully in pig sacrifices at the Fu-jen *kung,* and are generally indistinguishable from their Chang-chou neighbors. The only remaining sign of Kuan-yin *t'ing*'s identity as a Hakka temple is the popularity of the temple as a pilgrimage destination in neighboring Hakka areas. Proximity to Ta-ch'i, combined with isolation from other Hakka populations, has resulted in the effective assimilation of this Hakka enclave. In contrast, Hakkas in Nan-hsing (which borders the Hakka-dominated township of Chung-li) have retained their ethnic identity and dialect, their only ritual connection with Ta-ch'i being their contributions to the Kuan Kung procession.

To generalize, other factors (ethnicity, ease of travel, and so forth) being equal, the greater the distance from town, the more troublesome it is to participate fully in communal activities there. Consequently, remote villages are likely to establish autonomous festivals earlier in their economic development than villages nearer town. This fact is apparent in the inverse relationship between the population of village-cult domains and distance from Ta-ch'i. For example, relative isolation almost certainly accounts for the existence of village-level sacrifices in Fu-hsing, a village with a very small Han population. According to residents of the village, they set up their own pig sacrifices as early as possible to avoid the inconvenience of transporting huge sacrificial pigs over winding mountain roads to Ta-ch'i.*

Pilgrimages and Economic Regions in China

Writing about pilgrimages in post-Conquest Mexico and in medieval Europe, Victor Turner (1974: 179) observes that "any region possessing a certain cultural, linguistic, or ethnic unity, often corresponding also to an area of economic interdependence, tended to become at once a political unit and a pilgrimage catchment area." In other words, a profound functional and historical connection has been recognized between the participatory dimensions of pilgrimage and such other spatially patterned aspects of social organization as economic regions, ethnicity, and administrative districts (e.g., Bhardwaj 1973: 146). However, relatively little empirical research (especially in the case of China) has been devoted either to tracing the details of these connections or to identifying the social and historical factors that give rise to and reproduce them (see also Whitney 1970: 171; Ward 1977: 182).

As previously noted, pilgrimages to Pei-kang's Ma Tsu temple play an important role in defining a sense of "Taiwaneseness." But what is the nature of the connection between the ritual community constituted by pilgrimages and the regional structure of economic interaction?

TAIWAN

Pei-kang—like Lu-kang, Hsin-kang, and other important centers of Ma Tsu worship in Taiwan—was an important port in the early period of Chinese migration to the island. These early ports suffered a relative commercial decline when silting harbors and changing modes of transport rendered their once advantageous locations a disadvantage. In contrast, Taipei, the apex of Taiwan's present-day economic and administra-

---

*In contrast, people from Shan-chu-hu, an isolated hamlet north of Ta-ch'i, go to great effort to transport their pigs through Ta-ch'i and over the hills to San-hsia. Shan-chu-hu is inhabited by Ch'üan-chou people, a minority group in Ta-ch'i. Their minority status accounts for the trouble they take in transporting their pigs to San-hsia, a town where their own group dominates.

tive hierarchies, was founded relatively recently, in the late nineteenth century (Feuchtwang 1974a). Although some temples in the vicinity of Taipei attract large numbers of visitors, none approaches the importance of the Ma Tsu cult centers. Ritual centrality does not correspond very neatly with economic centrality in present-day Taiwan.

This apparent anomaly is best understood with reference to the symbolic contrast between the old ports that serve as centers for the Ma Tsu cult, on the one hand, and Taipei, the regional metropolis, on the other. Taipei has always been a seat of central, alien power and authority in Taiwan. Founded as an official capital in the late Ch'ing dynasty, the city was also the seat of Japanese colonial administration, and since retrocession has been the capital of the mainlander-dominated Nationalist government. Consequently, despite its commercial and administrative centrality, Taipei is particularly unsuitable as a center for ritual expression of Taiwanese identity.

Moreover, generally negative government attitudes toward (and occasional active discouragement of) pilgrimages and flamboyant public ritual (both under the current government and under the Japanese) have inhibited the growth of ritual activity in areas where the government's presence is most strongly felt—namely, in Taipei and other large cities. Taipei is the center of a reemerging official cult based on the veneration of Nationalist heroes. Monumental shrines to Chiang K'ai-shek, Sun Yat-sen, and martyred soldiers emphasize a national, not a regional or ethnic identity. Conversely, the explicit association of old port cities with Taiwanese historical experience—and their implicit contrast with cities like Taipei—heighten the Ma Tsu cult centers' appropriateness as symbols of "Taiwaneseness."*

But this divergence of symbolic and economic/administrative centrality at the island-wide level does not mean that there are no functional connections between economic and ritual interaction. Taipei's economic hinterland is geographically coterminous with Pei-kang's pilgrimage catchment area; both include virtually the entire island. Moreover, the connections between economic and ritual region are not limited to this convergence at the boundaries. In traveling to pilgrimage centers like Pei-kang, pilgrims make use of the same transport networks that link economic central places. Thus, the first stage of a pilgrim's journey typically takes the pilgrim up the hierarchy of economic central places—from the village to the market town, from town to local city, and so forth. Only in the latter stages of the journey is this process reversed; as pilgrims near

---

*The location of Taiwan's Ma Tsu cult centers lends some support to Victor Turner's (1974: 227) suggestion that pilgrimage centers often arise in places of past commercial and political prominence.

the cult center, they typically travel down the local central-place hierarchy from city to town, and finally to the sacred site. In the case of pilgrims from villages surrounding Ta-ch'i, travel proceeds through the market town, the local city of T'ao-yüan, and the regional city of Chang-hua, culminating in the modest towns of Pei-kang and Hsin-kang.

Commenting on the economic consequences of institutionalized pilgrimages in Mexico and Europe, Victor Turner (1974: 210) points out that the growing popularity of a pilgrimage center may lead to "elaborate market, transportation, catering, recreational, and lodging arrangements . . . each social class, ethnic category, and cultural region having its own distinctive type of travel and accommodation." In other words, pilgrimages may create their own economic infrastructures.* Something like this seems to have occurred in Taiwan. Excursion companies rely on the business provided by the pilgrimage trade, and the economies of pilgrimage centers depend on providing goods and services to pilgrims. Indeed, the abundance of entertainments available in Pei-kang creates a carnival atmosphere during the height of the pilgrimage season and boosts the local economy.

In sum, Ma Tsu pilgrimages encompass a ritual catchment area that is essentially identical to economic and administrative regions dominated by Taipei. However, this convergence at the boundaries should not be read as evidence that ritual community is epiphenomenal to economic causes. To some degree, the ritual centrality of pilgrim centers like Pei-kang can precede or heighten economic centrality.

PREREVOLUTIONARY CHINESE MAINLAND

The importance of pilgrimages in Taiwan raises important questions regarding the role of pilgrimages in prerevolutionary mainland China. Partly because of the paucity of easily accessible data, relatively little research has been completed on pilgrimages in China. Since 1949, opportunities to conduct research on topics like pilgrimages have been severely limited on the mainland. Moreover, the Chinese government's restrictions on travel, combined with its hostility toward what are often viewed as wasteful and superstitious religious practices, have resulted in the elimination of the great traditional pilgrimages. Anthropological and sociological studies of Chinese society before 1949 concentrated on village-level ethnography (reflecting the methodology of "structural-functionalism" that dominated the field) and on statistical surveys, with little comment on wider fields of cultural and social interaction. Most of the Western-

---

*Chang Hsiao-mei (1978) describes in detail the variety of economic services required by pilgrims to O-mei Shan.

language information on pilgrimages is found in descriptive works published before the 1930s.

Chinese sources are myriad but frustrating. A wealth of historical/mythical lore is compiled in various gazetteers (see Geil 1926 for lengthy translations of passages from these), but such texts focus on the legends associated with sacred sites and the history of official (or imperial) interest in them, telling us little about popular participation in pilgrimages and associated rituals. Most promising are itineraries or guidebooks for pilgrims published by important temples and monasteries. Extracts from one such guidebook are translated in Johnston (1913). Another guidebook, *Ts'an-hsüeh Chih-chin* by the Buddhist monk, Hsüan-ch'eng Ju-hai of K'ai-hua Monastery, Hangchow, contains a wealth of information regarding popular pilgrimage destinations and routes, but little regarding the organization of popular pilgrimages (Brook 1981: 74; see also Chang Hsiao-mei 1978).

A thorough investigation of the history, sociology, and cultural context and meaning of pilgrimages in China is a research project of greater scope than I can attempt here. However, considering the importance of pilgrimages in China's social and cultural integration, and the neglect of the topic in academic discourse, some preliminary suggestions are in order. Let me begin by speculating in very general terms about some of the functional connections between pilgrimages and other dimensions of spatial organization in Chinese society.

An indispensable framework for beginning such an inquiry is provided by Skinner's regional analyses of Chinese social and economic institutions. Skinner sees the spatial organization of Chinese culture as closely paralleling the spatial organization of China's economic and administrative systems (1977b: 269):

The basic cultural cleavages in China were those of class and of occupation (complexly interrelated) and of region (elaborated nested hierarchy), not those between cities and their hinterlands. This conclusion, however, by no means implies a negligible role for China's cities. For the exchange of cultural material that perpetuated the distinctiveness of each nodal territorial system while at the same time keeping cultural differentiation in check occurred primarily in market towns and cities; and the mechanisms for the refinement and universalization of local-cum-rustic forms and their incorporation in literate traditions (and, conversely, for the coarsening and parochialization of elite forms and their incorporation into little-local traditions) were, once again, concentrated in the hierarchically ordered central places of China's regional systems.

How, then, do the extensive pilgrimage networks of prerevolutionary China fit into this schema? Pilgrimage fields frequently seem to be organized into nested hierarchies (Srinivas 1966; V. Turner 1974: 179; Bhardwaj 1973; Obeyesekere 1963, 1966; compare Sopher 1968: 407). This raises the question of whether or not each pilgrimage center's catchment area corresponds to a particular level in the similarly structured nested hierarchy of economic (or administrative) regions. But the nodes of economic regions are central places—market towns and cities situated at the nexus of regional commerce and transport. In contrast, pilgrimage centers such as Pei-kang are often located in peripheries (C.-K. Yang 1961: 87; V. Turner 1974). Thus pilgrimage centers must be added to Skinner's economic and administrative central places as loci of intensified cultural interaction.

The fact that pilgrimage centers are often located some distance from major cities need not imply a lack of convergence at the boundaries between pilgrimage catchment areas and economic regions. I have been unable to discover information pertaining to the catchment areas of China's great traditional pilgrimage centers, but the case of Ma Tsu pilgrimages in Taiwan is instructive in this regard. Ta-ch'i's pilgrims begin their journey to Pei-kang by proceeding up the hierarchy of central places. The largest city they visit is Chang-hua, after which the journey progresses down the central-place hierarchy as pilgrims near the sacred center at Pei-kang. Descriptions of pilgrimages in prerevolutionary mainland China suggest a similar sort of progression (e.g., Day 1940: 32; Chang Hsiao-mei 1978).

Extensive pilgrimage networks on the Chinese mainland required elaborate support services. Many Buddhist monasteries and shrines, including not only those located at important sacred sites, but also those along the major pilgrimage routes, derived significant portions of their income from providing food and lodging for pilgrims (Johnston 1913; Hsien-ch'eng 1827). Moreover, traveling officials, merchants, and even aspirants in China's imperial examination system also frequented these Buddhist hostels (K. Ch'en 1964: 263; Welch 1967: 10). By the same token, the guidebooks for pilgrims published by monasteries and temples included important information regarding routes, lodgings, local customs, and so forth, and undoubtedly facilitated the journeys not only of pilgrims but of other travelers as well (Brook 1981).

In sum, although pilgrimage centers were often located far from economic central places and administrative capitals, they depended in large part on the same transportation networks that linked economic and administrative systems. Just as pilgrims might take advantage of transport facilities set up mainly for commercial purposes (for example, traveling by boat on China's highly developed system of inland waterways, or, more recently, by train or regularly scheduled bus), so secular travelers might find the food and lodging provided for pilgrims at temples a great convenience.

Unfortunately, I have been unable to uncover sufficient information to conclude that these overlapping networks resulted in a close correspondence between pilgrimage catchment areas and economic regions on the Chinese mainland (as they do in the case of Taiwan's Ma Tsu cult). Nonetheless, descriptions of popular pilgrimages in prerevolutionary China suggest that the largest may have extended up to what Skinner terms the level of the macroregion (C.-K. Yang 1961: 88). It is unlikely that significant numbers of lay pilgrims ventured beyond the relatively well-developed transport networks of their own economic macroregions. The time and expense required to journey beyond these boundaries would have been prohibitive.

For wandering monks and those of wealth and leisure, such considerations were less of an obstacle. Indeed, a widespread aspiration, especially among monastics, was to visit as many of China's sacred sites as possible, a value graphically communicated in what Welch (1967: 306) identifies as the usual expression for wandering, "*ts'an-fang,* which may be translated as 'traveling to every quarter of the country.'" High on the list were the four sacred mountains associated with the bodhisattvas Ti Tsang, Kuan Yin, Wen Shu, and P'u Hsien. Perhaps equally important were China's five famous Taoist mountains (Geil 1926; Kupfer 1911; Mullikin & Hotchkis 1973). These famous sacred sites served as nodes for at least two kinds of pilgrimage. First, they attracted large numbers of lay pilgrims from within their respective macroregions, and second, they were important stops in the travels of wandering monks and other religious adepts, being part of a network that conceptually encompassed the entire cosmos.

A brief speculation regarding the structure of religious integration in China at the level of the empire, as it relates to political and economic integration, may be appropriate here. Even the formally institutionalized Buddhist sangha never developed elaborate bureaucratic structures comparable to those of the medieval Catholic church (see C.-K. Yang's 1961 distinction between "institutionalized" and "diffused" religion in China). The ineffectual administrative framework that nominally governed monastic affairs was imposed upon largely autonomous monasteries by a central government concerned with keeping religion firmly under control (K. Ch'en 1964: 253–57). Thus Chinese Buddhism maintained a degree of ritual and doctrinal unity not through formal organization and bureaucratic discipline, but through informal institutions such as the pilgrimages of wandering monks and lay devotees. Since both types of pilgrimage converged on the same sacred sites, these sites—and pilgrimage ritual in general—provided an important point of contact between monastic institutions and local religion.

Furthermore, the organization of pilgrimages may have been as important in the spatial integration of Chinese religion as the better-understood and better-documented official cult. The official cult was designed at least in part to sanction and reify political authority at all levels and to bring local territorial cults under central ideological control (C.-K. Yang 1961; Feuchtwang 1977). Consequently, official temples were located mainly in administrative capitals.*

Official rites and cosmology exerted a profound influence on popular consciousness. As we have seen, as a ranked bureaucracy headed by the Jade Emperor, the pantheon structured local territorial-cult iconography. However, it was only at the lowest level of official rites—the county-level City God cult—that there was significant nonofficial participation in official religion. The most widespread popular participation was in pilgrimages to sacred sites, not in official rites corresponding to high-level administrative districts. Significantly, as one moves toward higher levels of popular participation, the deities associated with communal ritual become less bureaucratic.

This fact is evident in the iconographic representations of the cosmos that adorn domestic altars in northern Taiwan. Seated in meditative repose at the top of the painting, twice as large as any of the other figures, is Kuan Yin. To her lower right is Ma Tsu, and to her lower left Kuan Kung, the red-faced legendary general. Below Ma Tsu and Kuan Kung are the white-bearded, Santa Claus–like Place God (T'u Ti Kung) and the Stove God (Tsao Chün; also known as Tsao Wang Yeh and Tsao Shen), respectively. The prominence accorded Kuan Yin and Ma Tsu, who are central in pilgrimage cults, is evidence of the dominance of the social identities or, to use Obeyesekere's (1966) phrase, "moral communities" expressed in popular pilgrimages, over those defined in official religion, with its stricter reference to administrative structures of hierarchy and control.

Clearly, then, one cannot assume that official religion's administrative districts historically or functionally preceded the pilgrimage cults' catchment areas in defining the boundaries of China's "cultural" regions.

---

*To avoid further clouding an already complicated description, I gloss over the connections between official religion and the cult of ancient sacred mountains in such customs as imperial sacrifices. An association between mountains, the limits of empire, and imperial authority is quite ancient in China. As in the case of the other cults treated in Chapter 10, one can assume that the state's notion of the religious significance of mountains differed from that of many pilgrims, although the two interpretations were to some degree mutually authenticating (see Geil 1926; Baker 1925).

Similarly, one cannot assume that social identity is strictly isomorphic with density of economic interaction (Sopher 1973: 109–10). Here William A. Christian's (1972: 11) comments regarding the complexity of historical factors impinging upon the segmentary, situational structure of social identities in rural Spain are apropos:

Shared identities must be based on shared activities or a shared code for interpreting activities. Either the code itself or the actual activity provides a common experience. People can either be related because of proximity, and hence interaction, or because they share the same political or cultural hub, the same capital, which for economic or political reasons, in short because of the power and control it exercises over the lives of those in its hinterland, demands that all activities on the periphery be translatable into the terms of the center (e.g., all Spaniards must understand Castilian, use the decimal system, and participate in the capitalist economy).

It is thus reasonable to assume that social and economic interaction requires some measure of shared culture and that, to some degree, this interaction may even produce and reproduce shared codes. But interaction does not necessarily lead to social identity. At the level of domestic groups, for example, it is clear that interaction (along with the "politics of language") reproduces difference not only in the social roles of men and women, but to some degree in their worldviews (e.g., Bourdieu 1977; F. Myers & Brennis 1984). The same can be said for social class and status hierarchies. As long as such social distinctions are evenly distributed in space, Skinner's assumptions regarding the cultural effects of interaction are descriptively appropriate. However, such characteristics as tribal or ethnic identities may spatially "distort" the patterns predicted by a purely interactionist model.*

In the preceding sections we have documented such distortions at the marketing-community level, where the social (and spatial) boundaries of ritual and economic community are not strictly isomorphic. In the history of Taiwan's Chinese settlement, place of origin on the mainland was ritually reified as an important determinant of social identity, because most of the settlers brought with them allegiance to the territorial-cult deities of their respective homelands. These allegiances subsequently structured the competition for resources in Taiwan. But in making the point that common social identity may give rise to, as well as result from,

---

*Hart (1888: 214–15) noted that Tibetans, border tribes, and Han Chinese converged at the same temples at O-mei Shan in Szechwan. Much more research would be required to establish the dynamics of ethnic interaction at places like O-mei Shan, but it seems clear that even profound cultural differences may persist under the encompassing cult of such sacred sites.

social interaction, it would be a mistake to underestimate the significance of their functional/historical connections.* In sum, pilgrimages on mainland China are probably not most usefully conceived as "expressions" of economically determined regional identities; indeed, as we will later see, they may have played an important role in constituting and reproducing such identities. Nonetheless, it is clear that economically defined regions and the "moral" communities constituted by pilgrimages were complexly linked both functionally and historically.

If this assessment of the significance of pilgrimage cults in defining and expressing wider spheres of social identity is correct, a third hierarchy of regional systems—the ritual—must be added to those defined by official administration and economic circulation. Complex functional and historical connections undoubtedly generate a tendency toward spatial convergence among political, economic, and ritual regions, but any "objectivist" history must keep at least these three aspects of human interaction analytically distinct. Specifying their respective roles in China is an important task for future research.

This "objectivist" project does not, however, exhaust the possibilities for deepening our understanding of the Chinese past or of Chinese culture. Characteristic interactions among economic, administrative, and ritual "structures" are mediated and reproduced by notions of the nature of this same interaction—in a word, by Chinese notions of history. If in the process of constructing our own history of Chinese society we factor out native Chinese sociologies as being mere "myth" or "ideology," we are likely to overlook how such sociologies play an objective role in shaping the interactions among economy, polity, and cosmology. In Part III, I consider the dialectical reality of the Chinese people's construction of their own past and present, in the historical idiom of local religion and iconography.

---

*One could plausibly argue, with Skinner, that in the long run social divisions that crosscut economic regions tend to fade. Wang Shih-ch'ing's (1974) study of a multiethnic community in north Taiwan lends some support to such a position.

Part III

Efficacy, Legitimacy, and the Structure of Value

Cosmology socially reproduced in rituals is the language that confers concreteness, even "reality" upon Taiwanese social relations. This assertion runs counter to sociocentric explanations of Chinese religion. Take, for example, the following argument: because officials in imperial times were the most powerful people in peasant experience—holders of apparently arbitrary, capricious, and unlimited authority—it makes a great deal of sense that gods should be modeled after them. But does it? Although it is clear that in many respects Chinese do think of gods as resembling officials or emperors, what is not clear is the logic that explains why and in which contexts they do so. In other words, it is not necessarily "natural" that Chinese should construct an imaginary supernatural world that is a mirror image of the world of concrete experience; to explain why religious symbols take the forms they do, one must attempt to explain the process that produces them.

Even if we consider only formal features of symbols, the same kinds of difficulties that Lévi-Strauss (1962; 1966) identifies in Durkheim's (1915) theory of totemism apply to the notion that Chinese cosmology is a direct projection of concrete social categories. The crux of the issue here is which is more useful, to focus on symbolic relations as motivated (one cultural category resembles or "stands for" another similar cultural category) or to focus on similarities in the structure of contrastive differences. For Lévi-Strauss, the logic underlying totemic symbols like "bear" or "raven" lies not in any inherent qualities their referents may possess (strength, bravery) that are extended to some social category, but rather in the ways in which the contrasts between one totemic category and another resemble the contrasts between social categories. Thus the relevant focus of analysis shifts from the resemblance between "bears" and the "bear clan" to resemblances between the contrast bear/raven and the contrast bear clan/raven clan.

What follows here is inspired in part by this basic structuralist insight. I argue that the social efficacy of Chinese religious symbols is illuminated by assuming that structures of relations among officials provide a model or code for thinking about similarly structured social relations.* This is preferable to assuming that the Chinese pantheon resembles a bureaucracy mainly because gods are imagined as officials. Moreover, I suggest that the imperial bureaucracy provides more than a felicitous metaphor for social relations; rather, social relations are in part formed in rituals and identities that are defined in cosmological terms. As far as Taiwanese are concerned, to be neighbors means to worship at the same T'u Ti Kung shrine, a settlement is not a village until it has a village temple, and so forth. This is not to say that economic and other forms of secular social interaction are historically irrelevant in patterning ritual relations; only that the relationship between ritual and social relations is dialectical.

Of course, as we have seen in Part II, discrepancies do arise between existing ritual relations and evolving patterns of social interaction. One can then speak of a process of accommodation or adjustment between the two, in which ritual organization appears as a "dependent" variable. But it could just as easily be the other way around; evolving patterns of ritual organization can lead to changes in economic or political interaction. Indeed, changes in ritual forms may be correlated with the sorts of changes in economic and administrative patterns of interaction documented in Part II. For the most part, however, these changes are best viewed as transformations of a fairly stable underlying set of culturally grounded assumptions regarding the relations between social life and cosmos. In any case, the connection between social and ritual relations is not that between an objectively existing "reality" and its symbolic, perhaps distorted or mystified, expression. In the chapters that follow, I attempt to

---

*Similar arguments have been made regarding the connection between kinship ideology and social organization among such classic "segmentary societies" as the Nuer of Sudan. Putative patrilineal kinship serves as a code for a nested hierarchy of feuding relations among what are in fact territorially defined settlements (Gough 1972). In other words, Nuer genealogy and Chinese celestial bureaucracy are metaphoric codes at the level of actual social relations. Indeed, in China and other Asiatic states, there may be a historical connection between the two, with ancestors becoming gods as tribes became states. See Friedman (1975); Friedman & Rowlands (1978); Robert J. Smith (1974). But compare Baity (1975), who argues that ancestors can never become gods.

show how religious symbols are a concrete part of the process of social reproduction, not just reflections of it or some sort of maintenance mechanism for it.

Many "religion-as-reflection-of-society" arguments explain away obvious correspondences between social categories and supernatural images as people's natural predisposition to project their experience into an imaginary world, which then becomes the justification for the real world upon which it is modeled. This framework provides a basis for mapping similarities between cosmology and social structure and for exploring ways in which religious ideas act to maintain, reinforce, or legitimate social order. Such functionalism has contributed significantly to a sociological understanding of religion. Nonetheless, I argue that there are good reasons for rejecting the notion that collective religious symbols are produced by somehow assembling various religious ideas produced by individuals. The alternative I propose is that collective representations are reproduced in social interaction and, dialectically, reproduce society. Stated in such an abbreviated way, this proposition can probably be reconciled with a wide spectrum of current social theory. The more difficult task is to give it concrete specification in analysis.

In insisting that the analysis of collective religious symbols be sociologically rather than psychologically grounded, I do not mean to imply that individuals can be entirely ignored. Although it is a commonplace that to some degree everyone thinks in terms of cultural categories acquired as a member of society, it is also clear that there is considerable room for individual variation and creativity. Many innovative ideas, although building on collective representations, are the creations of individuals. But it is only those symbols and ideas that achieve social efficacy that persist and become collective representations.

As Talcott Parsons and those influenced by him have taught us, individual internalization of these collective representations is important for the stability of the social system. This function does not explain their reproduction in social process, however. The hierarchically ascendant or encompassing level in a society is social, and it cannot be derived from or reduced to a product of individual imagination.

A crucial point here is that a focus on the social reproduction of collective representations is not incompatible with the notion that collective representations also reproduce social institutions. This is so precisely because it does not rely on an intervening explanatory appeal to individual psychology. In Gregory Bateson's (1972; 1979) terms, society, including collective representations and social institutions, is a self-reproducing cybernetic system (see also T. Turner 1977b, 1979a, b). The fact that describing this system seems to require an analytical distinction between social structure, institutions, or society on the one hand, and culture, collective representations, or symbols on the other, carries with it the constant temptation to reify the analytic in its object—that is, to see as separate entities what are only part of a single process. When, for example, we write of the functional relationships between culture and society in terms of "mutual interaction," "influence," "reinforcement," or "reflection," our language leads us astray. Social theorists as divergent as Max Weber and Karl Marx have long been aware of this problem, and it is a problem that seems even more difficult to overcome when discourse moves from abstract theory to concrete analyses.

Consider the persistence in Taiwanese religion of the imperial–administrative model of the pantheon. Fifty years of Japanese colonial rule and 35 years of Republican administration have intervened since the demise of imperial bureaucracy in Taiwan, yet there has been no perceptible diminution of this religious model. If gods are modeled on peasants' images of officials, why officials so different from any in most peasants' experience? In my view, the answer lies in what Lévi-Strauss calls an underlying structure: both gods and officials are in a sense symbolic functionaries in a similarly constructed, culturally fundamental notion of order and relationship that transcends cosmic, social, and administrative hierarchies. Thus, although it may be true that officials were real men and gods an illusion, the significance of both "official" and "god" stems from their analogous positions in an ultimately cultural model of cosmic order. In other words, as material things, men may be real, but "official" and "god" are equally culturally constructed categories.

In developing these points with reference to the meaning of religious symbols in Ta-ch'i, I seek to demonstrate that gods, rituals, and pantheon are codes not merely for categories of people, but for relationships (both spatial and historical) among them. But my purpose goes beyond demonstrating this by now structuralist commonplace; I want to show that Chinese cosmology and values are manifestations or aspects of the same structures of reproduction (what Bourdieu 1977 terms "structuring structures") as the social categories and groupings that they supposedly mirror.

In very general terms, then, Part III begins with the Durkheimian insight that collective representations are social facts. The analytical distinction between culture, collective representations, and symbols on the one hand, and social institutions, social structure, and "society" on the other, is viewed as encompassed within a structured cybernetic process—that is, within society or social reproduction (Augé's 1982 "social logic"). The differences between Durkheim's two meanings of society thus pertain to a logical relation of hierarchy (compare Lukes 1973; Schwartz 1981; Merquior 1979; Boon 1982: 54–68). Society is opposed to culture at one level of analytical contrast, but encompasses both at another.* Or, following Bateson (1972; 1979), social reproduction is of a higher "logical type" than "culture" or "social structure" as commonly used.

The focus of inquiry here is the concept of power or efficacy (*ling*), which is the underlying premise of much of Chinese ritual activity. I attempt to show how the concept is not only a key operator underlying the logic of relations among religious symbols, but also both a product and a generator of the social relations reproduced in ritual activity. To anticipate my main point, in Chinese thought magical power is attributed to the mystical process that mediates order and disorder (yang and yin). *Ling*, which is conceived as the power possessed by some supernatural agent, is at once the fetishized product of the reproduction of social relations and a cultural logic that gives social relations meaning and value. Thus social institutions both embody Chinese notions of order and reproduce them.

To substantiate these claims, the meaning of the territorial-cult deities discussed in Part II must be located within a wider set of religious symbols, including ghosts and ancestors. The connection between these symbols and social reproduction hinges on the relationship between cosmological notions and the legitimacy of social institutions and authority. I attempt to show how both cosmological notions and the legitimacy of social institutions embody what I term "structures of value."

Direct observation of the process I seek to describe is especially difficult because of the complexity of Chinese society. An exhaustive model of the sort that might be developed for a small-scale society is impractical. Thus the analysis can aspire at most to provide glimpses of the sorts of processes that in some broadly similar fashion must pervade a much wider range of institutions. Nonetheless, if the general framework developed here is convincing, even an analysis of institutions in a small part of China during a short period of time may contribute to a fuller understanding of Chinese civilization.

---

*Other writers (e.g., Sahlins 1976, 1981; L. Dumont 1980a,b; Geertz 1973, 1980) choose to label the encompassing level "culture." The choice seems to depend on the degree to which one is interested in differentiating oneself from sociocentric or from cultural-deterministic reifications.

7

Yin and Yang:
Disorder and Order

Chinese religion as practiced in present-day Taiwan defines yang as the principle of order and yin as the principle of disorder. Creation, reproduction, change, transformation, and efficacy (*ling;* or in the sense developed by Weber, charisma) are viewed as aspects of the interaction of yin and yang. These ideas, of course, have their parallels in China's textual "great tradition." In popular ritual and cosmology, the impressive subtlety and variety of philosophical speculation are expressed in a wide range of apparently heterogeneous rituals and beliefs, but contrary to superficial appearances, this corpus of ritual and cosmology constitutes a consistent epistemology.

In what follows I attempt to demonstrate that yin and yang—the contrast between disorder and order—are fundamental premises of this epistemology, and that it is this epistemology that gives meaning and structure to Chinese rituals.* My argument has three objectives: first, to show the relevance of these seemingly esoteric philosophical concerns to the religious ideas of common people; second, to illuminate aspects of meaning in ritual that are inaccessible to behaviorist or functionalist analysis, particularly regarding the Chinese attribution of efficacy to supernatural entities; and third, to show how this set of basic assumptions about reality

---

*Others make this point, but portray "peasant" or "folk" religion as "dualistic" (Overmyer 1980; Saso 1972, 1976; Baity 1975). My own interpretation of yin/yang in Chinese religious thought does not neatly divide the cosmos into good and evil, pure and polluted; such dualisms are always contextually or hierarchically relative.

serves to legitimize characteristically Chinese patterns of social order and political authority.*

The Relativity of the Yin/Yang Contrast

In Chinese thought, yin and yang are not attributes affixed to entities as, for example, a standard list of correspondences like female: male :: ghosts:gods :: dark:bright might imply.† Rather, they are, taken together, a statement about the nature of things in general. Thus, for example, both women and men have both yin and yang organs, and these organs themselves have both yin and yang aspects (see also Saso 1977: 14–15). Or, to cite an example more to the present point, all celestial deities are unambiguously yang when contrasted with the likewise unambiguously yin ghosts and spirits of the underworld; that is, deities embody structured order in contrast to the unstructured chaos of the ghostly underworld. But within the category of "bright spirits" (shen-ming), yin/yang contrastive logic continues to apply, and the yin world too is structured in yin/yang terms. Thus female deities, who are yang when opposed to ghosts and underworld officials, are yin when opposed to male celestial bureaucrats because their gender affiliates them with reproduction and disorder (Ahern 1975; Seaman 1981; Sangren 1983).

The relationship between yin and yang is not only relative, it is hierarchical. As Louis Dumont (1980a: 239) puts it, "Hierarchy is not, essentially, a chain of superimposed commands, nor even a chain of beings of decreasing dignity, nor yet a taxonomic tree, but a relation that can succinctly be called the 'encompassing of the contrary.'" The first example he cites is the story of Eve's creation from Adam's rib. Initially, Adam is man undifferentiated into genders, but with Eve's creation, Adam's maleness is opposed to femaleness (p. 240):

In his entirety, Adam—or "man" in our language—is two things in one: the representative of the species mankind and the prototype of the male individuals of this species. On a first level, man and woman are identical; on a second level, woman is opposite or the contrary of man. These two relations characterize the

---

*In respect to this third objective, Part III may be viewed as an attempt to give substance to "two simple and connected propositions" suggested by Freedman (1974: 21): "First, Chinese religion entered into the unity of a vast polity. Second, it was an intrinsic part of a hierarchized society."

†For fuller treatments of this common misperception, see L. Dumont (1980a); R. Needham (1973). As Needham (p. xxviii) formalizes the point, "a:b :: c:d does not entail that a = c or that b = d." My application of this basic structuralist insight to the analysis of the symbolics of divinities is inspired, in part, by L. Dumont (1970) and Leach (1962,

hierarchical relations, which cannot be better symbolized than by the material encompassing of the future Eve in the body of the first Adam. This hierarchical relation is, very generally, that between a whole (or a set) and an element of this whole (or set): the element belongs to the set and is in this sense, consubstantial or identical with it; at the same time, the element is distinct from the set or stands in opposition to it. This is what I mean by the expression "the encompassing of the contrary."

The yin/yang relation, as evident in many ritual contexts, is one in which yang hierarchically encompasses yin. In other words, the order/disorder contrast is itself a kind of order.

The relative nature of these contrasts is expressed with striking clarity in domestic worship.* Images of deities, whether placed in temples or on domestic altars, face south (at least in theory), absorbing yang from the sun. Hence, worshipers, facing north, are yin relative to the deities' yang. On domestic altars, ancestors and deities—both yang relative to worshipers—are relatively differentiated according to direction; the deities, placed stage left (i.e., east, toward the rising sun), are yang to the ancestors' yin (stage right, west, toward the setting sun). This logic is carried further to the relative placement of ancestor tablets and deity images.[†] Worshipers themselves assume a relatively yang position when they face southward to make sacrifices to soldier-underlings of local territorial-cult celestial bureaucrats and to ghosts. The ghosts and spirit soldiers, both yin relative to worshipers, also stand in yin/yang relation to each other. The soldiers, whose ritual function is to control the ghosts, receive their sacrifices just inside the threshold; ghosts just outside.

Figure 3 schematically summarizes the relative yin/yang contrasts associated with household ritual. Note how the spatial structure of domestic worship translates to a horizontal plane the vertical structure of cosmology. North, which is yang because it faces south and absorbs light and warmth from the sun, is equivalent to up, south (facing north) to down. Thus, if the figure is pivoted on an east-west axis, the tripartite divisions of the cosmos—heaven, earth, and underworld—are clear. In sum, heaven:earth :: earth:underworld :: yang:yin.

1983). As Dumont (p. 194) puts it: "A characteristic [in this case, of a deity] does not exist here except in relation to its opposite. . . . Nothing is true by nature and everything by situation."

*This analysis of the semiotics of space in domestic rituals follows closely that developed by Feuchtwang (1974b), but rather than emphasizing, as he does, relative interiority/exteriority, I emphasize yin/yang (disorder/order). In so doing, I am inspired by Saso's (1972) analytic descriptions of *chiao* and Granet's (1973) classic essay on left and right in China. On the ruler:ruled :: yang:yin relationship, see W.-T. Chan (1963: 277). See also A. Wolf (1974a); Baity (1975).

†Ancestor tablets of the directly patrilineally ascendant line are placed stage left of those of collateral or matrilateral lines without direct patrilineal descendants.

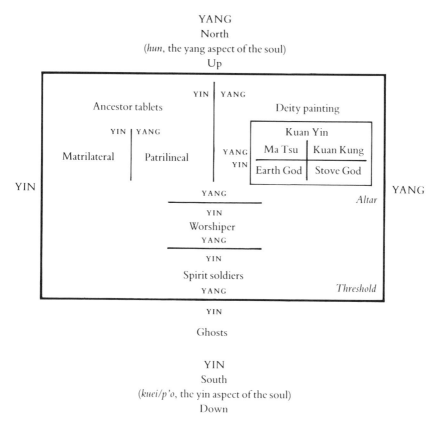

Fig. 3. Yin and yang in domestic space

An iconic representation of part of this cosmos is vertically present in the painting of deities that hangs over the domestic altar (see Fig. 4). In northern Taiwan, this painting most frequently includes Kuan Yin, Kuan Kung, Ma Tsu, Tsao Shen (the Stove God), and T'u Ti Kung.* Figure 4 raises some complex issues only partially addressed in the subsequent analysis. The relative positions of the deities conform to yin/yang logic. In the cases of Kuan Kung, a general/bureaucrat, and Ma Tsu, a female virgin-savior, the yin/yang relationship is clear. The vertical contrast between Kuan Kung and Ma Tsu on the one hand, and the Stove God and the Place God on the other, seems to replicate the yin/yang contrast be-

---

*See Maspero (1981: 123) for descriptions of different kinds of icons and domestic altars in China. Even in Taiwan there is considerable variation. Many icons omit Kuan Kung or represent Kuan Yin alone. In the storefront-homes of some merchants, Kuan Kung alone presides over the censer.

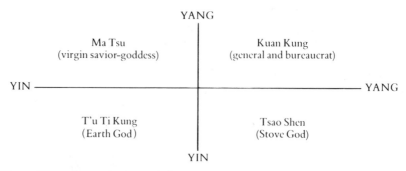

Fig. 4. Yin and yang in domestic icons

tween earth and heaven; that between the Stove God and the Place God
may refer to the mediating and transformative role of fire (messages sent
to gods are burned, food is cooked, etc.) vis-à-vis earth (see also A. Wolf
1974a). Kuan Yin's ascendant position is more problematic; as a female she
should be yin, but informants insist that she is relatively superior to the
other deities, hence she belongs on top. Because Kuan Yin's ascendant
position here may represent a mildly heterodox construction of the cosmos, I return to this problem in Chapter 9.

To summarize, the contrastive yin/yang logic is consistently applied in
the spatial organization of domestic worship and in cosmological conceptions. Similar contrastive logic informs a wide spectrum of Chinese
traditional knowledge, including calendrical constructions (Feuchtwang
1974b; J. Needham 1965: 228–29), Taoist meditation practices (Saso
1977), alchemy (Eliade 1962; J. Needham 1956; Boehmer 1977), geomancy
(Feuchtwang 1965), medicine (Kleinman 1980), architecture (Meyer 1976),
the staging of operas (Ward 1979), and so forth (see also Richard J. Smith
1983). In other words, what represents order at one level of contrast may
represent disorder at another. The consistency and ubiquity of this logical
framework in a multitude of symbolic, ritual, and iconographic manifestations testify to its pivotal importance in Chinese thought.

The Disorderly Oblivion of Decay and the Orderly
Anonymity of Heaven

That yin stands to yang as disorder to order is especially evident in the
rituals, symbols, and myths associated with death. A central theme of
Chinese funerary practices appears to be a "yangification" of the deceased
through a progressive ritual separation and elimination of yin elements of

the deceased's identity. This yangification is evident at several levels—in the long-term transformation of the dangerously entropic corpse to disembodied ancestral tablet; in the rites performed to prevent that aspect of the deceased's soul believed to journey through purgatory from becoming an anonymous ghost (*ku-hun, kuei*); and in the cleaning and reburial of the deceased's bones after all the yin flesh has rotted away (Watson 1982; Ahern 1973; Baity 1975).

The immediate concern of survivors upon the death of a relative is to aid the deceased in her/his transition from the world of the living to the world of the dead, which stand to each other as yang to yin. Yet even in the world of death there is order. The deceased must pass through an underworld populated by judges and officials, whose role is to punish and control the undifferentiated mass of ghosts (*kuei*). These officials of the underworld, who are yang in relation to the ghostly yin masses, are assisted by monstrous demons whose gruesome tortures of ghosts are often vividly depicted in temple murals.

In a perceptive article entitled "Domestic and Communal Worship in Taiwan," Stephan Feuchtwang (1974b: 128) notes that "within the metaphor of gods and kui itself, the kui in purgatory as an unstructured mass are contrastingly paired with the gods' structure, a structure that is, moreover, a hierarchy and the organ of domination over the kui." Thus Feuchtwang implies that the relevant metaphor is not the generally cited gods = officials, ghosts = bandits and strangers, but gods:ghosts :: social order (i.e., community):undifferentiated individuals (see also Ahern 1975: 208). A key point seems to be that underworld ghosts (as opposed to ghosts who haunt the yang world of the living) are not imagined as monsters. The monsters are the spirits who must impose order upon the chaotic masses, whereas the ghost masses, who are pure yin, are not anomalous but anonymous. The object of many of the rituals performed before burial is to ensure the safe passage of the deceased through the realms of the various underworld officials—that is, to keep her/him from becoming an unworshiped, unremembered, and hence undifferentiated ghost (i.e., yin). To effect this categorical separation, underworld officials must be bribed, and karmic debts must be paid.*

As the deceased's body decays in the grave, it becomes progressively less threatening. Eventually, when the yin flesh disappears and only the yang bones remain, the body is reburied in a jar, with great attention to

---

*Among the most vivid of debts is the one that all women acquire because of their association with the yin pollution of procreation and menstruation. During the ritual of the bloody pond, sons metaphorically drink their mother's menstrual blood, and thereby shift her to the relatively unmarked yang status occupied as a birthright by males (Sangren 1983; Ahern 1975; Seaman 1981; deGroot 1885).

geomantic influences, which are also defined in yin/yang terms (Feucht-wang 1965; Ahern 1975; deGroot 1885). But the body in the grave con-tinues to be yin in relation to the yang of the commemorative tablet placed on the domestic altar (and sometimes later on the altar in the lin-eage hall). As Feuchtwang (1974b: 119) observes, a process of selection and progressive fading from memory weeds out many souls: "Those weeded out, without wealth or status, are in limbo, orphan souls."

As those who remain become progressively purified of yin, they also become progressively anonymous. The most yang of ancestors (*tsu-hsien*)—those enshrined in lineage halls—are, like ghosts, purged of identity, having become nodal ciphers in the hierarchical structure of lin-eage relations. Moreover, the higher an ancestor is in the hierarchy, the more anonymous and yang that ancestor becomes. Contrasting ghostly masses in purgatory with distant ancestors, both spirit categories purged of personal identity, amounts to contrasting pure undifferentiated, un-civilized humanity with pure patrilineal structure.

In sum, the power that is life depends on the interaction of disorder and order. What has sometimes been described as Chinese belief in mul-tiple souls—the soul in decaying flesh in the earth that is led by T'u Ti Kung to the underworld, the soul in the ancestral tablet, and the spirit in the grave—is more accurately characterized as the progressive dissolution of life's volatile combination of yin and yang. As the deceased gradually disappears from living memory, she/he moves simultaneously nearer the poles of entropic yin and pure yang structure. Once living memory fades, the only trace of the deceased lies in the still problematic combination of yin and yang associated with the grave.

An homologous yangification process marks ascendance in the ranked bureaucracy of male deities. As we have seen, the structure of the pan-theon is often conceived as similar to the structure of China's traditional imperial bureaucracy. Like officials, celestial bureaucrats have specialized functions and are responsible to higher celestial authorities. Moreover, like officials in the earthly bureaucracy, meritorious deities can be pro-moted up the hierarchy of celestial offices. At the apex, T'ien Kung, sometimes referred to as the Jade Emperor (Yü Huang Ta Ti), reigns over the heavenly bureaucracy much as the emperor reigns over all under heaven (*t'ien-hsia*).

It is noteworthy here that the higher positions in the celestial bureau-cracy are the least personalized. In many Taiwanese temples, heaven is represented by a plaque with written characters, whereas all the other de-ities in the temple are represented by carved images. Middle- and lower-level officials are associated with the nested hierarchies of local social organization—that is, with aspects of social/cultural order directly meaningful to common people. At these middle levels, local gods are often said to be deified historical personages who were rewarded for meritorious service, which makes explicit a distinction between office and officeholder. At the higher levels, however, office and officeholder tend to merge, and the highest offices become essentially depersonalized ciphers.*

Common people, although acknowledging the hierarchical superiority of heaven, concentrate their piety on lower-level gods. This fact is generally attributed to the greater accessibility of real-world lower-ranking bureaucrats, presumed to be the models for low-ranking celestial officials. Chinese informants themselves sometimes rationalize their behavior in essentially these terms. Nonetheless, it seems to me that the relative ritual importance of lower-ranking celestial bureaucrats stems from a more complex logic. In brief, the efficacy and accessibility of lower-ranking celestial officials are in part a function of their mediating yin and yang qualities in the celestial hierarchy.† As long as the office is distinguished from its holder, and the officeholder is thought to be a deified historical personage, divinity retains yin aspects vis-à-vis the pure yang abstract order of heaven itself. Thus the same logic that converts ancestors, once living memory of them as individuals is lost, to depersonalized, pure yang status also accounts for the progressive hierarchical yangification of the celestial bureaucracy. The higher a deity is in the celestial bureaucracy, the more devoid of individuality and the more purely yang he is. Moreover, the higher a deity's position, the lower his practical efficacy.

A related reason why lower- and middle-level celestial bureaucrats figure more prominently in local religion pertains to the fact that power, or *ling,* is itself constituted in the process of social reproduction. Consequently, those deities that correspond to the forms of social order most important in peoples' lives are bound to be thought of as the most relevant and powerful ones.

In my view, there is an association between pure yin and undifferentiated anonymity that logically parallels the association between pure yang and abstract order. For example, an important ritual associated with the Fu-jen *kung's p'u-tu* involves the worship of a blue-faced, paper image of Ta Shih Yeh, who is a transformation of Kuan Yin evoked to control the ghosts invited to the festival. Indeed, the entire *p'u-tu* festivities are in

---

*There is also some tendency for the lowest-ranking celestial bureaucrats (e.g., T'u Ti Kung and the Stove God) to lack clear-cut connections to formerly living personages, a fact that I see as indicative of their associations with the most abstract transformative notions of earthly decay and fire. However, many informants believe that these gods, like most others, were appointed to their offices in reward for their meritorious lives.

†See Leach (1983) for an enlightening discussion of mediation.

part an attempt to objectify, control, and eliminate antisocial, disruptive yin forces in the community. The ghosts invited to the feast are specifically the spirits of the socially anomalous—people who, when alive, were wanderers without roots or descendants. Ta Shih Yeh, monstrously represented as a blue-faced, horned devil with bulging red eyes, coerces these ghosts into behaving according to the rules of communal order. Ta Shih Yeh's image stands between the icon of this order (the votive lamps placed on the temple altar) and the sacrifices offered to the ghosts (which are placed on long tables in front of the temple doors).

A Taoist priest also stands between the temple altar and the collected ghosts. Speaking in an unintelligible "ghost language" (*kuei-hua*), the priest magically multiplies the offerings, such that "one becomes ten, ten becomes one hundred," and so forth. He also performs spells to make it possible for headless and fire-spitting ghosts to eat. (Temple paintings of Chinese purgatory vividly portray many such fiendish afflictions.)

Both Ta Shih Yeh and the Taoist priest mediate the disorder represented by the ghosts and the order represented by the gods and the votive lamps; in a sense, their combined task is to lure the unstructured, potentially disruptive ghosts into the harmonious order of community structure. Conceptually, gaining the release of souls from purgatory and effecting their admission to heaven is one way to get rid of them. The burning of the paper image of Ta Shih Yeh, which concludes the ritual, temporarily exorcises the disruptive forces he controls by sending them back to purgatory.*

In sum, ancestors and gods become increasingly anonymous and purified of yin as they ascend the hierarchical structures of patrilineal genealogy and celestial bureaucracy. At the opposite pole of yin/yang contrast are the ghosts in purgatory. Like the purely yang distant ancestors and heaven, these ghosts are anonymous; but their anonymity is the yin negation of any ordering principle, not the orderly anonymity of patrilineal and heavenly yang.

*I witnessed a form of exorcism similar in some respects to the burning of Ta Shih Yeh. A woman who complained that she could not control her three-year-old daughter was instructed by a local spirit medium to burn a straw effigy and thus eliminate her own dislike of her little girl.

8

The Power of Supernatural Spirits

That order and disorder are pervasive concerns in Chinese culture is self-evident and need not detain us here. However, the idea that the logic of order and disorder is also the logic of Chinese cosmology and rituals requires elaboration. My argument is that the power attributed to supernatural entities (*ling*) is an implicit function of the mediation of order and disorder. In other words, supernatural entities are perceived as powerful and efficacious—as having the ability to act—only in contexts in which they mediate other entities, who stand for order (yang) and disorder (yin). *Ling* is thus an attribute of the construction of order out of disorder, or of the dissolution of order into disorder.

Because order and disorder are contextually relative, the power attributed to any mediator is also contextually relative. Context is defined with implicit reference to other categories of spirits or social collectivities. Neither spirit nor social entity escapes this logic of the social determination of power. Consequently, the power of supernatural entities is not based directly on motivated correspondences with real-world categories. This is not to deny entirely the relevance of such correspondences; analogies between gods, ghosts, and ancestors on the one hand, and officials, strangers, and kin on the other, are frequently drawn by native informants. However, such exegeses fail to explain the kinds of power attributed to various spirit categories.

The notion that *ling* is an attribute of the mediation of order and disorder only begins to suggest the complexity and open-ended productivity of the logic that underlies Chinese cosmology. Order and disorder are very general and abstract notions, and one need only consider the magnitude of Chinese philosophical discourse on yin and yang to appreciate some of their conceptual complexity. Very generally speaking, in Chinese thought order emanates from nature or heaven, and disorder is the negation, inversion, or dissolution of order. More subtly (and most generally), order consists in the very dichotomy order/disorder. This point is obscure even to most Chinese, but this very obscurity plays an important role in maintaining yin/yang logic as an ideology.

Most ritual is concerned with the reproduction of social order, which of course has many dimensions. The Chinese Empire, which the Chinese called "all under heaven" (*t'ien-hsia*), was conceived as a pervasive order, in contrast to the chaotic world of barbarians outside its domain. Similarly, community constitutes a bounded order in contrast to outsiders, and patrilineal kin ties and filial piety are the proper elements of ordered relations between sexes and generations. More problematic is the order constituted by life, in contrast to the decay or disorder of death. Despite attempts by Chinese philosophers to create encompassing systems, in each of these domains order is somewhat differently conceived. What they have in common is the centrality of the order/disorder contrast itself.

This multiplicity of domains of order complicates the interpretation of Chinese religious symbols, because the same symbol may occupy different positions relative to order and disorder in different domains or contexts. Ancestors, for example, unambiguously represent order in the domain of patrilineal kinship, but as sojourners in the realm of the dead, they belong to the yin world. Thus supernatural entities shift meaning depending upon the context in which they are addressed. In attempting to make sense of the apparently contradictory beliefs regarding these entities, a first step is to define the contexts in which their power becomes intelligible.

For example, it is not sufficient simply to document the ethnographic fact that Chinese believe the ghosts of people who have drowned are dangerous to the living; one must also explain why they are so conceived. In what follows, I argue that such explanations are to be found in a cultural logic that situates this category of spirit in implicit contrast to other spirit categories. The multitude of Chinese spirit categories and the complexity introduced by shifting contexts preclude exhaustive analysis, so my argument is offered by way of illustration and example.

All spirit categories mediate yin and yang in some contexts, and it is this mediation that constitutes their power. But it is not enough to argue that power or efficacy is culturally defined as a function of the relationship of order and disorder; equally important is the fact that the relationship between order and disorder is a hierarchical one. This modification of the structuralist emphasis on binary opposition must be credited to Louis Dumont (1980a; see also T. Turner 1984 for a relevant critique). As previously noted, order hierarchically "encompasses" disorder—that is, at one level of cultural contrast, order and disorder are in complementary binary opposition, but this opposition is itself an ordered one. (I explore some of the implications of this structure in later chapters.) Thus the hierarchical nature of mediation means that efficacy or power attributed to any supernatural entity stems from the way it can shift in status from yang (relative order) at one level of contrast to yin (relatively unstructured status) at another.

This last assertion means that mediation and *ling* are attributes of matrices of symbolic contrast. At least two dimensions of contrast are necessary to specify mediation. In what follows, I employ a schematic device to illustrate how these two dimensions can link sets of four or more symbols. My objective is to illustrate how particular supernatural entities acquire *ling*. I do this by juxtaposing them with other entities to which they stand in implicit contrast. These sets of symbols provide the semiotic contexts within which meanings are specified. Experts may object to the quality of my evidence for defining the groups of entities that constitute the relevant symbolic contrasts, but my main point is to explicate the key role that *ling* plays in the ordering of all such contrasts. I do not wish to deny the relevance of other interpretations of the meaning of the entities themselves. Indeed, this approach suggests multiple meanings for any religious symbol.

My analysis thus differs significantly from what might initially appear to be similar arguments in Mary Douglas's widely influential work (see especially Douglas 1966). Rather than associating magical or dangerous power with disorderly, anomalous entities, I argue that Chinese culture defines power as a function of the mediation of order and disorder. Anomalous characteristics associated with powerful mediating spirits (e.g., virgin mothers, blue-faced devils) express the power of mediation, not vice versa. In other words, the power of imaginary spirits cannot be attributed to their supposed anomalies; rather, anomalies are manifestations of their mediating power (see also Leach 1983). This means that we must shift focus from characteristics attributed to supernatural entities and

analyze the concept of efficacy, or *ling*, itself. *Ling* is the key cultural operator (Boon 1973; Lévi-Strauss 1966) structuring Chinese religious logic.

Ancestral Spirits and Other Ghosts

Seemingly contradictory Chinese beliefs regarding the afterlife of the
soul are a source of confusion for Western exegetes. Souls of the departed
are thought at once to reside in the grave, to inhabit ancestral tablets on
domestic and lineage altars, to journey through a netherworld populated
by corrupt officials and their demonic henchmen, and to attain salvation
in the Western Paradise of Amitabha, the Buddha of Boundless Light.
Some of the complexities and contradictions of this apparent hodgepodge of beliefs stem from their historically disparate origins in ancient
Taoist, Buddhist, Confucian, and other traditions. Yet *ling* constitutes a
grammar that may allow us to begin to see a logic in this apparently chaotic syncretism.

Consider first the following kinds of deceased souls: ancestral spirits
enshrined on domestic and lineage-hall altars; spirits of kin not so enshrined (who may be further divided into spirits of the recently deceased
and spirits of forgotten kin); ghosts of people who died by violence; and
spirits who have no living kin and are thus forgotten and unworshiped.
Consider further the following ethnographic fact: within this set of spirits, the two categories that Taiwanese consider most *ling*—and dangerously so—are forgotten kin and ghosts of people who have suffered violent and premature death.

Spirit mediums (*tang-ki*) frequently attribute the maladies of their patients to ritual neglect of deceased kin. Moreover, the categories of kin
most likely to be overlooked, and thus to haunt the living, are those that
do not fit neatly into yang patrilineal structure—for example, children,
collateral relatives without descendants, maiden aunts, and daughters
who die unmarried (see also Baity 1975). Each of these categories of
kinsmen is denied incorporation into a continuing patriline and the concomitant worship of descendants. Thus such kin cannot be wholly purified of yin, but as relatives they do not belong to the pure yin category
of forgotten ghosts. In short, they mediate yin and yang.

Even more feared are the ghosts of those who have drowned, been
murder victims, or committed suicide.* Unlike other souls, such ghosts

---

*Note the relevant discussion of "good" and "bad" deaths as they relate to the regenera-
tion of social order in Bloch & Parry (1982: 15–18).

remain in the yang world, where they seek vengeance on the living. Michael Loewe (1979: 10) notes that, as early as the Han dynasty,

in normal circumstances the *p'o* [yin aspect of the soul] and the *hun* [yang] were believed to separate at the moment of death; but . . . in cases of death by violence this norm is frustrated. In exceptional circumstances of that type *p'o* and *hun* remain bound together; although they are separated from the body, they retain the power of assuming another bodily form. This capacity permits them to avenge the violence practised on the body which they formerly inhabited; such vengeance is exacted by various forms of malevolence.

These beliefs persist virtually unchanged in present-day Ta-ch'i. In sum, the souls of those who die violently, like those of unworshiped kin, mediate yin and yang.

All kin are yang in relation to spirits of non-kin, but kin who die without patrilineal descendants to worship them are yin in relation to ancestors who have a definite place in a patriline. By the same token, spirits of non-kin are yin relative to spirits of kin, but people who die violently tend to be remembered, and are yang relative to the spirits of forgotten strangers.

Figure 5 juxtaposes these two dimensions of yin/yang contrast: first, according to whether the spirit is that of a person remembered or forgotten, and second, according to whether the spirit is kin or not (see also Baity 1975). Worshiped ancestors, who are doubly yang in this set, seldom interfere with their descendants. (When they do, the ascribed mo-

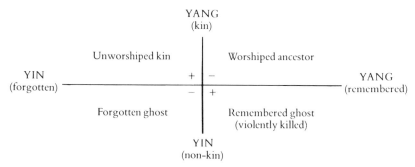

Fig. 5. Yin and yang in ancestors and ghosts. In this and subsequent figures, *ling* (efficacy or magical power) is indicated by a "+"; categories marked "−" are not *ling* relative to those marked "+". *Ling* is the mediation of yin and yang, so entities in the upper left and lower right positions are *ling*, whereas those in the upper right and lower left are not.

tive is always the ancestors' anxiety that their descendants are neglecting to perform the proper rituals on their behalf.) Only the conscientious performance of ritual duties by descendants prevents ancestors from devolving to the category of forgotten kin or ghost. In the case of worshiped ancestors, the trajectory of efficacy or power is from descendant to spirit; through commemorative worship and sacrifices, it is the living who act upon the ancestors by providing for their needs. However, in the cases of unworshiped kin and spirits of the violently killed, it is the spirit category that acts malevolently on the living.

A fourth category of deceased souls, those anonymous ghosts residing in purgatory, is doubly yin: they are neither remembered nor kin. Paradoxically, the anonymous ghosts in purgatory, who are the formal opposites of the doubly yang, worshiped ancestors, are quite like ancestors in some respects. Except during the seventh lunar month, when the gates of purgatory open and they are freed to roam the yang world, such ghosts are not perceived as threatening. And again it is the living, through the *p'u-tu* (a ritual designed to free ghosts from purgatory) and its associated ceremonies of "feeding the hungry ghosts," who act upon these anonymous ghosts, rather than the ghosts who act upon the living.

Applying a similar schematic framework, Figures 6 and 7 summarize the mediating role of the living vis-à-vis the deceased relatives and ghosts who are propitiated at *p'u-tu* ceremonies during the seventh lunar month. In Figure 6, descendants (who are *ling* in this context) are yang in relation to the recently deceased and ghosts but yin in relation to the more distant patrilineal ancestors enshrined on tablets. Descendants are obligated to mediate actively on behalf of recently deceased relatives to ensure their successful transformation to pure yang ancestral status. This transformation is effected through funerary rituals, with the result that the recently deceased are purified of yin and become orderly. If appropriate rituals are not performed, the spirit of the deceased devolves to the yin, disorderly,

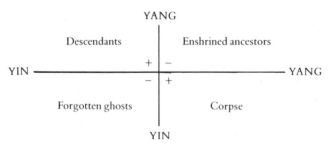

Fig. 6. Yin and yang in ancestor/descendant relations

Fig. 7. Yin and yang in community/ghost relations. The *p'u-tu* is a ritual to feed hungry ghosts and free them from purgatory.

anonymous, and even malevolent status of ghost. Thus efficacy in this context adheres to descendants who mediate the pure yang of generalized patrilineality and the yin that is associated both with death and with the crossing of the boundary between yang and yin worlds.* But the recently deceased spirit is also *ling* because it has not yet been purified of yin. Consequently, if proper rituals are not performed on its behalf, the spirit may makes its displeasure known by intervening in the lives of its descendants in a variety of unpleasant ways.

A homologous structure of relationships is depicted in Figure 7. During *p'u-tu* ceremonies, the community (an undifferentiated collectivity) intercedes actively on behalf of hungry ghosts. In addition to literally feeding and clothing ghosts, the ceremony attempts to obtain salvation for them (see Overmyer 1980). Taoist or Buddhist priests acting as mediators ritually purify the ghosts of yin pollution, the cause of their having been sentenced to the tortures of purgatory, and seek to gain their admission to paradise (or, at least, their reincarnation in a higher level of existence in the yang world).

The community, as sponsors of the ritual, are *ling* in this context. However, the ghosts, who are normally safely confined in the yin world, are allowed a brief sojourn in the yang world during the seventh lunar month. As we have seen, ghosts in the yang world can be dangerous. Thus it is that during the seventh month special rituals of a propitiatory

---

*Life is to death as yang is to yin. Since patrilineal ancestors are on the other side of the life/death boundary, they ought to be yin relative to their descendants. However, in Figure 6 enshrined ancestors are in a position that is yang relative to descendants. One way to escape this contradiction is to claim that the contexts are different; during the deceased's funeral, the new ancestor is yin relative to her/his descendants, whereas in ancestor worship the relationship is the converse. But this line of reasoning disguises an important contradiction in how Chinese culture reconciles assertions of the stability of patrilineal institutions and the facts of death and procreation. These issues are addressed in Chapter 9.

nature must be performed to prevent the temporarily *ling* ghosts from creating harm and disorder.

Juxtaposing rituals performed on behalf of ancestors with rituals performed on behalf of ghosts may help to explain what at first appears to be an anomaly: *p'u-tu* ceremonies performed on behalf of ghosts are also believed to redound to the benefit of ancestors. If, as is generally argued, ghosts and ancestors correspond to very clearly differentiated categories of real people (i.e., strangers and kinsmen), how can ancestors benefit from rituals performed for ghosts? One explanation offered by Taiwanese is that the Buddhist merit (*kung-te*) accumulated by the community also benefits the community's ancestors. But there is nothing in orthodox Buddhism that justifies such indirect transfers of merit. A more convincing if less linearly "causal" explanation seems to lie in the closely parallel logics that inform both sorts of rituals. When Taiwanese manifest a belief that *p'u-tu* rituals benefit ancestors as well as ghosts, they may be confusing their roles as descendants and as members of a community, and thus the distinction between ancestors and ghosts. This "confusion" is understandable, however, because their structural position is identical in both kinds of rituals: in both cases they are acting as *ling* mediators to prevent the devolution of the dead to pure yin status, and thus to ensure the stability of yang order.

Female Deities and Mass-Grave Spirits

A similar argument illuminates the special efficacy of two other categories of Chinese spirits: female deities and spirits entombed in mass graves. It is quite common in Taiwan to find communal sacrifices offered to spirits in mass graves (often termed *ta-mu-kung* or *yu-ying-kung*) during the seventh lunar month. Typically, these graves are said to contain the victims of battles with competing ethnic groups, with the aborigines, or with the Japanese. In short, they contain the spirits of local militia or soldiers (*yung*).

Unlike the free wandering spirits that are propitiated at most *chung-yüan* and *p'u-tu* ceremonies, these grave spirits are sometimes said to answer prayers, much as gods do. Moreover, as Stevan Harrell (1974b) notes, grave spirits are often perceived as more approachable and efficacious than celestial officials. He suggests that such spirits are more approachable because, among other things, their power stems from sources outside the structures of orthodox patriarchal and bureaucratic authority.

In this respect, there is an important similarity between the efficacy of *ta-mu-kung* and that of female divinities, particularly Kuan Yin. Elsewhere I have argued that female divinities are thought to be more responsive to individual requests than celestial officials are (Sangren 1983). Moreover, female deities are thought to be responsive to all—even to the structurally anomalous and socially disenfranchised in China. Harrell suggests a similar appeal for *ta-mu-kung* and the like. These facts conflict with the idea that Chinese peasants imagine the supernatural world to mirror the mundane: women (the mundane equivalents of female deities) and local militia (the mundane equivalents of the mass-grave spirits) do have power, but it is formally quite insignificant compared with the power and authority exercised by patriarchs and officials. Why, then, does popular imagination so often endow female divinities and mass-grave spirits with power that is in some ways greater than that attributed to celestial bureaucrats?

To answer this question, it is necessary to abandon the idea that women's qualities are projected directly onto female deities, or that the dangerous power of soldiers and militia is attributed to mass-grave spirits. Rather, we must assume that *ling* is a function of a spirit's mediating role in the disorder/order, yin/yang logic already suggested. Or, to use conventional notation, it is less that

$$\text{women} = \text{female deities}$$

and

$$\text{militia, soldiers} = \text{mass-grave spirits}$$

than that

$$\text{women:patriarchal authority :: female deities:celestial bureaucracy}$$

and

$$\text{militia:community :: mass-grave spirits:celestial bureaucrats.}$$

With this in mind, we can now consider Figure 8, which shows the relations among male territorial-cult deities, female deities (especially Kuan Yin), mass-grave spirits, and ghosts in purgatory. Female deities and celestial bureaucrats, as bright spirits in heaven, are yang to the yin of mass-grave spirits and ghosts. But female deities are yin to male deities' yang. In this particular set, the significance of female deities' and ghosts' yin seems to be the absence of territorial boundedness in contrast to the ordered, yang boundedness of the male territorial bureaucrat and the spatially specific spirits in mass graves.

The connection between the male territorial-cult deity and the spatially

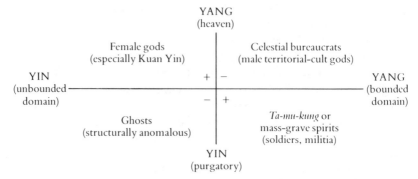

Fig. 8. Yin and yang in the relations among male and female gods, spirit soldiers, and ghosts

bounded community is so obvious that it need not be belabored. Because *ta-mu-kung* are located in a grave site that mediates yin and yang worlds (see Ahern 1973: 240–41), they are tied to a particular locale. It is precisely this spatial particularism that makes them yang relative to the spatially undefined ghost masses of the underworld, although they remain yin relative to the celestial bureaucrats' yang. Since the spirit soldiers in mass graves are usually believed to have died defending community boundaries against threatening outsiders, the relationship between celestial bureaucrats and mass-grave spirits is that of territorially bounded community to local militia.*

Whereas the mass-grave spirits are metaphorically conceived as the ancestral defenders of boundaries (but as no one's ancestors in particular; see Baity 1975), the ghost masses of the netherworld are unbounded, uncivilized, undifferentiated humanity. The relationship of these ghost masses to Kuan Yin parallels the mass-grave spirits' relationship to the territorial-cult god (ghost masses:Kuan Yin :: mass-grave spirit:territorial-cult god). In Chinese myth, Kuan Yin is coterminous with Miao-shan, a princess whose father had her killed when she rejected his demand that she marry. In purgatory, she revealed herself to be Kuan Yin and, overthrowing karmic justice, led all the imprisoned spirits to heaven (Sangren 1983; Dud-

---

*In Wei-liao, a hamlet near Ta-ch'i that lacks a Place God (T'u Ti Kung) shrine, a *ta-mu-kung* serves as the ritual focus for a neighborhood-level community, and thus in effect stands for the absent bureaucrat. This absence of one of the key parts of the relevant contrastive set is a real anomaly. I suspect it is a temporary one created by the mass grave's having been imposed on the community at just about the time in the process of ritual intensification when a territorial cult ought to have been instituted. I would be surprised if Wei-liao does not eventually form a separate neighborhood cult focused on T'u Ti Kung.

bridge 1978). This legend coincides with Kuan Yin's important role in the universal salvation (*p'u-tu*) rituals performed at *chiao,* and during the seventh-month *chung-yüan* ceremonies (Liu 1967; Saso 1972; Sangren 1980; Pang 1977; deGroot 1885; Baity 1975; Feuchtwang 1974b).* Like the mass-grave spirits, Kuan Yin is thought to answer personal requests, but her efficacy, unlike that of the mass-grave spirits, is not limited to a particular locale. In sum, both Kuan Yin and *ta-mu-kung,* unlike the doubly yang celestial bureaucrats and the doubly yin ghost masses, mediate yin and yang, and it is this mediation that constitutes their power or responsiveness.

When contrasted with female deities and mass-grave spirits, celestial bureaucrats are relatively "locked into" a rather rigid, hierarchical pattern of symbolic relationships; in theory, they ought to act as little more than nodal ciphers in the structural hierarchy.† What power they have is directed toward defending order and, more specifically, toward defending the boundaries of community from threatening outside forces. Consequently, no bureaucrat, patriarch, or celestial official, however highly placed he may be in the branching pyramid of authority, has the power to respond ex officio to individual requests that might subvert community (see also Baity 1975).

I do not want to overstate the consistency of this distinction, however. A key phrase in the preceding argument is "ex officio." In fact, male bureaucratic gods sometimes receive personal requests, but should they choose to grant them, they do so for "unofficial," usually slightly illegitimate reasons (e.g., bribery, nepotism). Generally speaking, however, personal requests are taken much more frequently to female deities like Kuan Yin.

In contrast to the orderly hierarchy of celestial bureaucrats, female deities and mass-grave spirits seem to derive power from their abilities to represent the regenerative force that is latent in disorder. In many personal requests—for example, that one's children be favored over others in college entrance examinations, that one's business succeed in competition

---

*The conceptual transcendence of social boundaries inherent in the symbol of Kuan Yin is evident in the constituencies that worship her (see Sangren 1983). The concept of universality and unboundedness is itself a cultural category, and is yin to the yang of particularism and boundedness. Thus my analysis departs significantly from Victor Turner's influential notions of structure and anti-structure, categories assumed to be universal and independent of any particular cultural construction.

†In another context, Granet (1975: 60) points out the similar constraints in the analogously structured authority of a feudal noble family. Authority is limited not only because one's immediate superior is, in turn, subordinate to the next higher level, but also because all the members are constrained by the "eminent rights of the domestic community" as a whole; that is, the ultimate authority is hierarchical order itself.

with others, or that one recover from disease—what is desired is an ally who has the power to manipulate order, rather than one obligated to uphold it. Those of lowly estate in the mundane structures of hierarchical authority (e.g., women, the poor, the landless, outsiders) are concerned less with the abstract maintenance of order than with finding or constructing a secure and culturally valued place within it. And of course, even real-world officials may seek personal relations with spirits in non-official contexts.

In short, those who beseech the help of Kuan Yin or a mass-grave spirit implicitly ask that the order immanent in the administered cosmos be altered in their favor; or, more precisely, they desire a reproduction of new order rather than an affirmation of existing order. Consequently, such requests occur in contexts other than public festivals. The cultural logic that defines the meaning of specific religious symbols in wider context thus limits the "power" of celestial bureaucrats, their hierarchically superior positions notwithstanding. If one requires special treatment, celestial bureaucrats will not do.

The power of female divinities is to the power of celestial bureaucracy as the power of mothers is to formal patriarchal authority in the household (Sangren 1983).* Both mothers and female deities act as partisan advocates of their clients' (i.e., children/supplicants) interests, whatever the justice of those clients' causes in the larger structure of rights and authority (or, for that matter, karma).† It is because of this power to circumvent generalized order and thus accomplish particular ends that personal requests are addressed much more often to female deities than to celestial bureaucrats. And because such appeals are partially illegitimate, or at least problematic in terms of cosmic order's claim to stability, their granting is all the more miraculous—*ling*.

The categorically liminal mass-grave spirits are also approached with very personal, even selfish requests for special treatment, and for similar reasons. Without known descendants, the spirits in mass graves lack the social identity that would convert them into the doubly yang category of distant patrilineal ancestors, even though, like ancestors, they are histori-

---

*Louis Dumont (1970: 192) notes a similar division of labor between two South Asian gods: the female divinity relates to internal relations (like a mother), while the male divinity relates (like a father) to external ones.

†Not all such mediators are conceived of as female. Ti Tsang, for example, poses an interesting contrast to Kuan Yin. Ti Tsang is a bodhisattva closely associated in Chinese myth with Mu-lien, who is said to have achieved a degree of enlightenment sufficient to journey to hell to save his mother. The strikingly symmetrical gender inversions in the Mu-lien and Miao-shan myths are undoubtedly susceptible to illumination through structural analysis.

cally connected to particular locales.* Consequently, they are not locked into the ordering principles that underlie patrilineal ancestor worship or bureaucratic hierarchy. But as souls tied to a particular locality in the yang world, mass-grave spirits do possess a kind of unchanneled power, which through the initiation of reciprocal ritual communication can be harnessed for the benefit or the detriment of the living.

For example, one informant attributed his lineage's ascendance to wealth to a rather curious set of circumstances. Several generations before, the lineage corporation's founder heard a strange noise as he walked through the forest at night. Investigating, he discovered two human bones. He carried the bones home and later placed them in a proper grave, providing the unknown spirit with the usual sacrifices due an ancestor. But unlike "real" ancestors, this unknown spirit proved especially grateful and powerful, rewarding the lineage founder with great wealth. Through worship, the spirit was, in effect, transformed from a forgotten ghost to the equivalent of a mass-grave spirit. The same informant attributed the lineage corporation's recent decline to ritual neglect of this unknown spirit.

In sum, the efficacy attributed to mass-grave spirits may stem precisely from the fact that they are neither ancestors nor celestial bureaucrats. Unlike ancestors, such spirits can never be purified of yin and are thus permanently endowed with the power inherent in the mediation of order and disorder. But they are not like ghosts in purgatory, either, for the attachment of their yang bones to a particular locale prevents their devolving to pure, ineffective yin.†

To digress a little, I suspect that a similar logic accounts for the fact that of the three loci of an ancestor's soul (the grave, the tablet, and the underworld), it is the soul in the grave that most directly affects the lives of the living. The soul in the grave cannot become pure yang (like the tablet of a distant ancestor) because it is in the ground, and it cannot become pure yin (like a forgotten ghost) because it has a physical presence in a specific

---

*Baity (1975) argues that since gods should not be tied particularistically to descendants, they must originate as ghosts. I doubt whether this rule is universal because, as in the case of the Ch'ens of Chung-liao (Chap. 6), one person's ancestor can be another person's god. But Baity is probably correct about the characteristic pattern of development in the majority of deity cults. More to the point, however, a deified historical personage cannot be thought of as having living descendants. This argument may account as much for Confucius's resistance to deification, as does the secular orientation of his teachings. His descendants, of course, publicly share in his charisma by staking a particular claim to worship him.

†I speak, of course, of Chinese conceptions: if all memory of the grave is lost, such a devolution ("objectively speaking") obviously occurs, but Chinese do not include this devolution in their conception of the status of these spirits.

locality. This potent mix of yang and yin may account for descendants' concern with the geomancy of the grave.

In the same vein, most female deities are thought to have been either unmarried virgins (Kuan Yin and Ma Tsu) or, literally, "Unborn Mothers" (Wu Sheng Lao Mu).* Like the mysterious benefactor of my informant's ancestor and the spirits in mass graves, such women cannot be cleansed of yin. Thus they permanently escape assignment to any fixed position in the nested hierarchy of ancestor worship, although as bright spirits they are also immune to becoming pure yin.

These latter points emerge more clearly in the contrastive set of female ancestors, Kuan Yin, Ta Shih Yeh, and the spirits of deceased women tortured in purgatory's bloody pond (see Fig. 9). In a sense, female ancestors become male (and yang) by merging with their husbands and losing their individual identities.† Their surnames but not their personal names are inscribed on tablets as adjuncts to their husbands, whose personal names are included. In contrast, Kuan Yin, by refusing to marry, can never become an ancestor, and thus can never be purged of yin because she can have no descendants.‡ However, in her sojourn in hell, Kuan Yin too undergoes a gender transformation, assuming the form of the male demon-god, Ta Shih Yeh.§

As we have seen, Ta Shih Yeh plays an important role in *p'u-tu* cere-

---

* *Wu-sheng* in Buddhist terminology means "not subject to life and death"—that is, beyond transmigration. The use of this term in Wu Sheng Lao Mu's name seems to place her outside the idiom of yin/yang contrast. Indeed, as in the ancient Taoist notion of *hun-tun*, the term is meant to suggest something beyond and superior to yin/yang and change. Nonetheless, because the deity is female, the implicit contrast with yang masculinity is unavoidable.

† Pratt (1928: 399) quotes a popular Buddhist pamphlet ("Guide Book for Those Not Advanced in Pure Land Knowledge") as follows: "There is no woman in Western Paradise because women who are saved are born there as men. For womanhood implies pain, and there shall be no pain there." Although framed in Buddhist terms of pain and suffering, this doctrine is entirely compatible with yin/yang logic. To win salvation, spirits must be purified of yin. Femaleness is yin in this context and must be removed.

‡ Note the important patrilineal asymmetry here. A man is a member of his father's line, but a woman gains membership in a line only when she marries. A man who does not produce descendants may be assigned one (e.g., by adoption) whether he marries or not, whereas a woman without issue must find not only assigned descendants, but also an assigned husband (as in the custom of "ghost marriage," in which a woman is "married" posthumously so that her spirit can enjoy the benefits of worship by descendants). Even the members of the marriage-resistance cults in nineteenth-century Kwangtung found it necessary to transfer membership to men's lines (Topley 1975). Some of the *pu lo-chia* ("women who do not go down to the family"), instead of joining their husbands, bought their husbands concubines, whose children were then obliged to worship the *pu lo-chia* as their mothers.

§ There may be some textual basis for Ta Shih Yeh in the wrathful tantric manifestations of Avalokiteśvara, the male Indic bodhisattva who is himself transformed into Kuan Yin in Chinese Buddhism.

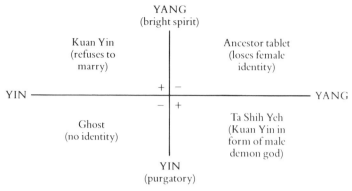

Fig. 9. Female gender and mediating power

monies. Represented as a blue-faced devil, Ta Shih Yeh's paper image is brought to life (made *ling*) in an "eye-opening" (*k'ai-kuang*) ceremony in which the image's eyes are painted in with chicken's blood, to the accompaniment of magical incantations and dances performed by a Taoist priest. During the rest of the *p'u-tu*, Ta Shih Yeh controls the masses of ghosts while they feast on the sacrifices provided by the sponsoring community.

Ta Shih Yeh is considered an especially problematic and powerful figure. I was told that it is crucial that the paper figure be totally consumed in flames once the ceremony is complete because, once brought to life, Ta Shih Yeh is extremely potent. During the ceremony itself, this power is channeled by the Taoist, a celestial bureaucrat.* Outside the strict control exercised by the Taoist priest, however, Ta Shih Yeh's power can be quite dangerous. For example, I heard a rumor that during a *chiao* performed on the occasion of the rebuilding of Ta-ch'i's P'u-ch'i *t'ang,* an unburned piece of Ta Shih Yeh's blue face was secretly taken to a domestic altar, where it was worshiped. The offender's family subsequently became rich, but the family of the *chiao*'s sponsor, formerly one of the richest in the township, suffered a dramatic change in fortune. The sponsor (*lu-chu*) himself sickened and died, and the town in general stagnated economically. All this misfortune was attributed to the illegitimate worship of the very *ling* fragment of Ta Shih Yeh's face.

As I understand this rumor, what accounts for Ta Shih Yeh's excessive efficacy is a kind of triple mediation of yin and yang, disorder and order. Kuan Yin, as we have seen, mediates yin and yang in the yang realm of bright spirits. Her wrathful form, Ta Shih Yeh, can be seen as doubly mediating, in that she is transformed from female to male and operates, not

*Taoist priests have ranks modeled on the ranks of imperial officials (Saso 1972; 1977).

in the yang world of heaven, but in the yin world of purgatory. The third mediation occurs when this already problematic spirit is removed from its proper relationship with the masses of ghosts in purgatory and placed permanently in the yang world of the living.

The fertility clandestinely enjoyed by Ta Shih Yeh's beneficiary is not returned to the community, and is achieved only at the community's expense. This image of limited good arises because the proper distinction between outsiders and insiders—constituted symbolically as that between the masses of ghosts and the community—is subverted. During the *p'u-tu* ceremony itself, the source of fertility is the community, and Ta Shih Yeh and the Taoist (sometimes Buddhist) priest mediate between the community and the masses of ghosts by giving the ghosts the community's offerings. But this flow of fertility is strictly limited to the sacred time of the ritual (compare Leach 1961). Indeed, one of the ritual's objectives is to ensure that during normal secular time, fertility flows into the community. When Ta Shih Yeh is not sent back to his proper place in the yin world after the *p'u-tu,* the result is that the outward flow of the community's fertility (in this case, diverted to the thief) continues into secular time. The intrusion of negative reciprocity into the bounded circle of insiders fundamentally threatens the morals of the community.

This rumor is a further manifestation of the cultural logic connecting reciprocity, community, and fertility discussed in Chapter 4 with reference to *ch'iu-kuei* rituals. Because the benefits of magical fertility are returned, with "interest," to the community defined by the territorial-cult, the *ch'iu-kuei* custom legitimizes "negative reciprocity" by defining it as an ethic of exchange suitable to dealings with outsiders. Within the community, "balanced" reciprocity ought to govern exchange. When it does not, as when Ta Shih Yeh is illicitly worshiped for private ends, the consequences for the community are disastrous.

Celestial Bureaucracy and Community

The efficacy attributed to territorial-cult deities raises some difficult problems for this line of analysis. Foremost among these is a contradiction between the cultural logic that accounts for any particular territorial-cult god's efficacy and the nested, hierarchical embeddedness of smaller communities in larger ones. In brief, any territorial-cult god's *ling* is conceived with reference to an absolute distinction between insiders and outsiders, whereas the notion of the pantheon as a bureaucratic hierarchy is based on the contextual relativity of this distinction. Two conceptions of order are thus condensed in territorial-cult ideology and ritual: one, relatively egalitarian, locates order in the difference between insiders and out-siders; the other defines order as nested hierarchical structure. In my view, the order that emerges in the process of ritually bounding a com-munity of conceptual equals (*ling*) predominates in local-cult ideology. Yet the contradiction is left unresolved or ambiguous, and this endows territorial-cult ideology with the capacity to legitimate both egalitarian and hierarchical relationships. In Chapter 11 I argue that the mutual au-thentication of state and local cults, so crucial for imperial China's cul-tural integration, depended upon the ambiguity of a similar contradic-tion—that between *ling* and virtue. What I wish to stress here is that the structure of this contradiction is already present in local-cult ideology.

INSIDERS AND OUTSIDERS

As we have seen, celestial bureaucrats are believed to affect the mun-dane world, mainly by intervening on behalf of the community and thus protecting it against the attacks of various external enemies. In my view, the efficacy attributed to territorial-cult deities consists precisely in this mediation of the distinction between insiders and outsiders.

The notion that spatial boundaries, civilization, and social and cosmic power are connected dates back at least to the *feng-chien* system of the Chou dynasty (1122 B.C.?–256 B.C.). K.-C. Chang (1983: 16–17) notes that in the ancient context *feng-chien,* which is commonly translated as "feudalism," is better rendered as "to put borders to [a piece of land]," or "to establish [a rulership over the land]." Merit, as authenticated in history/myth, accrues to the hero/lord who civilizes—that is, who es-tablishes boundaries and order. Juxtaposed with the present analysis, Chang's argument suggests an important connection between the origins of the Confucian notion of merit or virtue (*jen*) and the popular notion of efficacy or magical power (*ling*).

The myths associated with many present-day territorial-cult heroes manifest a similar association between divinity and the bounding of un-civilized territory. For example, K'ai Chang Sheng Wang's name is roughly translatable as Sage-King Who Opened [Civilized] Chang-chou. More-over, one of the common festivities included in celebrations of territorial-cult gods' birthdays in Ta-ch'i is the *yu-ching* procession. The term *yu-ching* means to inspect the boundaries of the ritual community. The territorial-cult deity's efficacy consists precisely in this bounding of otherwise un-differentiated humanity. In other words, the territorial-cult god stands for the ordering process implicit in the distinction between insiders and outsiders, between the order of bounded community and the disorder of undifferentiated humanity, between yang and yin.

Diagraming the *ling* attributed to territorial-cult deities presents special difficulties. Real communities are not undifferentiated, but only appear so when contrasted with the structured world of gods (Feuchtwang
1974b). Moreover, the definition of the boundary between insiders and
outsiders is relative—that is to say, there is a nested hierarchy of ritually
defined communities. However, in the context of particular territorial-
cult rituals, the boundary between insiders and outsiders, between civilization and chaos, is thought of in absolute terms.

Figure 10 attempts to illustrate "*ling* logic" in the territorial-cult god's
mediation between insiders and outsiders. In addition to supernatural entities, Figure 10 includes "outsiders," "insiders," and "community."
These categories, no less than various kinds of spirits, are cultural constructions. The notion of community here is that of abstract, ordered society; its essential element is the contrast between insiders and outsiders
mediated by the territorial-cult deity. In this regard, the notion of *ling*
attributed to territorial-cult deities clearly resembles Durkheim's characterization of primitive notions of the "sacred." But the power attributed
to the territorial-cult god is a direct projection not so much of "society"
as of the process that creates order (in this case, community or society) by
distinguishing it from disorder. Thus it is not surprising that the in-
sider:outsider :: order:disorder contrasts resemble Lévi-Strauss's charac-
terizations of the nature:culture contrast so central to primitive thought.
Nor is it too speculative to suggest that the *ling* attributed to territorial-
cult deities constitutes a kind of tribal-level epistemology. Efficacy in this
epistemology is, of course, attributed to the god; it mediates the boundary between insiders and outsiders, order and disorder. But insiders, too,
acquire a kind of efficacy. Unless insiders perform proper rituals, the
boundary against outsiders may crumble and chaos result. Hence men

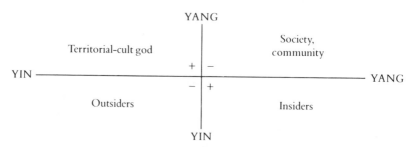

Fig. 10. The territorial-cult god as mediator. Community in this instance equals
abstract, ordered society. Note that the community appears as *both* abstract social
order (upper right, doubly yang position) and efficacious creator or mediator of
this order (lower right, mediating yin and yang). This double function manifests
the circular mystification of community's power in its own creation.

must actively solicit the god's help in order to preserve society. In this sense, both insiders and the territorial-cult god are *ling*—that is, both are efficacious agents in the construction of the order that constitutes community.

In this epistemology, the line between insiders and outsiders is an absolute one (i.e., people one meets are either members of the community or outsiders), so there is no place for hierarchically relative elaboration. In reality, of course, Chinese social life is rife with relative distinctions, but in territorial-cult rituals, the conception of community is indeed that of encompassed equality. Internal differentiation must be denied if the crucial line between insiders and outsiders is to be ritually reproduced.

Figure 10's analysis of the *ling* attributed to territorial-cult gods challenges the celestial bureaucrat = official equation on two counts. First, celestial bureaucrats act as advocates and defenders of local interests against those of outsiders; in a sense, power "bubbles up" in this structure (see also Ahern 1981a: 94–95). In contrast, of course, imperial officials were identified more with outsiders' interests; though not unidirectional, efficacy in real bureaucracies tends to trickle down rather than up. From a structural point of view, then, the celestial bureaucrat resembles the *lu-chu* more than the mundane official, despite his donning of some of the symbols of office of the latter.

Second, the celestial bureaucrat is not really thought of as "governing" a real community. Although informants may sometimes refer to the territorial-cult deity as a supernatural governor, the kind of "governing" such bureaucrats do is not strictly parallel to that of real-world officials. The celestial bureaucrat is a symbolic mediator between undifferentiated community at one level and the outside world. In protecting the community from natural disasters, ghosts, and so forth, his power is directed outward, whereas the officials' major concerns were internal social control and tax collection.

HIERARCHY AND COMMUNITY

In preceding discussions of the ethics of exchange and importance of *kuan-hsi* (relationship), I noted that the distinction between insiders and outsiders is of crucial importance in Chinese culture. But I have also stressed that this boundary is context-dependent; people who are treated as outsiders in some situations may be treated as insiders in others. As we saw in Part II, for example, inhabitants of other villages are outsiders in the context of village rituals, but insiders in the context of multivillage rituals in the market town.

The dependence of community boundaries on context is also apparent in many nonritual situations. To cite just one example, when faced with attack from aborigines, Japanese, or other Chinese ethnic groups, the people of Ta-ch'i have acted as a unified, undifferentiated community; in other circumstances, however, the marketing community has been rife with internal distinctions and even hostilities. Thus "community," like yin and yang, is relative.

If the preceding analysis of the *ling* attributed to territorial-cult deities is not off the mark, the relativity of community boundaries poses a problem for this logic. This problem is mitigated by conceiving the pantheon in the hierarchical terms of past imperial bureaucracies. Figure 11 attempts to illustrate how insider/outsider contrasts are reconciled in Ta-ch'i's hierarchy of territorial-cults. This schematization differs from preceding ones in that instead of only four categories, the nested nature of categorical relationships connects eight categories (logically, the structure could be hierarchically extended further). But within this nested hierarchy, focus is again on yin/yang contrasts along two dimensions, horizontal and vertical. The diagram condenses what could also be represented in several four-part diagrams. Each diagram would encompass four categories, as juxtaposed in Figure 11, but each horizontally contrasting pair would appear on two different diagrams—once as the lower, or yin, pair

Fig. 11. The efficacy of territorial-cult gods

and once as the upper, or yang, pair. This feature of the diagram is indicated by the yang/yin contrast designated at each intersection of four categories.

Figure 11 approximates more closely than Figure 10 conventional wisdom (and many informants' rationalizations) regarding the iconography of territorial cults. In the right column the gods are arranged in proper hierarchical order with superior gods in the yang position relative to their inferiors. Each level of community or social solidarity is arranged, as during communal festivals, in the yin position (left column) relative to its respective territorial-cult deity. Note also that *ling* is attributed to territorial-cult deities as they mediate between the communities they represent and a wider (in this case, external) environment.

A close scrutiny of Figures 10 and 11 reveals an important inconsistency, however. I have argued that in territorial-cult rituals, outsiders are yin relative to insiders. But in Figure 11, more encompassing communities stand in a yang relationship to less encompassing ones. For example, households appear as yin to neighborhoods' yang and neighborhoods appear as yin to villages' yang. This is a problem because the efficacy attributed to territorial-cult deities consists in their differentiating the community from the outside world. From the point of view of the neighborhood, T'u Ti Kung is a defender of its boundaries against other neighborhoods; thus higher levels represented in Figure 11 (e.g., village, standard marketing community) ought to be yin, not yang.

To be consistent with this latter observation, the order of categories at the left side of Figure 11 would have to be inverted, making smaller collectivities yang relative to larger, encompassing ones. The household would thus be yang to the neighborhood's yin, and so forth. Such a reordering would also be consistent with most people's experience of social order; intimate communities like the household have a more profound effect on peoples' lives than broader ones, and lower-level gods are worshiped more frequently than higher-level deities. However, such an inversion of hierarchical relations among social collectivities would contradict the assertion of encompassed equality that is implicit in the meanings of higher-level cults. In other words, lower-level social orderings must be denied in the process of asserting community at a higher level. In hierarchical iconography, this is expressed in the precedence granted to the gods of territorially more inclusive cults.

Thus we cannot model a set of symbolic relations that is consistent with both *ling* defined in yin/yang terms and hierarchy bureaucratically conceived, because of the contradiction between notions of community embodied in the two metaphors themselves. In particular ritual and social contexts, clear-cut distinctions between insiders and outsiders prevail;

however, nested hierarchical structure is necessary in the construction of a broader, contextually relative perspective.

In sum, there is a fundamental ambiguity regarding the basis of the power of territorial-cult deities. As I argue at greater length in Chapter 9, this ambiguity means that competing interpretations of the nature of social relations embodied in territorial-cult iconography may coexist. Moreover, the fact that there are many cases in Taiwan in which patently nonbureaucratic deities function as foci of territorial-cults suggests that it is *ling* more than bureaucratic hierarchy that is indispensable.

T'U TI KUNG AND THE STOVE GOD

The preceding discussion indicates that almost any territorial-cult deity's meaning may be defined with reference to two different symbolic matrices—one, broadly speaking, having the structure of a bureaucratic hierarchy, and the other pertaining to the mediation of insiders and outsiders in the magical definition of community. Territorial-cult deities may also be endowed with particular attributes that add other dimensions to their meaning.

Take, for example, the question of the ranking of the Place God (T'u Ti Kung) and the Stove God (Tsao Chün). When Arthur Wolf (1974a: 138–39) asked an informant about the apparent inconsistency of placing the Stove God in a position superior (yang) to T'u Ti Kung on standard domestic icons, even though the Stove God is T'u Ti Kung's subordinate in bureaucratic rank (see Figs. 4, 11), he was told that since the Stove God is the Jade Emperor's younger brother, he can report directly to heaven without following normal bureaucratic lines of authority.* According to Wolf this case indicates that the "view of the gods as bureaucrats is so pervasive that evidence to the contrary is itself explained away in bureaucratic terms" (p. 138).

Although it is not bureaucratic hierarchy per se that is evoked to gloss inconsistency, but an image of nepotistic behavior attributed to celestial bureaucrats, this nepotism is apparently modeled on that displayed by real-world officials. Does the fact that Wolf's informant produced a rationalization of apparent inconsistency in these terms mean that Chinese spirit categories can be explained as straightforward projections of "real" mundane counterparts? I think not. Although there is no denying the informant's statements, somewhat different conclusions can be drawn from them.

---

*On a trip to several parts of Taiwan in the summer of 1984, I was given similar accounts of the Stove God's special relationship to heaven. Sometimes, however, the Stove God is said to be the Jade Emperor's nephew.

For one thing, Taiwanese make no attempt to alter domestic icons in order to align them more perfectly with a bureaucratic hierarchy. If the gods are modeled on bureaucrats and nothing more, why not apply the metaphor consistently? And even if T'u Ti Kung's subordination to the Stove God can be explained as nepotism, there are still the superior positions accorded to Ma Tsu and Kuan Yin—two female, nonbureaucratic deities—to be explained (see Fig. 4). Moreover, gods can just as clearly constitute a model for mundane officialdom, not just a reflection of it. According to Gary Seaman's central Taiwanese informants, "The gods in heaven judge merit and dispense fortune according to a truly honest appraisal of a man's actions and intentions, not according to official whim and crass political considerations as do the powers of this world" (1978: 7). In short, the very fact that contradictions of the sort Wolf cites do not appear as such to Chinese (until so framed by the anthropologist) is itself evidence that their meaning is contextually defined. Moreover, these contexts are themselves best understood in terms of the contrasts I have attempted to outline here.

In discussing Figure 4, I introduced an alternative interpretation, suggesting that the positions of the Stove God and the Place God may refer to fire's role in mediating heaven and earth. Hence the Stove God (representing fire) is in the *ling* position between the Place God (representing earth) and the higher gods in heaven. Here Henri Maspero's observations on the ancient association of fire with civilizing order are relevant. One of the great heroes of ancient myth was Yi, the forester, who was in charge of burning mountains and marshes, thus converting wilderness into civilization: "If fire was thus indissolubly linked to the ordering of the world after the great waters, *hung-shui*, had flowed away, this is because fire was the chief element in clearing the land, the preliminary condition for all agriculture" (Maspero 1981: 206–7). Although this ancient myth is not directly associated with the Stove God in present-day Taiwan, fire's efficacy in bringing order to the land persists in the iconic positioning of the Stove God relative to T'u Ti Kung. Fire is efficacious not in itself, but for what it does; it converts undifferentiated wilderness (earth?) into civilization.

In addition, the mediation of heaven and earth is symbolized in the oil lamp kept burning in front of virtually all temple altars, in the incense and inscribed paper messages burned and thus sent to the gods, and so forth. Fire's transformative power in the preparation of food hardly needs to be noted; Chinese consider the consumption of raw vegetables thoroughly uncivilized. Echoes of the raw:cooked :: uncivilized:civilized distinctions are found in the terms for unassimilated ("raw" *sheng*) versus assimilated or civilized ("cooked" *shu*) aborigines, and in the term for "maturity" (*ch'eng-shou*, i.e., "to become cooked").

In contrast, the Place God is associated with earth and to some degree with decay. Arthur Wolf (1974a: 138) points out that the Place God is responsible for guiding spirits of the recently deceased to the borders of the underworld. The Place God is also loosely associated with snakes. I was told by one informant that the deity's daughter is a snake, and that to kill a snake carries the danger of incurring his displeasure (although I did not note that this inhibited people from killing snakes; Taiwanese seem to find snakes as objectionable as Americans do). Snakes—anomalous creatures that live both above and below ground—are probably also mediators between the underworld and the yang world of men.

In my view, the ordering of divinities on domestic icons refers to this set of mediating operations rather than to the hierarchical bureaucratic relations summarized in Figure 11. If my analyses are correct, Chinese religious symbols are "multivocal"—that is, the same symbol may stand for different ideas. The most productive way to think of this multivocality is in reference to the different contrastive sets within which a symbol may act as an operator. An interpretation of any symbol's meaning must take into account the set that defines the symbol's use in a particular situation. For example, the Place God is at once a mediator between insiders and outsiders in neighborhood-level communal rituals, a mediator between the yang and yin worlds of the living and dead during funerals, and a functionary in a nested hierarchy of progressively encompassing levels of social solidarity. The symbol's meanings in each of these domains are defined with reference to other symbols in the same domain. But because these domains are concerned with different issues, the search for a single, motivating referent is misguided.

Nonetheless, there is some relevance to correspondences between social and religious categories; many forms of ritual communication with the supernatural seem to follow from such "motivated" metaphors (compare Ahern 1981a). In other words, gods *are* conceived and treated as officials. However, the relevant metaphoric correspondence is a structural one: imperial bureaucracy and communal relations are both nested hierarchies. It is less that gods resemble officials than that the conception of relations among gods and officials resembles the actual structure of relations among communities—in both cases the structure is that of nested hierarchy.

Once such a set of metaphoric correspondences is in place, a transference of attributes between corresponding entities (e.g., officials and celestial bureaucrats) is not surprising. But this transfer is by no means unidirectional; officials acquire some of the magical efficacy of gods, just as gods acquire real-world officials' nepotism. Yet these correspondences cannot explain the system itself, nor do they exhaust the meanings of religious symbols in other contexts.

This point can be somewhat differently stated by thinking of Chinese religious symbols as a semiotic code. Just as in language words may sometimes act as entities (subjects, objects) and sometimes as operations (predicates), so religious symbols can stand for both entities and operations. In the somewhat imprecise terms of this analogy, if we wish to relate religious symbols to the social processes that produce them, we must focus on their functions as operators. In these terms, Wolf's informant was asked to give a substantive definition of what was, in the context, an operation. Native informants intuitively think of religious symbols like territorial-cult gods as both entities and operators. If called upon to reconcile a contradiction in usages, such as the Place God's relative position on domestic icons and in bureaucratic theory, they may produce a rationalization in substantive terms. They would be very unlikely, however, to abandon the use of the symbol as an operator, because it is as operators mediating order and disorder that such symbols are *ling*. In subsequent discussion I attempt to show that *ling* is itself a product of social reproduction. Thus the logic of conceptual relations embodied in territorial-cult iconography and ritual does replicate the logic of social relations in the "real" world—but the "real" world of local social relations, not that of imperial bureaucracy.

9

Orthodoxy and Heterodoxy

Mystification and Value in Ritual

Chinese religion is inseparable from the entire spectrum of discourses and texts through which meaning is produced, reproduced, and fought for, and in which individuals create themselves socially (i.e., in which society socializes individuals). In addition to written and printed texts, this spectrum includes all kinds of rituals, shamanism, architecture, economic transactions, knowledge, and even daily conversation. The meaning generated in all forms of symbolic action is premised on and perpetuates what is almost always an unspoken, unconscious epistemology. This is among the central insights of the deconstructionist movement in Western academia (see Sturrock 1979).

An important corollary of this view of things is that such epistemologies—and the institutions in which they are embodied and reproduced—depend on suppressing the consciousness of their own genesis in social reproduction. This suppression is not consciously motivated; rather, it is a necessary condition of the process of social reproduction itself. Values, forms of collective consciousness, and the social institutions that embody them require the legitimation that they are, to use Geertz's (1973) phrase, "uniquely realistic."

This latter point is probably nowhere clearer than in ritual where, as Moore and Myerhoff (1977: 18) put it:

Underlying all rituals is an ultimate danger, lurking beneath the smallest and the largest of them, the more banal and the most ambitious—the possibility that we will encounter ourselves making up our conceptions of the world, society, our very selves. We may slip in that fatal perspective of recognizing culture as our construct, arbitrary, conventional, invented by mortals. Ceremonies are paradoxical in this way. Being the most obviously contrived forms of social contract, they epitomize the made-up quality of culture and almost invite notice as such. Yet their very form and purpose is to discourage untrammeled inquiry into such questions. Ceremonies convey most of their meaning as postulates.

Ritual here is usefully defined as behavior formally and explicitly concerned with the restoration or reproduction of order. Any notion of order implies a notion of disorder or chaos; it is in the precise nature of the relationship between the culturally constructed notions of order and disorder (or, in some cultures, nature and culture; see MacCormack 1980) that the most fundamental of Moore and Myerhoff's postulates lie.

That the yin/yang relationship in Chinese thought is intimately connected to a pervasive concern with the basis and structure of cosmic order is widely recognized (see Richard J. Smith 1983). This concern is quite explicit both in local rituals and in philosophical writings. But despite its sophistication, the notion of order displayed and reproduced in Chinese rituals demonstrates just the sort of denial of which Moore and Myerhoff write. In other words, the arbitrariness of granting order a kind of valued priority over disorder is implicitly denied in the very act of asserting that priority.

To give substance to this assertion, it is necessary to probe more deeply the relationship between order and disorder in Chinese thought. The logic of yin/yang is not only susceptible to structuralist analysis; it also bears a remarkable resemblance to it. But there is an important difference: although structuralist analysis and Chinese yin/yang logic both find significance in systems of contrasts, for the Chinese the nature of the oppositions is seen as a natural property of micro- and macrocosm, rather than a universal property of the functioning of the human brain (or, following Bateson 1972, 1979, as I would prefer to view it, mind).

Moreover, the Chinese oppositions are asymmetrical. That is to say, at one level yin and yang constitute a binary opposition, but this opposition is itself encompassed within a whole that is ordered, and hence yang. In Louis Dumont's terms, the relationship between yin and yang is hierarchical, and "unlike the mere distinctive relation, hierarchical relation includes the dimension of value" (1980a: 244). Yang, the principle of order, although in some sense incomplete in itself, is positively valued; yin, necessary in the production, reproduction, and restoration of order, is not. This does not equate disorder with evil, but it does equate order with good. And because disorder (especially that associated with reproduction, fertility, decay, and death) dissolves proper categorical distinctions—

including the stability or dominance of order itself—it is always poten-tially threatening, feared, and problematic. The asymmetry in the dis-order/order, yin/yang contrast is clear in the ambivalence toward and even fear of yin that is evident in many rituals and associated beliefs. Aside from yin's obvious association with death and decay, however, the logic of this asymmetry is less than clear.

In sum, Chinese yin/yang theory, which is self-consciously "natu-ralistic" (J. Needham 1956), can also be read as a statement about value—albeit a very abstract and instrumentally disguised or mystified one. In my view, the ideological nature of this epistemology is directly related to the asymmetrical or hierarchical relation that places order over the com-plementary opposition order/disorder—that is, order/disorder is itself a kind of order. The legitimacy of social institutions depends on the denial of the arbitrariness of order's hegemony. Order is seen as inescapable in both logic and nature. It is in this sense that Chinese ideas regarding the origins of order are not only a value but also an ideology. It is important to note, however, that the "instrumentality" here inheres in the social sys-tem, not in the consciousness of individual ideologues or interest groups. As Peter Hamilton (1974: 29) puts it, "Ideology . . . is not produced to 'cover up' reality in a conspiratorial fashion, but is systematically gener-ated by the structure of social relationships."

To this point, I have been concerned mainly with what might conven-tionally be termed "religion as a cultural system." But to explain the dominance of yang as a value in Chinese society, it is necessary to look outside the logic of the cultural system as such and examine the func-tional connections that link culture and society into a single hierarchically encompassing, self-reproducing system. Departing somewhat from the structuralist inspiration of preceding sections, my argument remains within a generally Durkheimian tradition, but with an emphasis on the encompassment of collective representations by social institutions. As J. G. Merquior (1979: 3) puts it:

If as Durkheim often does, we conceive of [society] as a "collective conscious-ness," consisting of mental representations shared by all the socii, then the deter-mination of thought by society is a kind of spiritual Parthenogenesis, hardly able to inspire empirical research: if thought as society is taken to engender thought as the conceptual order, there is little for the empirical social scientist to undertake here. If, however, society refers to a morphological and/or institutional structure, then the thesis of a determination of thought by society becomes the basis of really interesting, testable hypotheses.

The latter stance approaches Marxian and Parsonian/Weberian construc-tions. However, the notion of "determination" in Merquior's statement must be interpreted as meaning that collective representations are re-produced in the social processes of which they form an integral part—not that they are in some sense epiphenomenal or external to society.

"Value" in this perspective is viewed as a property of the reproduction of society, and is expressed both in social structure and in collective representations. Louis Dumont (1972, 1980a,b) has succeeded perhaps better than any other analyst of complex civilization in showing how institutions embody value. Nonetheless, the consistency between the values embodied in institutions and those embodied in collective representations calls for explanation. What is the process that leads to this consistency? Attention to the ways value is socially reproduced is, of course, one of the hallmarks of Marx's analysis of capitalist culture. Despite the lamentable reification of some of Marx's categories in Marxist discourse (in which his supporters and detractors are equally implicated), Marx's discussion of capitalism's "fetishism of commodities" stands as one of the best illustrations of how social institutions both embody *and* reproduce value.*

Terence Turner's recent critique (1984) of Dumont's analyses of hierarchy and value is instructive in this regard. Turner manages to construct a remarkably coherent model of the reproduction of structures of authority and value among the Kayapo of central Brazil. His critique of Dumont's theory of hierarchy includes its failure to develop the connection between ideology and social reproduction. He faults Dumont for downplaying what he sees as a dimension of hierarchy that crosscuts Dumont's important insight that hierarchy and totality are essential aspects of binary opposition. Summarizing his critique of Dumont's model of hierarchy, Turner (p. 337) argues that

it takes the oppositions in question at their face value, as what they appear to be: expressions of conceptual relations between elements overtly specified in the terms of the opposition, with the proviso that one of these is also identified with, and thus symbolically represents, the whole constituted by the two elements of the opposition. I shall argue, to the contrary, that moieties and symbolic polarities of an analogous type cannot properly be understood as expressions of relations between their overt elements, but rather as symbolic transformations of oppositions located on a different structural level, between terms which do not both appear as themselves in the symbolic "representation." The point of the transformation linking the two forms of the opposition is the imposition of an asymmetrical pattern of weighting, or broadly speaking of dominance and subordination, upon the terms of the opposition "represented" by the symbolic form, and the repro-

---

*Debate over Marx's distinction between use value and exchange value has obscured what I consider a subtle ethnography of value as a specific property of capitalist culture and social institutions. Louis Dumont and Marx do not appear as divergent on this score as is generally perceived.

duction of that pattern in a collectively standardized form as the common frame-work of social life. The logical structure of symbolic polarity, and of moiety structure as a special case of it, thus has an intrinsically functional aspect, as well as a hidden symbolic complexity, which are obscured by the decontextualized, positivist approach Dumont attacks but which, in this case, he also absorbs to a dangerous degree into the terms of his own critique.

In my view, Turner's critique is convincing. But in defense of Dumont, it should be noted that the analysis Turner accomplishes so admirably for central Brazilian societies is much more difficult for complex societies like China and India, whose institutions, ideology, and religion are more differentiated in Durkheimian terms. Thus one might argue that the pro-cesses, functional specifications, and reproductive transformations that Turner elaborates also occur in complex societies, but in much more in-stitutionally diffuse, less formally elegant, and more socially pluralistic patterns.

Consequently, the task of demonstrating the descriptive utility of this perspective in an analysis of Chinese culture and institutions is formidable. I begin by analyzing two kinds of rituals and the ways they embody, legiti-mate, and reproduce structures of authority and value. The same themes are later approached in an analysis of pilgrimages, with particular empha-sis on the social construction of identity. Finally, in Chapter 11, I discuss the interactions of sacred power, history, and social reproduction.

Chiao

The hegemony of hierarchical order is ritually most eloquently ex-pressed in what Michael Saso (1972) has termed the "rite of cosmic re-newal" (chiao), a complex series of rituals performed by Taoist practition-ers on behalf of a territorial-cult community whenever a new temple is dedicated or an old one rebuilt (see also Liu 1967). One of the main themes in these rituals is the Taoists' intervention to reverse what is be-lieved to be the progressive expansion of disorder and entropy (yin). Un-less order succeeds in encompassing disorder, people will fail to maintain proper social distinctions, crops will fail, and chaos will result. In short, the reproduction of social and cosmic order requires ritual intervention. Taoists reestablish order (yang), compelling disruptive yin forces to sub-mit to yang's ordering authority. To this end, various exorcistic and ma-nipulative rituals are performed. Chiao thus constitute what is essentially a paradigmatic ritual; most other communal rituals are abbreviated ver-sions of chiao.

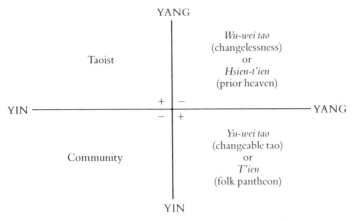

Fig. 12. The Taoist as mediator. The Taoist restores heavenly (*t'ien*) power by mediating between heaven and prior heaven (*hsien-t'ien*).

One of the most revealing and central of the many rituals included in
chiao involves the physical manipulation of deity images in the temple.
All the gods in the temple (who represent the entire Chinese pantheon)
normally face south, absorbing yang (Granet 1973). During the *chiao*,
however, they are moved back toward the temple doors, facing north, in
the position normally occupied by worshipers. The gods' normal positions are then occupied by the Taoist gods of "prior heaven" (*hsien-t'ien*).
These gods, mysterious to nonspecialist Chinese, are thus yang in relation
to the regular pantheon's temporary yin status. To restore cosmic order,
order must be temporarily conceived as relative disorder. But control is
maintained by positing a kind of metaorder, that of "prior heaven." According to Saso (1972), the order in the cosmos is recognized as a change-
able one (*yu-wei tao*)—in other words, disorder and order, both yin and
yang, are part of daily reality.

But in asserting a metareality in which changelessness (*wu-wei tao*)
reigns, the Taoists ultimately align themselves with the camp of ordered
hierarchy.* At one level, disorder and order are dialectically inseparable,
but in the last analysis order is hierarchically encompassing. As Saso
points out, it thus makes a great deal of sense that Taoists claim to be
celestial officials. Like officials, their role is to assert the primacy of order
by dispelling disorder (see Fig. 12).

To readers familiar with the complexities of philosophical Taoism, this

---

*I speak here of present-day Taoist practice. Ancient Taoist philosophy was apparently
more heterodox, prizing *hun-tun*, chaos, and primal disorder (compare Girardot 1983).

conclusion may seem to overlook more complex, less positivist counter-tendencies in Taoist thought. For example, in a definitive essay entitled "Right and Left in China," Marcel Granet explores an intriguing range of contexts in which yin and yang imply their opposites. He concludes that there is no fixed predominance, but rather an alternating preeminence (1973: 57).

> The uneven, which is yang, is a synthesis of even and uneven, of Yin and Yang. [Note that uneven incorporates even, but even does not incorporate uneven.] Similarly, the sorcerer, because of the hierogamies which he knows how to effect, is both man and woman, and a woman when he wishes to be (the theme of sex change is common). Moreover, when the sorcerer holds the set-square which produces the square, he possesses the round (Chinese geometers think that the square engenders the round). The round figures the Sky, the square figures the Earth. The set-square, badge of the sorcerer, who holds it in his left hand, thus evokes the Yin, but it is considered to conceal and to produce the Yang: the theme of exchange of attributes is always associated with that of hierogamy.

But Granet's evidence does not in my view preclude Dumont's notion of encompassment, at least as yin and yang appear in popular rituals and beliefs. Dumont's "encompassment" is expanded in Chinese yin/yang thought into what at first appears to be an infinite series: yang encompasses yin, which encompasses yang, and so forth. But in the *chiao* this entire framework is itself encompassed at a transcendent or "meta" level by the principle of changelessness, order. This principle is no longer termed yang, but it occupies the same position in the structure of categories, relatively speaking. Moreover, the essentially ideological nature of Chinese epistemology, despite its consciousness of itself as naturalistic or positivistic, is revealed by the Taoists' imposition of their metacosmological level, *hsien-t'ien* (prior heaven).

Similar arguments apply to the philosophical postulation of other categories of reality that either underlie or lie beyond yin and yang. For example, immanent tao (*t'ai-chi tao*) and transcendent, eternal tao (*wu-chi tao*) are important contrasting categories referred to in *chiao* rituals (Saso 1972). These categories lie beneath illusory appearances, at a deeper, more fundamental level of reality than yin and yang. But the fact that tao, the monistic principle of reality in Taoist philosophy, must itself be bifurcated suggests a philosophical contradiction—for the arbitrariness of according yang (or, in this case, *wu-chi tao*) precedence at one level of contrast necessitates postulating a metacategorical level to justify it. Indeed, no matter how many metalevels are posited, order and structure must somehow achieve hegemony (see Fig. 13).

This paradox seems to explain practical Taoism's complex multiplica-

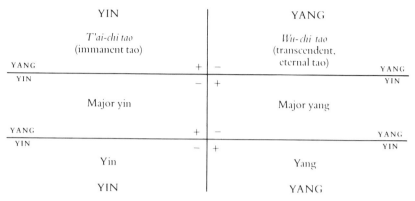

Fig. 13. The Taoist structure of metacategories of order. The "Appended Remarks" of the *I Ching* (Part 1, Chap. 11) distinguishes major and minor yin and yang: "The Great Ultimate . . . generates the Two Modes (yin and yang). The Two Modes generates the Four Forms (major and minor yin and yang)." (Chan 1963: 267.)

tion of naturalistic metacategories; they represent attempts to deny the arbitrariness of assigning value to order.* In other words, the fact that social order is ultimately a human construction is avoided by being embedded within ever more abstract metacategories. If this analysis is correct, the "structure of value" embodied in peasant ritual and cosmology is essentially similar to that embodied in many philosophical texts.[†] This reverses the common idea that unsystematic ritual complexities are codified and simplified in philosophical texts. Rather than bringing system to ritual, philosophical Taoist texts seem concerned with solving unsolvable epistemological paradoxes whose structures are more clearly outlined in rituals than in written form.

Fertility and Decay

The hegemony of yang is somewhat differently asserted in rituals associated with death. As several observers have noted, a number of Chinese practices reveal an intriguing connection between notions of reproduc-

---

*Manifest in this paradox is what Terence Turner (1977b: 69–70) sees as "an analogy to the principle embodied in Gödel's famous proof that any relatively complex system of logical propositions is necessarily incapable of serving as the basis for deducing all of the logical axioms necessary to demonstrate its own logical consistency."

[†] See Tambiah's (1970: 34–35) pertinent arguments regarding the relations among ritual, texts, and cosmology.

tion and fertility on the one hand and notions of death, decay, and pollution on the other. For example, James L. Watson (1982: 180) mentions an unspoken but unmistakable association of women's procreative power with the disorderly decay of human flesh in Cantonese management of death pollution. This connection is asserted in the green cloth worn as part of mourning dress by the deceased's daughters-in-law. Green, symbolizing fertility, is believed to absorb death pollution (p. 174). This same cloth is later fashioned into back-strap harnesses used for carrying infants. In addition, daughters-in-law are expected to rub their unbound hair against the coffin, hair also being thought to absorb pollution.* Noting that the green cloth is worn at the funeral so that it covers the reproductive organs, Watson argues convincingly that daughters-in-law are expected to expose themselves to the pollution of death as a means of reproducing the patriline.

In the same vein, Granet (1975) notes that in ancient China the subterranean world of decaying corpses (the "Yellow Springs") was also the source of great creative/regenerative power. An ancient custom was to bury family members in the southwest corner of the house beneath the spot where seed grain was stored and the conjugal bed was located. The connection between decay and fertility could hardly be more explicit. What is more, this suggests that elements of yin/yang thinking predate the formal (i.e. textual) construction of yin/yang theory itself.[†]

The ancient Chinese association of decay with agricultural fertility lives on in at least one custom I observed in Taiwan. In rural Wei-liao hamlet near Ta-ch'i, farmers make sacrifices to the Feng-ling mass grave, which contains the bones of unknown dead disinterred when Ta-ch'i's main graveyard was converted into a public park. They do this every year before planting and after harvest.

In sum, both decay and fertility seem somehow to be associated with

---

*The fact that married-out daughters too are expected to perform this penance presents something of a problem for interpretation, since they do not contribute to the reproduction of the deceased's patriline. Clearly, the complexity of Chinese symbolism regarding fertility and continuity requires further study. On the basis of Watson's information, it appears that daughters-in-law and married-out daughters are equivalent to unmarried daughters at one level of contrast (that indicated by their rubbing of unbound hair on the deceased's coffin), whereas they are contrasted with each other at another (only daughters-in-law wear the green cloth).

†According to W.-T. Chan (1963: 244), it is not clear exactly when yin/yang theory was first textually formalized: "Tsou Yen (305–240 B.C.) is often mentioned as the representative thinker of this school, but his work is lost and all that we have about him is a brief account of his life and thought in the *Shih chi*." The yin/yang idea is present in the *Tso chuan, Lao Tzu, Chuang Tzu,* and *Hsün Tzu,* but not in the *Analects,* the *Book of Mencius,* the *Doctrine of the Mean,* or the *Great Learning (ibid.).*

yin and disorder.* But merely asserting this association in Chinese culture does not explain it. In light of the preceding arguments regarding the hegemony of order, what is one to make of the apparently valued place accorded to yin as the disorder necessary in reproduction? This question seems to me to pertain to what Maurice Bloch and Jonathan Parry see as a general problem in the legitimation of authority (1982: 11): "[In systems where] positions of authority are conceptualized as belonging to an eternal and unchanging order [e.g., China], . . . individuality and the flow of events pose a problem for this theoretically static world and a threat to its continuity in that different role holders are patently different and the social order is not eternal." Bloch and Parry argue that the resolution of this contradiction implies that "individuality and unrepeatable time are problems which must be overcome if the social order is to be represented as eternal" (p. 15); consequently, death must be represented as part of a cyclical process of renewal. Thus the Chinese bifurcation of flesh, decay, and yin on the one hand and bones, ancestors, and enduring patrilineal order on the other is quite typical of hierarchical societies. Just as the flesh decays, so is the individual transient; like bones, what endures is patriarchal order.

Bloch and Parry make a number of revealing observations that illuminate aspects of Chinese burial practices. Most pertinent here are their suggestions of a bifurcation between disorderly female sexuality and orderly male fertility, and the necessary assertion of the hierarchically encompassing status of the latter if structures of social authority are to preserve legitimacy.

The fascinating Cantonese customs that Watson documents seem to constitute just such an assertion. In exogamous patrilineal societies practicing virilocal residence, women from outside (hence, yin) must be procured to reproduce patrilines, but ultimately their sexuality must be shown to depend upon the fertility of encompassing patrilineal order if the legitimacy of the latter is to be maintained. A similar logic may underlie geomantic beliefs regarding the power of ancestors' bones to steer fertility in the direction of living descendants (Feuchtwang 1965).

Emily Ahern (1975: 210) approaches Bloch and Parry's position, noting that "the central dilemma might be expressed this way: how can we keep families pure and homogeneous and their members loyal when, in order to grow, they need outsiders (women with competing loyalties and

---

*Boehmer (1977: 78) notes that yin has two meanings: "one, the visible, which is associated with dissipation; and the other, the invisible, which is the esoteric source from which yang is reborn."

children whose loyalties are unformed) and when, in addition, all family members must eventually die?" Ahern's answer is that the pollution associated with the disorderly penetration of boundaries (e.g., menstrual blood, death, marriage, birth) can be ritually cleansed in various rites of purification. My argument here is that the logic of this purification involves an assertion that order encompasses disorder.

Bloch and Parry identify the crucial connections between religious beliefs and practices and the processes of social reproduction and legitimation of authority, as manifested in death rituals. Moreover, the hierarchical structure of categories in which female sexuality is symbolically encompassed by male fertility is essentially identical to the encompassment of disorder by order in the metacosmological categories evoked in *chiao* rituals. In other words, the structure of categories pertaining to order/disorder embodies the same valued asymmetry in both cases. In both cases it also serves to legitimate existing structures of authority and the institutions in which they are reproduced, while denying actors themselves consciousness of these very functions (Bloch & Parry 1982: 42). The legitimacy of institutions (e.g., patriliny, local social structure) depends on this mystification of the connection between institutions and the ideas that legitimate them; if the values embodied in a conceptual order are seen as properties of the reproduction of social institutions, these same social institutions can hardly be legitimated with reference to these values. It is in this sense that Cantonese customs regarding fertility and death pollution properly constitute ideology. This ideological function of funerary customs almost certainly explains why Watson's villagers "do not even attempt to explain" the "mysterious transformation" in which "the passive aspect of death pollution is essential for the biological reproduction of the agnatic line" (1982: 174).

Heterodoxy

Structures of value that prize order and legitimate existing social institutions and authority define Chinese orthodoxies, both official and local.* Conversely, it is the denial of order as an ultimate value that defines heterodoxies.

*I avoid the terms "elite" and "popular" here because they impose these value structures too directly onto social classes. Such contrasts tend to divide culture too sharply along class lines. The terms "official" and "local," although less than ideal, suggest that orthodoxy is more closely linked to institutions than to individual members of social groups. For example, imperial officials acted both as representatives of official institutions and as leaders in their native localities. Moreover, nonofficial, classically educated local elites had consider-

This definition of orthodoxy precludes too rigid a restriction of the term to, say, a philosophical tradition like Confucianism. Broadly speaking, institutions as diverse as ancestor worship and the imperial bureaucracy are orthodox in Confucian terms. However, a notion like *ling,* which plays an essential role in legitimizing institutionalized communities, has no place in Confucian philosophy. In Chapter 8 I argued that there is an important inconsistency between the notion of community as an absolute contrast between insiders and outsiders central to *ling* and the notion of society as a nested hierarchy of relatively defined communities. Yet both of these notions are orthodox ones, because both legitimate elements of social order, albeit from different perspectives. Heterodoxy, in contrast, undermines the legitimacy of any order.

Although I wish to focus primarily on orthodox worldviews, some comparison with heterodox cosmologies may better define the orthodox.* For example, yang's hegemony in Chinese ritual and pantheon must be qualified by noting the value placed in ancient Taoist texts on *hun-tun*—the cosmogonic, mystical union of yin and yang in a state of prestructure or disorder.

N. J. Girardot locates the clash of values between early Taoism and early Confucianism in their respective attitudes toward history. Whereas "in the Confucian tradition with its golden age idea attached to the genealogical lore of the sage kings and civilizational heroes, the 'essential' was not fixed at the Creation of the World but after it, at the time of the aristocratic ordering of human civilization" (Girardot 1983: 41), ancient Taoism valued an "idealized neolithic culture" defined as the time of *ta-t'ung* ("great equality"):

It can be said that the mystical return to an experience of primal unity implies a necessary cosmological interrelation of body and spirit, the reunion or marriage of *yin* and *yang,* the coexistence and copenetration of the one and the two, non-being and being, the uncreated and the created, egg and chicken. All of this in the early Taoist texts is rooted metaphysically in the cosmogonic mystery of the third term or central gap—the "betwixt and between"—of chaos (*ibid.*, p. 43).

Figure 14 expresses this notion schematically. In valuing chaos, ancient Taoist mysticism is heterodox not only because it confounds Confucian

---

able influence on the organization and ideology of local ritual, and there was a large segment of population that fell somewhere between "elite" and "peasant" status. Thus there was constant interaction between elites and peasants, and both peasants and elites had recourse, to some degree, to both local and official orthodoxies (see Sangren 1984a).

* Strickmann's (1980) critique of Saso (1978) makes the important point that orthodoxy is defined from the point of view of interested actors. Here, however, orthodoxy pertains not to the particular claims of contending aspirants (e.g., Saso's various Taoist schools) to a privileged position in the structure of authority, but to the legitimacy of the structure itself.

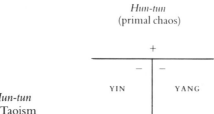

Fig. 14. *Hun-tun*
in ancient Taoism

orthodoxy, but also because it precludes the possibility of legitimizing any social institutions or structures of authority. This suggests the essentially dependent or derived nature of such heterodoxies; the transcendence of order/disorder categorizations presupposes their existence. In denying hegemony to order, early Taoism denies itself the potential for achieving institutional hegemony, because it defines itself in counterpoint to the structure of value that legitimizes social institutions.* Early Taoist rebellions (e.g., the "Yellow Turban" and "Five Pecks of Rice" rebellions of the Han dynasty, 202 B.C.–A.D. 220) appear to have been no more successful in creating institutionally viable alternatives to an orthodox ordering of society and culture than were later movements inspired by heterodox ideologies in the "White Lotus" tradition.

Girardot (1983: 279–81) argues that after the Han period the "old utopian and revolutionary implication of the *hun-tun* theme" was replaced by a much more orthodox set of concerns: "The vast liturgical apparatus of sectarian Taoism was primarily directed toward the maintenance and regeneration of ordinary society (the *chiao* rites), the protection of the normal social order through exorcistic ritual, and the procurement of heavenly blessings for the dead (the *chai* rites). For the layman the attainment of these goals was the result of good works and grace mediated by the liturgical performances and magical rites of the priests (*Tao-shih*) on behalf of the divine Lao Tzu (Lao Chün) and the celestial hierarchy of gods" (Girardot 1983: 279; see also Loewe 1979; Stein 1979).

Insofar as Taoist texts and ideas inform the religious ideas and activities of common people in Ta-ch'i, they conform to an epistemological structure that values order. However, if Girardot's analysis of early Taoism is correct, Taoism in the pre-Han period assumed a much more heterodox role. In any case, after the Han dynasty, elements of Buddhist

---

*Early Taoism is reminiscent in this respect of such poststructuralist thinkers as Roland Barthes and Michel Foucault (see Sturrock et al. 1979). Both schools see all constructions of reality as arbitrary and mystifying, and both lapse into vagueness regarding the social implications of this insight. No Taoist or poststructuralist critique is possible except in counterpoint to that which it subverts. In short, Taoism:Confucian orthodoxy :: deconstruction:scientific (or "logocentric") orthodoxy.

thought replaced Taoism as the major source of skeptical detachment from values legitimating social order. In this regard, Figure 14 can be compared with Figure 4, in which Kuan Yin assumes a role comparable to *hun-tun* in Figure 14. Both figures mystically combine order and disorder, yin and yang, but assert the hegemony of denying the differentiation. In the case of Kuan Yin, this denial is made most explicit in the placing of a female above the other deities (i.e., in the yang position), and perhaps also in the ambiguities associated with her gender.

Although Kuan Yin is generally thought of as female, in Buddhist texts a given bodhisattva can be either male or female in form. Many people in Ta-ch'i are aware of this, so even though they usually speak of Kuan Yin as female, the deity's ambiguous gender may not be irrelevant to its role as domestic icon. As a figure that can be either male or female, Kuan Yin, like *hun-tun,* unites yin and yang.

Although Kuan Yin's popularity as a savior goddess does not threaten the hegemony of yang order, placing her at the top of the cosmos is potentially subversive. Textually defined as a bodhisattva, Kuan Yin is to most Chinese a member of a pantheon that includes all deities, regardless of sectarian textual origin. At the same time, however, most Chinese are aware of Kuan Yin as a symbol of personal salvation—salvation that can be achieved only by renouncing the world. Thus placing Kuan Yin above all others implies the ultimate futility of earthly categorical distinctions, including the hierarchical relations among men and women, fathers and children, rulers and the ruled that are so fundamental to Confucian orthodoxy. Under the circumstances, it is not surprising that, as C.-K. Yang (1961: 192–204) argues, the Chinese state has historically viewed Buddhism with ambivalence, seeing it as a threat to its own legitimacy.

Here Louis Dumont's (1980a: 273–78) arguments regarding the renunciatory role of Buddhism in India are instructive. According to Dumont, Buddhism in India provided a conceptual arena where individualism could be expressed in counterpoint to the holistic, hierarchical values of the society—but only in a context defined as outside the social world (see also C.-K. Yang 1961: 216–17). The role of renunciation in the historical development of Chinese thought clearly takes us far afield, but early Taoism and, later, Buddhism in China may indeed have been renunciatory counterpoints to the hegemony of order.*

Such renunciation is tolerable to authorities only as long as it is confined to individual rather than social ends. Thus, in late traditional times, the state defined the role of Taosim as alchemical cultivation for medicinal purposes and that of Buddhism as otherworldly salvation. Only Confu-

---

*See Mote (1971) for another formulation of the complementary roles of Confucianism and Taoism in Chinese thought.

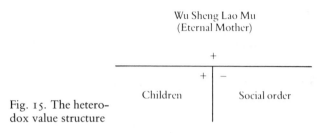

Fig. 15. The hetero-
dox value structure

cianism was granted authority in the conduct of social relations. The vio-
lation of these boundaries could bring harsh suppression (C.-K. Yang
1961; deGroot 1903–4). Consider, for example, the White Lotus and related millennial sects that periodically inspired antiestablishment rebellions in late imperial times (Overmyer 1976; Naquin 1976). In sectarian ideology, the foremost heterodox divinity, Wu Sheng Lao Mu (the
"Unborn Mother"),* stands outside both history and the legitimizing/
authenticating idiom of bureaucracy/nested hierarchy. In a very literal
sense, she represents the subversion of both political legitimacy and hierarchical cultural order. This heterodoxy is schematized in Figure 15.

In contrast to orthodox cosmology (as represented, for example, in
Fig. 8), where female deities are hierarchically subordinate to male, yang
order, in heterodox ideology the Unborn or Eternal Mother is said to be
the mother of all in creation, including men and gods. But since this hierarchically encompassing symbol is female and cannot be purified of yin,
the hegemony of hierarchical order (i.e., of yang) is undermined. Moreover, this hegemony is undermined not only at the apex of the pantheon,
but in all cultural distinctions. As evidence of this last point, one need
only note that some of the more radical heterodox cults deny even such
fundamental cultural distinctions as male and female.

A corollary of this undermining of basic distinctions is the subversion
of hierarchy's legitimacy; as the Eternal Mother's children, all worshipers
have direct, unmediated access to ultimate power. No other authority,
mundane or supernatural, can claim to mediate. The heterodoxy of Eternal Mother cults is thus a threat not just to established political authority,
but to authority at all levels of society. Consequently, Eternal Mother
cults, currently very active in Taiwan, are perceived as heterodox (*hsieh*)
by both the government and the common people.[†]

---

*This deity is also known as Wu Sheng Sheng Mu, Yao Ch'ih Chin Mu, Wang Mu
Niang Niang, and, in more orthodox cosmologies, Hsi Wang Mu.
[†]My assistant's mother required her to wear a special charm to protect her from
the black-magic enchantment attributed to members of an Eternal Mother sect we were
investigating.

The undermining of authority implicit in these heterodox movements may explain their tendency to splinter. Despite essentially identical ideologies, White Lotus cults in Taiwan have proliferated into numerous contending sects because branch leaders refuse to recognize the authority of cult superiors. Probably the largest and certainly the most public of Eternal Mother cults in Taiwan is the Tz'u-hui *t'ang* (Overmyer 1974; Sangren 1980, 1983). The cult's center is near Hua-lien, but there are over 100 branches throughout the island. Much of my knowledge of cult organization and ideology comes from observing a branch temple near Pai-chi in the rural foothills east of Ta-ch'i.

If rumors regarding other related cults are credible, T'zu-hui *t'ang* practices are relatively tame. Meetings feature the spirit possession of many members (not just of the specialist medium), most of whom don the cult's blue uniform. The annual pilgrimage to Hua-lien (a small city on Taiwan's remote eastern coast), unlike Ma Tsu pilgrimages to Pei-kang, brings the entire body of worshipers together at the same time. When I attended this annual celebration, it was apparent that the government was keeping a close watch on the proceedings; policemen were much in evidence among the crowds, and cult leaders quietly exhorted members to confine the more ecstatic of their performances to discreet locations.

Despite their longevity and occasional political effervescence in Chinese history, the values condensed in heterodox cosmologies are less logically robust than orthodox ones. This fact is apparent when one takes note of the attribution of efficacy to any of the ascendant heterodox entities (e.g., *hun-tun,* Kuan Yin, or the Eternal Mother). Heterodox structures seem to locate efficacy not in mediation, but in entities that stand outside hierarchy and history. But this efficacy makes sense only with implicit reference to the mediating role of the heterodox hegemonic symbol in an orthodox structure. For example, the supremacy of the Eternal Mother in White Lotus ideology depends on an implicit appeal to the mediating position of female divinities in orthodox structures; otherwise, the choice of a female symbol as the negation of male order would make no sense (Sangren 1983).

Although this argument is difficult to support with direct empirical evidence, consider the fact that some heterodox sects place images of Kuan Yin on their altars. Only after an initiate is accepted into sect membership and indoctrinated into secret dogma is Kuan Yin revealed to be, in fact, a "stand-in" for the Eternal Mother. By the same token, members on a pilgrimage to the T'zu-hui *t'ang*'s founding temple stopped en route to worship Kuan Yin at a famous orthodox Buddhist shrine. However, the sect branch's leader instructed the members to perform special ritual gestures (the equivalent of crossing one's fingers behind the back when making a promise with no intention of keeping it), indicating the differences in their estimations of Kuan Yin's cosmological status from orthodox views.

Moreover, within the social organization of these cults, hierarchy and authority often taken traditional forms, men generally assuming leadership roles, and authority following a teacher/pupil grid (see Naquin 1976; Topley 1963). It is also relevant that sectarian rebellions seem to have become more orthodox as they became more successful. The classic example is the rebellion led by Chu Yüan-chang, founder of the Ming (r. 1368–98). In the course of overthrowing the Mongols, the rebellion abandoned its millennial White Lotus ideology in favor of reestablishing Confucian institutions (Dardess 1970; Taylor 1963). Heterodox movements in China seem to have been unable to imagine a viable social application of their own heterodoxies. Short of world renunciation, some form of social order is inescapable.

In sum, cultural and political chaos—the *luan* nightmares of both formal Chinese political philosophy and local exorcistic ritual—seem the inevitable results of divesting *ling* of its connection to hierarchical order and locating it in an autonomous entity such as the Eternal Mother or *huntun*. Or, to return to our schematizations, *ling* must ultimately inhere in a symbol that mediates hegemonic order (yang) and encompassed disorder (yin). Otherwise, social stability and legitimizing social institutions and authority are impossible. That heterodox movements like Chu Yüan-chang's moved toward orthodoxy as they achieved political and military control suggests that this Durkheimian conjuncture of the social and the cosmic was a necessary condition for the building of secular order in China. Chinese cultural orthodoxies and the heterodoxies they implied were incapable of legitimizing radically new political structures; the cultural alternatives were limited to two, social order or world renunciation.

Despite its remarkable complexity and flexibility, the structure of orthodox Chinese epistemology amounts in the last analysis to the acceptance of culturally constructed order as the dominant value. Order as defined in yin/yang terms is valued because to most Chinese it is self-evidently better that microcosm and macrocosm, individual and society, be ordered. In Durkheimian terms, this value and the ritual forms through which it is expressed and reproduced are sacred because to the Chinese, this value is the basis for the existence and regeneration not just of "Chinese" society, but of society or civilization in general. Yet what I term the "hegemony" or "dominance" of yang is more than the power of society as culturally conceived and objectified—it is an unconscious commitment to a particular view of reality that is unaware of its own culturally constructed nature. In this expanded sense, then, Durkheim was right. But it is not social categories that are crudely imagined to be transferred to supernatural worlds. Rather, it is the socially produced set of collective representations about the nature of reality that provides people with both the means to think and the values to live by.

Social Relations and the Politics of Symbols

In terms of practical social efficacy, then, yang and order reign supreme. Nonetheless, the hegemony of yang and order does not preclude yin and yang from being an effective language for contesting as well as expressing social and political arrangements. And because deities can embody either order or disorder under different circumstances, the definition of context can become an arena for conflicting interpretations. Yang embodies order and proper hierarchical relations, and hence serves established authority. Consequently, one of the ways in which authority at once co-opts and legitimizes popular cults is to construct contexts that emphasize the yang aspects of their focal deities.

This was accomplished most directly by appointing the deity to celestial office. The best-known example of this co-optation involves the female deity Ma Tsu. By endowing her with official titles and including her in official rites, the state consistently attempted to impose an essentially yang perspective on the cult. To some degree, this "yangification" of Ma Tsu was amplified as her cult developed strong associations with elements of established local society. As a patroness for Fukien merchants who sojourned widely in China, Japan, and Korea, Ma Tsu's character must be seen as mainly a yang one because she served as the ritual focus for stable voluntary associations, and hence for order. In short, centuries of legitimation into ordered social hierarchies, both state and local, have resulted in placing her in an encompassing hierarchical order. In Sants'eng (a village in Ta–ch'i's marketing community), Ma Tsu even serves as the main deity in a village-level territorial cult, a post generally occupied by a male celestial bureaucrat.

Still, in some contexts Ma Tsu remains yin. No matter how many official titles and honors are bestowed upon her, Ma Tsu's female gender holds the potential for contrast with male celestial bureaucracy. I have written about some of the dimensions of this contrast elsewhere (Sangren 1983), and Ma Tsu's role in pilgrimage is treated at length in Chapter 10. What I wish to emphasize here is the tension—sometimes explicitly manifest in a struggle over meaning and interpretation, but more often instrumentally sublimated—between Ma Tsu's yin and yang aspects. The dimensions of this struggle can be extremely subtle and complex, both in broad historical contexts (see Watson 1985) and in specific local situations.*

As an example of the latter, consider Ma Tsu's role as territorial-cult patroness in San-ts'eng. Since territorial cults usually focus on male celestial bureaucrats, a female deity as supernatural governor seems at first the cultural equivalent of a grammatical mistake. In this case, the bestowal of honorific titles like *T'ien Hou* ("Queen of Heaven"), although linking Ma Tsu to the orthodox celestial hierarchy, still cannot make her into an official. One way of explaining such an anomaly would be to argue that essentially random historical events are at play—in this case, the fact that one of San-ts'eng's early settlers happened to have an image of Ma Tsu obtained from the cult's founding temple in Mei-chou, Fukien. The situation could then be attributed to peasant ignorance or lack of interest in cosmological subtleties, and it could be argued that there is no anomaly because peasants recognize none.

But this does not explain why such deities continue to be worshiped and are not replaced with more appropriate ones. When questioned about the apparent contradiction of a female in the role of celestial bureaucrat, San-ts'eng informants would generally turn the discussion to either the cult's history or the devotion of the villagers to the goddess. But in many conversations there seemed to be an undertone of resentment surrounding the village's relations with Ta-ch'i's townspeople. Subtle historical information of a sort most San-ts'eng natives might consider somewhat sensitive (and hence not an appropriate topic for conversation) would be necessary to establish this point, but I suspect that the choice (or at least the continued use) of Ma Tsu as a territorial-cult deity symbolizes the village's ambivalence toward its relations with the town.

As an officially sanctioned deity, Ma Tsu is orthodox and yang, but as a female, she is ambiguously located in the male celestial bureaucracy. In many ritual contexts, San-ts'eng recognizes its hierarchical subordination

---

*Jordan (1976) notes an attempt by the government to interpret a local religious festival in terms it finds ideologically acceptable by emphasizing the idea that the festival's purpose is to honor Koxinga as a Chinese nationalist hero. That interpretation is irrelevant to the local people's understanding of the festival, but it accounts for the government's tolerance of the ritual.

within Ta-ch'i's sphere of influence, but unlike many other villages in the marketing community, San-ts'eng refuses to see its village temple as a satellite.* Were Ma Tsu less than satisfying to San-ts'eng villagers, they could always invite a celestial bureaucrat to fill her place, putting her on a side altar, as most other villages do. Indeed, there is nothing immutable about the deities worshiped in Chinese communities; new deities frequently replace old ones, and the Chinese pantheon provides a very flexible idiom for expressing changing sociological circumstances. Despite the serendipities of local history, symbolic inconsistencies, if meaningless, are easily corrected.

In sum, I suspect that San-ts'eng's choice of Ma Tsu is meaningful, not mere historical happenstance. By worshiping a female deity as a celestial bureaucrat, San-ts'eng villagers can implicitly deny their hierarchical subordination to Ta-ch'i at the village territorial-cult level, while explicitly affirming it by participating in town-centered rituals. The veneer of orthodoxy is maintained because Ma Tsu, although female, has been officially legitimized in the state cult.

If religious symbols had only one meaning, Chinese religion would not be capable of encoding the complexities of Chinese social life as fully and as subtly as it does. By shifting from a predominantly orthodox, yang fitting of Ma Tsu into the hierarchical celestial bureaucracy to a yin emphasis on her female gender (thereby removing her from clear-cut bureaucratic subordination), San-ts'eng villagers manage to "have their cake and eat it too." At village festivals, Ma Tsu acts much like any celestial bureaucrat, but her gender makes it difficult to see her as bureaucratically subordinate to the township-level god.

In the politics of Chinese social relations, this contextual shifting is expedient precisely because it provides a means for both parties in a relationship to understand the nature of their relationship differently. Townsmen include San-ts'eng unambiguously in Ta-ch'i's ritual sphere, but villagers may or may not, depending on the context.

An important lesson to be drawn from this example is that what I term "heterodox structures of value" appear in the categories of thought and public religious symbols of most Chinese. Here heterodoxy and orthodoxy are not sociologically polarized. Depending on the context, nearly all Chinese have access to both. It is always useful to have an idiom ca-

---

*There is also an element of class division implied here: to villagers, the town represents the home of merchants and landlords. Indeed, it is wealthy townsmen who control township-level rituals. Rural Ta-ch'i people often express resentment about the townspeople's condescension toward them.

pable of questioning particular hierarchical orderings, but few can convert this idiom into a sustainable and encompassing worldview. Thus the "minor" heterodoxies constituted by Kuan Yin's domination on domestic icons and by San-ts'eng's female territorial-cult deity are best viewed as being encompassed within the orthodox orderings that define them as heterodox.

10

Pilgrimages and Social Identity

An essential part of my argument to this point is that *ling* (efficacy) must be viewed as a key cultural "operator" in the structure of value. A focus on operations or structural relations among supernatural entities provides a more consistent and parsimonious explanation of the structure of religious symbols than does a focus on people's presumed psychological disposition to imagine a supernatural world that replicates the "real" world of their experience.

It is time now to consider more closely the role of individuals in producing collective representations. Here Terence Turner's critique of structuralist analyses of narrative (1977a: especially 160–61) is instructive. In brief, Turner argues that although Lévi-Strauss (1969a: 12–13) is correct in insisting that collective representations are "independent of the conscious, self-reflective thought of any individual," he overlooks the ways in which people, through their individual activities, become the "unwitting architect[s] of the structures of [their] intellects" (1977a: 160).

These issues require elaboration. Lévi-Strauss's concern is to show how "systems of truths become mutually convertible and therefore simultaneously acceptable to several different subjects" (1969a: 11). For example, Stevan Harrell's (1974a) study of the religious beliefs in a single Taiwanese community reveals a striking range of variation. Few of Harrell's informants attempted to rationalize an apparent hodgepodge of personal beliefs into any coherent system, and there was no consistency among those who did. Yet despite this variation, virtually everyone participated in public rituals. Such a combination of private variation and public convention challenges any theory that seeks to ground collective representations (e.g., China's bureaucratic pantheon) in individual experience. Some other process must be posited to account for the persistence and relative stability of the basic forms of Chinese ritual and cosmology over vast stretches of time and space. On both logical and empirical grounds, it is reasonable to suppose that this process is social.

Nonetheless, in asserting the systemic priority of social process in an analysis of collective representations, individual actors cannot be left out altogether. As argued by proponents like Louis Dumont and Lévi-Strauss, structuralism makes us aware of the tautologies and teleologies of socio-centric functional explanations, but offers little in the way of alternative explanations to account for the relative conservatism of culturally specific collective representations. In other words, neither Lévi-Strauss nor Du-mont addresses successfully the question of how collective representa-tions are functionally linked to social institutions. As Terence Turner sug-gests in his critique and develops at length elsewhere, this question must be addressed if one is to understand the totality of the logic that encom-passes these representations.

In a criticism parallel to Turner's, Augé (1982: 109–10) argues that although

structuralists claim to identify symbolic configurations and to uncover the logic (mytho-logics, for example), it does not occur to them that this logic can only be fully apprehended when operating "beyond" these configurations, and that this is because they have eliminated every properly sociological consideration, and every reflection as to the nature of efficacy, from the anthropological framework.

He goes on to assert that

the problem is . . . to define the level at which an analysis might succeed in show-ing how it is that the anthropological logic of the system is also the differential logic of the society, and how social logics simultaneously define the intellectual order and the social order, the anthropological dimension and the social dimen-sion, the order of the symbolic and the order of ideology.

Neither Turner nor Augé rejects structuralist insights into the systemic relatedness of symbols; rather, both insist that the systemic properties of symbols can be fully understood only when the fact of their genesis in social process is taken into account.

To anticipate the themes of the subsequent discussion, collective repre-sentations are not the hierarchically ascendant level of analysis (as Dumont sometimes seems to argue), but part of a larger totality that encompasses collective representations and the social system. A key element in this larger totality is what Turner (1977a) terms the "cultural subject."

Religious pilgrimages are a particularly appropriate arena for address-ing these issues. Sometimes compared to rites of passage in primitive so-cieties, pilgrimages play an important socializing role for individual pil-grims. This socializing function is best understood as a social process rather than a psychological one; yet in making this case, the individual as "cultural subject" is not entirely abandoned.* The relationship between cultural subject and collective representations is dialectical. Pilgrimages are rituals in which individuals, in the process of acquiring social identi-ties, become the means for reproducing social institutions.

Pilgrimages and Cultural Categories

There is widespread agreement that institutionalized pilgrimages pro-mote social and cultural integration among locales that may otherwise lack a focus for common identity. In this regard, Victor Turner's notion of "communitas" has been most influential (1969: 177):

All human societies implicitly or explicitly refer to two contrasting social models. One . . . is of society as a structure of jural, political, and economic positions, offices, statuses, and roles, in which the individual is only ambiguously grasped behind the social persona. The other is of society as a communitas of concrete idiosyncratic individuals, who, though differing in physical and mental endow-ment, are nevertheless regarded as equal in terms of shared humanity. The first model is of a differentiated, culturally structured, segmented, and often hierarchi-cal system of institutionalized positions. The second presents society as an un-differentiated, homogeneous whole, in which individuals confront one another integrally, and not as segmentalized into statuses and roles.

Pilgrimages, in Turner's view, are the embodiments of the communitas spirit that "presses always to universality and ever greater unity" (1974: 179). He marshals considerable evidence in support of this idea. In the community of the pilgrims' quest, particularistic social distinctions based on caste, class, locale, and ethnicity vanish. Turner argues that pilgrims undergo a liminal experience akin to that of neophytes in primitive initia-tion rites (1974: 65, 182). Moreover, he explicitly contrasts pilgrimages

---

*Individual or human psychology undoubtedly finds expression in culture and religion. But this is not to say that culture and religion can be explained in psychological terms. If all of culture were reducible to psychology, all of the observable differences that engage anthro-pology would have to be explained away; history would be meaningless. Clearly, there are important logical similarities and perhaps functional connections in the cybernetics of indi-vidual repression and collective ideologies (see, for example, Becker 1973, 1975; Gabel 1975). But the historical/reproductive processes that give rise to cultural differences are not individual ones; they are social.

with local religion, the former expressing the "inclusive, disinterested, and altruistic domain" and the latter "crucial power divisions and classificatory distinctions within and among politically distinct groups," "selfishness," and "sectional interests" (1974: 185, 186).

Turner asserts that his dialectic of communitas and structure is "to be found at all stages and levels of culture and society" (1969: 113). Elsewhere, however, he defines communitas with specific reference to subjective orientations (1969: 127): "Communitas has an existential quality; it involves the whole man in his relation to other whole men. Structure, on the other hand, has a cognitive quality; as Lévi-Strauss has perceived it, it is essentially a set of classifications, a model for thinking about culture and nature and ordering one's public life." Communitas is thus at once an attribute of social institutions like pilgrimage and an individual psychological orientation. Armed with this notion, Turner can cite as manifestations of communitas both accounts from articulate pilgrims of their feelings of brotherhood with their fellows and such sociologically unifying effects as the fact that pilgrimages bring together people from diverse locales, statuses, and ethnic groups.

Turner has been most often criticized for imputing to pilgrims the subjective feeling of and desire for communitas (Pfaffenberger 1979). In the case of Ma Tsu pilgrimages, for example, pilgrims seldom articulate sentiments that might be interpreted as expressions of the communitas spirit (see also Sopher 1968: 423). This is not to deny the relevance of the subjective feeling of brotherhood, which is undeniably important in many pilgrimage cultures. But as Pfaffenberger (1979: 258) points out, "If a need for *communitas* figures in the decision to make the pilgrimage, it is at an unconscious or nonverbalized level, and therefore rather difficult to assess."

How, then, can we account for the undeniable role of pilgrimages in defining identities that transcend local particularisms, class, and status? In my view, at least part of the answer is to be found by shifting attention from the subjective dimensions of communitas to the significance of pilgrimage as a form of meaningful social action—that is, to aspects of the cultural meaning of pilgrimage that are, as Turner notes (1974: 127), essentially structural.

Here it may be useful to approach pilgrimages in the way that Lévi-Strauss approaches myths. It seems to me that both myths and pilgrimages are instances of communication or reproduction of categorical distinctions.* In contrast, Turner sees pilgrimage as a means by which, in a

*The similarities between myth and pilgrimage extend beyond their cognitive consequences (I hesitate to say "functions"). Many popular myths detail the adventures of mythic

kind of wish fulfillment, such categories are temporarily eliminated, if only to become reinstated in clearer form in a subsequent return to structure. But as James Siegel (1969: 281) remarks of Atjehnese pilgrimages, "At no point . . . can one say that there is necessarily a moment of unstructuredness. Nor is it correct to say that structurelessness inheres in the nature of man himself." Rather, Siegel argues, the existential experience of "unity" in pilgrimage rituals requires not that pilgrims experience structurelessness, but that they come to realize the difference between themselves and the world, "and therefore of their commonness and their potential for union" (p. 282).

In cultural terms, pilgrimage need not be seen as a cognitive dissolving of distinctions, but as a bringing to some degree of explicit awareness implicit cultural distinctions, including most profoundly the distinction between self and society. Moreover, this awareness involves gaining some appreciation not only of categories like "self" and "society," but also to some extent the hierarchical nature of the relation between them (T. Turner 1977b). In the sense elaborated by Sahlins (1976: 211), pilgrimages may be seen as one of the privileged arenas for "symbolic production" in agrarian civilizations.

Keeping the preceding points in mind, we shall now take up three themes: first, that pilgrimages embody and reproduce important cultural distinctions, not the least of which pertain to social identity; second, that social identity is not an entity, but a set of relative oppositions; and third, that pilgrimages are not just products of social history but also arenas for the cultural construction of social history.

Pilgrimages and Pedagogy

The importance of China's sacred places in a complex associative system of traditional Chinese categories suggests an immediate qualification to Victor Turner's claim that the cognitive aspect of structure is suspended in pilgrimage rituals. In fact, Chinese pilgrimages explicitly articulated and often baroquely elaborated cultural categories. Correspondences between sacred geography and temple architecture on the one hand, and the

---

heroes on epic pilgrimages. The Chinese example that comes most readily to mind is *Journey to the West*, a tale that played an essential historical role in accommodating Chinese consciousness to Buddhism. Moreover, a pilgrimage may, literally or metaphorically, retrace the hero's journey, and important shrines and sites on the route often represent important events in his life. For Taiwan's Ma Tsu pilgrims, the journey and its sacred sites relate not to the life of the cult's core symbol, but to the by now generalized myth of their pioneer ancestors.

cardinal directions, the four elements, cosmological hierarchies, and even aspects of human character on the other, were important in pilgrimage iconography (Edkins 1893: 236–37; Thompson 1980; Durkheim & Mauss 1963: 62–80; Johnston 1913: 368). For example, China's "four famous Mountains" (*ssu-ta-ming-shan*), which are important Buddhist pilgrimage centers, are each associated with a particular bodhisattva, cardinal direction, human virtue, and element.*

A similar logic seems to organize the "five old sacred places," or *wu-yü* (Saso 1972: 38–39, 42–43; Johnston 1913: 146; Doolittle 1865, 1: 277; Doré 1914–33, 10: 153–68), already important pilgrimage centers before Buddhism's introduction into China. In sum, the great pilgrimage centers of prerevolutionary mainland China were conceptually integrated into the kaleidoscopic maze of categorical correspondences and oppositions—so baffling to Westerners and fascinating to Chinese—that somehow connected divination, medicine, geomancy, cosmology, and physics into a single symbolic system.

The same sorts of categorical schemata are also apparent in aspects of temple architecture (Edkins 1893: 247–48), the arrangement of deities at various altars within temples (Doré 1914–33, 7: 247–49; Edkins 1893: 239–50; Burn 1926; Fitch 1929), and in iconography. For example, images of the presiding bodhisattvas of the four sacred mountains of China were sometimes placed at a single altar, highlighting through this association their connection with China's sacred geography. Thus, although few pilgrims could hope to visit all of China's four sacred mountains, some of the conceptual significance of such a journey was communicated through this iconographic juxtaposition (Fitch 1929: 36).

Perhaps the most fascinating example of representational elaboration of this sort is a practice reported by Joseph Edkins in which the interiors of large images were arranged according to Chinese notions of anatomy (1893: 251):

The heads are always empty. The chief viscera of the chest and abdomen are always represented. They are of silk or satin, and their shape is that found in drawings of the organs in native medical works. A round red piece of silk represents the heart, whose element is fire. It is the size of the dollar. It and the lungs, which are white, and divided into three lobes, are attached to a piece of wood, round

---

*Wu-t'ai Shan, in the northern province of Shansi, is associated with Wen Shu (Manjusri), wisdom, and air (or wind); O-mei Shan, in the western province of Szechwan, is associated with P'u Hsien (Samantabhadra), happiness, and fire; Chiu-hua Shan, in the central province of Anhwei, is associated with Ti Tsang (Ksitigarbha), filial piety, and earth; and P'u-t'o Shan, in the eastern province of Chekiang, is associated with Kuan Yin (Avalokiteśvara), mercy, and water.

which is wound a piece of yellow paper, having on it a Thibetan prayer. To the wood is attached, by silk threads of five colours, a metallic mirror called *ming-king*. This represents intelligence, the heart being regarded as the seat of mind. The lungs cover the heart as an umbrella or lid, as if to preserve it from injury.

In the abdomen the intestines are made of long narrow pieces of silk with cotton wool stitched along the concave border. This may represent fat or the mesentery. Embracing all, like the peritoneum, is a large piece of silk covered with prayers or charms. Inside are also to be found little bags containing the five kinds of grain, with pearls, jade, small ingots of silver, and gold of five candareens' weight, and bits of solder or various shapes to represent silver.

Undoubtedly, many of the more esoteric aspects of this elaborate symbolism are lost on the majority of pilgrims. Nonetheless, my conversations with pilgrims in Taiwan convince me that many take considerable interest and pride in acquiring this kind of knowledge—knowledge that, to use Joseph Needham's term, "resonates" among categorical classes at all levels of Chinese culture (1956: 283). Informed members of pilgrimage parties sometimes explain various aspects of architectural and iconographic symbolism to their companions, and most temples provide brochures explaining the cosmological and categorical significance of various icons and the place of the temple in the larger framework of a particular deity's cult.

In the case of the Tz'u-hui *t'ang*'s pilgrimage to Hua-lien, this pedagogical function of pilgrimage is even more explicit. One of the purposes of visiting the home temple in Hua-lien is the opportunity to be inducted into higher levels in the cult hierarchy, to "study treasures" (*hsüeh-pao*)—that is, to learn the secret symbolic correspondences known only to members more advanced in cult standing. Moreover, in highly stylized performances, sect members are possessed by many of the divinities of the Chinese pantheon. One of the themes of group-possession performances is to clarify hierarchical relations among divinities. In a state of apparent trance, cult members assume the identities of various divine entities, and in ritual battle (*fa-tou*), orthodox orderings of cosmological precedence are dramatically restructured. It is in this way, for example, that mainstream deities like Kuan Yin and Kuan Kung become subordinated to the sectarian Eternal Mother (Sangren 1983; Naquin 1976; Overmyer 1974, 1976). In my view, these performances are crucial to the initiates' conversion to a heterodox reordering of Chinese cultural distinctions. In sum, pilgrimage is better viewed as a "field" (to use the term of Victor Turner 1974: 17) for communicating, validating, and reproducing important cultural categories than as a means for escaping them.

The Dialectics of Identity

Much of the foregoing discussion of the categorical correlations and oppositions embedded in pilgrimage applies to other arenas of Chinese cultural performance as well. Although acquiring knowledge of these categories is an important and explicit goal of sophisticated pilgrims, a less systematized but equally important set of categories and oppositions makes pilgrimage special in the experience of most lay participants. These categories are precisely the local, regional, ethnic, and national identities that are transcended in the liminal pilgrimage experience, according to Victor Turner.

As noted in Chapter 4, the vast majority of Ma Tsu pilgrims undertake the journey not as individuals, but as members of village groups.* During the journey, most groups are distinctively identified, often displaying banners with their village's or association's name. During the height of the pilgrimage season in Pei-kang, the street leading to the temple is filled with a seemingly endless procession of clearly differentiated parties. Moreover, in their choices of ecstatic performances, dance, and costume, each group distinguishes itself as unique. In short, while ritually affirming a common identity as Taiwanese, each group nonetheless asserts its distinctiveness.

Celebration of "Taiwaneseness" seems to require or at least be embellished by a concomitant celebration of diversity. If all pilgrims came to Pei-kang independently, stripped of their ties to secular structure, they would be deprived of the stimulating spectacle of diverse local customs and performances that is one of the pilgrimage's main attractions. As it is, they gain not only an appreciation of the island's diversity, but also a heightened sense of their community's place in the larger society. There is nothing inherently "antistructural" about this; the ritual expression of solidarity at the pan-Taiwan level is accomplished partly through the expression of ritual differentiation at the level of pilgrimage (and hence village) groups.†

A similar message of diversity within hierarchically encompassing unity is apparent in secular rituals on the journey itself, most strikingly in

---

*Pilgrimages in prerevolutionary mainland China were often organized at the village level as well (Baker 1925: 9; Johnston 1913: 149; A. Smith 1899: 102–5).

†Boon (1982: 62) points out in this regard that Evans-Pritchard (1965: 68) errs in attributing to Durkheim the idea that social facts are grounded in "crowd psychology." Rather, says Boon, for Durkheim society is "less 'corporate group' than 'divisioned whole.'" And "even when a category . . . becomes momentarily a group [e.g., "Taiwanese" in pilgrimage procession], the rite heightens distinctions rather than collapsing them."

the highly developed market in local specialities (*t'e-ch'an*). The excursion buses that carry pilgrims to cult centers invariably visit other tourist attractions, including parks, large engineering projects (e.g., a new harbor being constructed on Taiwan's west coast), famous temples, and so forth. Even more frequent stops are made at ubiquitous shops and stands selling local products—most often nonperishable but edible delicacies. Among other things, such products are "markers" of the locales visited by the pilgrims (MacCannell 1976). In fact, many of these stands are located for convenient access some distance from the attraction or town whose specialty they feature. As much or more time is spent buying *t'e-ch'an* as is spent on explicitly ritual activities or on viewing attractions.* In many cases the products themselves have become a main "attraction," and at the conclusion of a pilgrimage of several days' duration, every conceivable space on buses is filled with the pilgrims' purchases.†

The utility or quality of such souvenirs is secondary to their perceived authenticity, and hence their representational value. Their value inheres in the validation they confer upon the pilgrim's experience.‡ Ta-ch'i, for example, is well known for its dried bean cake (*tou-fu kan*), but the rapidly increasing demand for the product (mainly from visitors to the tomb of Chiang K'ai-shek, located near the town) has inspired many entrepreneurs to import additional supplies and others to manufacture product of obviously lower quality. But tourist/pilgrims to the Chiang K'ai-shek shrine continue to be eager customers for all this; souvenirs like Ta-ch'i's *tou-fu kan* serve as a tangible cultural code for the "attractions," and are themselves part of a complex "ritual performed to the differentiations of society" (MacCannell 1976: 13). Thus quality in purely utilitarian terms is beside the point.

As Dean MacCannell argues in *The Tourist: A New Theory of the Leisure Class* (1976: 13), "Sightseeing is a kind of collective striving for a

---

* According to Geil (1926), "Each holy peak has one city or town near its foot, specially associated with it; and each holy city has within its walls one temple particularly connected with the peak. To Tai Shan the mountain belongs Tai An, the city; within the city is Tai Miao, the temple of the mountain" (p. 13). And of Tai Miao, he says: "Its courtyard [is] like a village fair, full of booths for trinkets, amulets, maps of the Shan, guide-books, magic maps, rubbings of the tablets, . . . peep-shows and . . . dancing girls" (p. 24).

† A semiotic analysis of these products would probably reveal some kind of conceptual order, but I lack the data to attempt one here.

‡ The pilgrims have their flags stamped on Hua Shan "so that the rest of their lives they may display at home the evidence that they have been on this sacred visit, not merely to the broad temple of the city, nor to the paradise at the Valley Mouth, but right through the Knife-blade Defile and across the dizzy ridge of the Green Dragon to Nan Feng Chang Ting, the Actual Genuine South Peak" (Geil 1926: 281). Kendall (1913: 195) documents a similar authenticating of pilgrimages to O-mei Shan.

transcendence of the modern totality, a way of attempting to overcome the discontinuity of modernity, of incorporating its fragments into unified experience. Of course, it is doomed to eventual failure: even as it tries to construct totalities, it celebrates differentiation." However, as I argued regarding Victor Turner's opposing structure with communitas, it is unnecessary to see a paradox in the fact that the cultural ordering of social life implies both differentiation and encompassing unity. On the contrary, it is only through contrast with encompassing unity that awareness of more particular dimensions of identity is achieved. Moreover, this cultural encompassing of diversity is not unique to modern society, as MacCannell argues. At least in terms of their operations as arenas for the symbolic production of social identities, modern tourism and religious pilgrimage are similar. Both provide a context within which cultural oppositions are communicated, elaborated, reified, and ordered by a similar hierarchical logic capable of both differentiating and unifying operations. Neither necessarily involves an existential or psychological transcendence of cultural order; both are complex rituals that intensify in spatially and temporally bounded experience the processes through which individuals internalize, discover, perpetuate, (re)create, and even change culture. In sum, social identity in Chinese culture is hierarchically and relatively constituted, and pilgrimages are one of the ritual processes through which this construction occurs. In the case of Taiwan's Ma Tsu pilgrimages, both local and island-wide communities are reciprocally authenticated in the implicit contrast between them that is one of the ritual's main themes.

Pilgrimages and China's "Little Traditions"

In light of the connection between social identity and its ritual production in dramas like pilgrimage, much of the debate over the integrity of Chinese religion seems misconceived (Sangren 1984a). To approach an understanding of cultural similarities and differences, analysis must shift from comparing collective representations (e.g., among localities or between elites and masses) to examining the relationships between collective representations and social processes.

Anthropologists writing about South and Southeast Asia have addressed the problems of cultural diversity and unity more successfully than have sinological anthropologists. For example, S. J. Tambiah's (1970: 34–35) discussion of how philosophical doctrine (text), cosmology, and ritual relate to one another clarifies at least some dimensions of disagreement. Tambiah argues that doctrinal notions are embedded in cosmology, and that rituals express basic cosmological structures. Thus, in China variations in local ritual forms are correlated with lineage form (Ahern 1973), occupation (Harrell 1974a), and historical settlement patterns (De-Glopper 1974; Wang 1974; Shih 1973), among other things. Nonetheless, basic cosmological categories and contrasts like yin/yang apply to a much broader spectrum of communities than would the specific deities honored in local ritual.

Consequently, pilgrims to Pei-kang who observe the sometimes (even to them) exotic ritual performances of groups from other locales may comment on their novelty, but would seldom consider them incorrect or evidence of fundamentally different religious beliefs. Taiwanese expect different localities to differ in the particulars of ritual practice because they have different histories. Moreover, a conversation between natives of different localities regarding their respective local cults and rituals presents no problem in cultural terms, because each shares an essentially similar cosmological model. The identity of territorial-cult deities may differ, as may some of the ritual forms used in their worship. But cosmology provides a common code for understanding the specific ritual statements that differentiate localities.

The hierarchical structure of the Chinese pantheon—like that in Sri Lanka (Obeyesekere 1966) and in India (Bhardwaj 1973)—facilitates the conceptual integration of local communities into more encompassing ones. Obeyesekere distinguishes "active pantheons" of local religion—namely, deities who have direct relevance to day-to-day village social relations—and "ideal pantheons" that play little role in local ritual but are the subject of worship in major pilgrimage centers. These ideal pantheons (according to Obeyesekere) are important in defining the larger "moral communities" that encompass localities. Obeyesekere's (1966: 22) arguments regarding the central role of Buddhist concepts of salvation in defining a single Sinhalese Buddhist moral community raise interesting questions about Buddhism's integrative role in prerevolutionary China as well:

The salvation idiom unites villages in a common world view, most matters of general concern being readily interpreted through these basic Buddhist concepts. Though "local deities" and "local beliefs" may differ from village to village, none can be called non-Buddhist, for all have been incorporated into a Buddhistic framework. . . . The differences among "local deities" . . . are more apparent than real, for the explanations of their powers, status, fortune, and attributes are uniform everywhere and invariably couched in terms of the "salvation idiom." Hence in a very fundamental sense Sinhalese Buddhists are a single moral community, for they have a common salvation idiom from which their world view is largely constituted. Far from being an abstraction, this "belonging" receives concrete sociological expression through . . . the mechanism of the "obligatory pilgrimage."

The importance in Chinese culture of Taoist and Confucian textual traditions—and, more fundamentally, of yin/yang logic—precludes applying Obeyesekere's arguments directly to China. Buddhism's "salvation idiom" did constitute a kind of heterodox (albeit partial) denial of Confucian and local-cult valorization of order and distinction, and in this sense Chinese Buddhism's salvation idiom was a unifying one. But thanks to the Chinese penchant for attributing the same kind of power (*ling*) to all divinities, every god—Buddhist or Taoist—was encompassed within the idiom of order:disorder :: yang:yin. Thus it is yin and yang that are most basic to China's culture, not Buddhism's salvation idiom.

The situation in Taiwan also differs from that in Sri Lanka because deities like Ma Tsu (a province-level deity in Obeyesekere's terms) and Kuan Yin (a civilization-wide deity) are also prominent in domestic and local ritual. Moreover, the prominence of female deities in Chinese pilgrimage cults limits the applicability of the feudal, hierarchical metaphor Obeyesekere suggests (Sangren 1983). Female deities like Ma Tsu and Kuan Yin may rank high in the Chinese pantheon in terms of prestige, but their gender places them outside the strictly hierarchical relations among celestial male bureaucrats. Nonetheless, as a provincial- (or macroregional-)level pilgrimage cult, Taiwan's Ma Tsu may be considered a rough analog of Ceylon's pilgrimages to the guardian shrines. At an even higher level of inclusivity were the great pilgrimage centers associated with the bodhisattvas and the five sacred mountains associated with the ancient boundaries of Chinese civilization (Doré 1914–33, 10: 153–68).

Obeyesekere and others (e.g. Bhardwaj 1973: especially 214) have noted that pilgrimages play an important role in integrating the so-called great tradition and little traditions in agrarian civilizations. There is no question that pilgrimages have important culturally integrating consequences, but framing the argument in terms like "great tradition" and "little traditions" may not be the best way to describe this process. The point is better put by saying that pilgrimages play an important role in reproducing basic and widespread collective representations through ritual action. This reproductive process occurs at many levels of cultural sophistication.

One obviously integrating effect is the role of the pilgrimage center as a transmitter of religious doctrine to pilgrims. Buddhist pilgrimage centers in China were invariably also the sites of famous monasteries, which were in turn repositories for more or less standardized versions of Buddhist sutras and other texts. Although it is doubtful that most pilgrims actively solicited instruction from monks during their visits, they were certainly encouraged to worship in ways consistent with established doctrine. Moreover, guidebooks published by monasteries for the benefit of literate pilgrims featured admonitions regarding appropriate conduct and aspects of Buddhist doctrine, as well as practical information regarding routes, etiquette, transport, and so forth (Johnston 1913: 150–68).

As a means of gaining merit (*kung-te*), patrons of monasteries and temples also sponsored the publication of morality tales, miracle myths, and other literature for distribution to worshipers. Such books remain popular among pilgrims to Taiwan's Ma Tsu centers, and are one of the ways in which cult centers compete for legitimacy. Although relatively few pilgrims might read esoteric sutras with sophisticated understanding, these more popularly oriented publications provide another channel for direct communication of exegesis. In sum, pilgrimages in China provided, and in Taiwan continue to provide, an important network for the dissemination of relatively standardized doctrine.

Yet it would be a mistake to overstate the homogenizing effects of pilgrimage in such simple-minded sociological terms, and an even greater mistake to see these effects as the raison-d'être for institutionalized pilgrimages. Differentiation is as much a theme in pilgrimage ritual as homogenization, and the largely unintended culturally integrating effects of pilgrimages must be distinguished from both the motives of individual pilgrims in embarking on pilgrimages and the cultural messages communicated through this experience. Thus Ta-ch'i natives who embark on a pilgrimage to Pei-kang do gain a heightened sense of their identity, both as Taiwanese and as Ta-ch'i natives, but few of them set out with this as their conscious goal.

Aura and Authenticity

What, then, *does* motivate the individual to embark on such a pilgrimage? Or, to borrow some terminology from Sahlins (1981), what are the pilgrim's "intentional" values and how do they relate to society's "conventional" ones? Once again, it is a socially constructed notion of power that plays a pivotal role. For one important "intentional" value, I believe, is the cultural power that one gains by making such a trip. To make this point, it is useful to explore the notion of "authenticity" in the context of pilgrimage-cult ideology.

MacCannell (1976: 48) makes an interesting point about what constitutes an "authentic" tourist attraction or work of art:

The work of art [or tourist attraction] becomes "authentic" only after the first copy of it is produced. The reproductions *are* the aura, and the associated ritual, far from being the point of origin, *derives* from the relationship between the original object and its socially constructed importance. I would argue that this is the structure of the attraction in modern society, including the artistic attractions, and the reason the Grand Canyon has a touristic "aura" about it even though it did not originate in ritual.

Like Victor Turner, MacCannell contrasts touristic functions with (generally undefined) religious functions of ritual (compare Johnston 1913: 132). But in the case of Ma Tsu pilgrimages, the relationship between the aura of Pei-kang's Ma Tsu and her markers (e.g., various branch images, pictorial representations, flags) is essentially the same as that between any tourist attraction and its aura. How else can the attraction be explained?

Clearly, the explanation is not to be found in formal religious doctrines. Buddhist enlightenment, for example, can be as easily achieved in one's own backyard as by means of the arduous pilgrimages to China's sacred mountains. To explain why so many pilgrims choose to visit these pilgrimage centers, some of which "lay several days or weeks journey from the nearest large city and attracted pilgrims from thousands of miles away" (Welch 1967: 372–73), one must look outside Buddhist or Taoist texts.

The pilgrimage center, in short, holds essentially the same attraction as any other culturally marked attraction—a chance, as it were, to authenticate, deepen, and reproduce an image of reality (or something closer to it). But the measure of what constitutes the "real" in this context is not immediately accessible to the senses; rather, the world of experience becomes real insofar as it conforms to a cultural construction of it. In providing an opportunity for pilgrims to create this cultural construction through the many metaphors for cosmos that pilgrimage provides, the drama of pilgrimage is, as Victor Turner argues, a kind of rite of passage. Like a rite of passage, pilgrimage socializes individuals by providing them with a model of cosmos and their places in it. However, pilgrims acquire this model not by transcending culture, but rather by recreating it in the semiotics and rituals of the journey.

In the case of Ma Tsu pilgrimages in Taiwan—and specifically regarding notions of cult branching (*fen-hsiang*) and efficacy (*ling*)—concern with authenticity is explicitly equated with spiritual power. Although Ma Tsu's spirit is believed to be immanent in all of her images, its efficacy is relative. To experience the "essence" of Ma Tsu—the manifestation that most closely approximates the deity's conceptual definition, as embedded in cult myths—one must visit the presence least diluted through divisions and most authenticated through miracles. Hence, the recounting of miracles plays a crucial role in establishing and maintaining the popularity of a pilgrimage center, not only because pilgrims may hope for similar celestial beneficence, but also because the tradition of miracles defines a particular manifestation as an "authentic" (*chen*) one.

There is thus a connection between a pilgrim's explicit concern with the efficacy of a particular manifestation of a deity and her/his implicit concern with categorical authenticity. This connection is consistent with a diffuse tendency in Chinese philosophical thought to distinguish between external appearances and inner essences. If this line of reasoning is correct, we must abandon the widely held view that peasant concern with "efficacy" or "what works" (i.e., that peasants worship gods who "answer their prayers") radically separates them from elites, who are more concerned with logical or ethical consistency. Rather, it is precisely the idiom of efficacy, transformed into different media, that links apparently divergent elite and peasant concerns at a culturally and logically "transcendent" level (T. Turner 1977b). For Chinese, efficacy, authenticity, and essence are not separate issues.

The fact that competition among rival pilgrimage centers is stated in the idiom of efficacy (e.g., as manifested in miracles) seems at first glance to support the view that peasants worship what works. But to argue that Chinese worship deities because they are efficacious is tautologous (see also Baity 1977); supernatural power is worshiped because people worship what they perceive to be powerful. The origin, persistence, and spread of cults and cultic devotion are not a result of the efficacy of the spirits involved, no matter what native informants may say. Whatever such propositions may tell us about the religious motivations of some individuals, they are neither a cultural or historical explanation of Chinese religious action nor a refutation of systemic consistency in religious symbolism. Clearly, they leave unanswered the question of why some divinities and particular manifestations of them are perceived as more efficacious than others. In my view, the answer to this question will be found, not in an analysis of individual (or class) psychology, but rather in an analysis of the deity's meaning in the cultural and social system of which it is a part. At least in the case of cultic devotion, "intentional" values are not independent of "conventional" values.

Although it may be true that relatively few individuals construct rationalized cosmologies or worldviews, it is generally the few "rationalizers" in any local tradition or cult who are most responsible for the form it takes. More to the point, as Seaman's (1978) study of a local spirit-writing cult in central Taiwan reveals, whatever the intellectual or psychological dispositions of the majority of their adherents, local cults are capable of developing highly differentiated and logically consistent cosmologies whose symbolic integration is in many ways more than the sum of the efforts of their rationally inclined leaders.

Seaman's description of the decision-making process preceding the construction of a temple provides a glimpse of the recursive workings of this sort of process (1978: 75):

At no time was there a formal vote, nor was there a gathering of "temple elders" or other informally designated leaders to consider the matter. Instead, the topic was informally initiated in idle conversation. It then disseminated along the lines of gossip and personal networks; more discussion and more feedback eventually led to a compromise of views. Finally the integrated scheme reached a point of acceptance where it was felt that it should be submitted to the gods for their opinion. In a seance, the gods indicated their approval. They also provided the geomantical calculations of position and dimensions for the structure. Consensus had been reached, not by a gathering of people in authority into one place, but by a complex system of gossip and feedback through personal networks.

In the same vein, Ahern (1981a: 94) quotes a particularly perceptive informant as follows: "When we say a god is *lieng* [*ling*] we mean the god really does help us. Word is then spread from person to person, each telling the other that the god helped. So it is really a matter of relations among men. . . . A change in the popularity of temples is not a result of change in gods' abilities. The abilities of gods don't change. People's attitudes toward them do, however."

At the social, public, cultural level, this momentum toward symbolic consistency stems precisely from the fact that both concern with efficacy in the idiom of local ritual and concern with consistency in philosophical texts are products of similar social processes. When the managers of the Ma Tsu temples in Lu-kang, Hsin-kang, and Pei-kang publish competing claims to cult supremacy, they are just as concerned to demonstrate that their respective deities are the "real" center of Ma Tsu's presence in Taiwan as they are to establish the deity's efficacy.

Indeed, as was already suggested, these are hardly separate issues. In the competing versions of Ma Tsu's arrival in Taiwan, historical consistency plays a key rhetorical role. Advocates of competing temples are energetic in publicizing not only stories of miracles performed by their deities, but also all sorts of documentary and archaeological evidence supporting their claims of past superiority over their present rivals. Moreover, to be convincing, the miracle stories designed to establish a temple deity's efficacy must be linked to the cult's wider myth-cum-history. Thus successful miracle stories are embedded in historical event and make reference to characteristics specific to Ma Tsu (her special concern for seafarers, her patronage of Taiwan, and so forth).

In sum, the various miracles attributed to the different manifestations of a deity can be seen as a form of support for their authenticity; a deity is shown to be powerful because it is a historically "authentic" one, as much as the converse. An unspoken premise is that historical precedence confers efficacy or power. To say that a particular manifestation of a deity is authentic is to say that it closely approximates the model of what that deity is supposed to be. What a deity is supposed to be is, in turn, determined by its resonance with historically meaningful social relationships, as constituted in the wider language of the entire spectrum of religious symbols.

Again, I return to the argument that individual pilgrims are impelled on their quests not by a presumed universal (i.e., acultural) desire for communitas, but for a culturally particular kind of power. In the case of Chinese pilgrimages like those to Pei-kang, this "power" encompasses such notions as *ling*. An important benefit of gaining greater conceptual control of culture is that it provides a means for authenticating one's individual value and identity in cultural terms—that is, a means of acquiring a cultural "hero myth" that perpetuates a sense of individual power (Becker 1975). Moreover, this power can confer obvious political advantages in manipulating the symbols that legitimate authority. Thus power that is magical (*ling*), in the sense that its genesis in social relations is mystified, can actually become power as we tend to think of it in more material terms. Such magical power can function as social power precisely because both types of efficacy have the same culturally mystified social origin.

The rewards of the knowledge gained in rituals like pilgrimages, in short, may include a very concrete kind of power (what Bourdieu 1977 terms "symbolic capital"). One need not be an interest-theory reductionist to suggest that this knowledge about power increases its holders' commitment to the reality upon which it is based. This process is clearest in the crucial symbiosis that wedded state power and Confucian ideology; Confucian ideologues reaped the reward of sharing in the magical power ("virtue") of the state, in the process of constructing the theory of reality upon which the state's legitimacy was based (see Watt 1972).

A similar reproduction of value is evident in the commitment of local religious leaders and their followers to the realities constructed in pilgrimage rituals. By embarking on a pilgrimage, the pilgrim mediates between her/his community and the magical efficacy attributed to the sacred site. Consequently, he or she also becomes endowed with a "trace" of the same magical charisma. As Jean-Paul Dumont (1984: 140) puts it, "The tourist [read pilgrim] is . . . an active participant in the construction of staged authenticity, an accomplice to his own entrapment. He is not only a consumer of what is produced for him but an active producer of what he consumes."

It is in this sense that I see a profound similarity between peasant and religious adept in the cultural consequences of pilgrimage (obvious differences in the sophistication of individual rationalizations notwithstanding). In seeking a deeper understanding of cosmic unity by visiting shrines devoted to the bodhisattvas, the Buddhist monk is not denying the differentiations of his culture, but emphasizing their encompassment within a larger field of meaning. Yet such encompassing systems of ideas are no less cultural than the mundane differentiations of social life, even when their point is to deny these very differences. The paradox here is, of course, that forms that transcend culture and category are themselves culturally located. Pilgrimage centers attract the seriously reflective devotee because they promise not only to deepen understanding of such ideas through contact with their most authentic embodiments, but also to provide access to power through this deepened understanding. Moreover, in the idiom of efficacy, lay pilgrims to Taiwan's Ma Tsu cult centers also seek an authentic confirmation of an encompassing cultural structure—namely, confirmation of the social significance of "Taiwaneseness" and control over their own identity.

Although I have been at pains to avoid attributing anything like Victor Turner's generalized desire for communitas to individual pilgrims, my argument does not wholly escape some assumptions about individual psychological motivation, for it assumes that the power of a religious symbol to inspire devotion (i.e., its efficacy) is grounded in its ability to bring order to or make sense of other cultural distinctions reproduced in social process (i.e., its consistency). But the assumption that people are universally drawn to symbols that effectively organize experience seems less problematic than Turner's assumption that people are universally motivated to abandon structure altogether (albeit to return to secular life with a heightened appreciation of its distinctions). The cultural connections among collective representations, social reproduction, and pilgrimages as they converge in the idiom of *ling* suggest that what is sometimes characterized as a purely cultural problem of "meaning" and an individual (implicitly acultural) problem of "power" or interest are, at the level of social reproduction, one and the same phenomenon.*

---

*In insisting that "interests" are always culturally constituted, Sahlins (1981) makes a similar point. But his dismissal of the logical priority of regenerative, reproductive, or cybernetic systems that constitute the interactions between "conventional" and "intentional" values leaves unaddressed the nature of the social process of transmission (i.e., the process by which "structures" are "received").

The fact that achieving a more encompassing and integrated view of one's own culture may be a personal revelation helps explain why many perceive such an experience as a transcendence of culture. The idea that our deepest personal transformations operate through socially institutionalized ritual structures is, perhaps, counterintuitive. But the growing consensus among cultural anthropologists is that even our intuitively natural (hence, apparently "noncultural") feelings and emotions are intelligible to us and others only insofar as they are endowed with meaning in a cultural system. The pilgrim may thus feel something akin to communitas as Turner describes it, and this feeling may entail a sense of transcendence of both social and cultural structure. However, this existential state is itself culturally meaningful—indeed, indispensable for the reproduction of cultural distinctions of a lower logical order—even though it may be culturally defined in mystical opposition to categorical differentiation (as tao is, for example). To put this more concretely, it is not necessary to negate structure to find grounds in most cultural systems for both social differentiation and solidarity; rather, it is necessary to conceive cultural distinctions in hierarchical terms.

Generally speaking, then, pilgrimage as cultural process is similar for both sophisticates and peasants: it involves a ritual intensification of cultural differentiation and integration. But the substantive elaboration of this process in cultural terms may vary greatly. The literate religious adept and the illiterate peasant pilgrim undoubtedly arrive at different syntheses in connecting mundane distinctions to encompassing generative processes, perhaps most importantly in terms of differences in relative awareness of the hierarchical nature of the process itself. Such a model is consistent with what appears to be a pattern differentiating intellectual and peasant religion in agrarian civilizations. For example, Clifford Geertz's (1960: 234–35) observations on elite (*prijaji*) and peasant (*abangan*) religion in Java might have been said of China as well:

As one traces *prijaji* patterns downward, they tend to shift in significance as they approach the *abangan* social context. Mystic practices tend to give way to a vivid and concrete polytheism; a concern for individual religious experience is replaced by a concern for group religious reciprocality. And the corollary holds too: *abangan slametans* [ritual feasts] become *prijaji* formal banquets. In any case, although the *prijajis* and *abangans* have, in many ways, very similar world-views, and although they share many concrete items of religious belief and practice, the ethics which can be deduced from these underlying world-views and which the items are arranged to symbolize differ rather markedly.

As a hierarchically organized generative process, pilgrimage ritual is fully capable of producing variant, even conflicting constructions. Yet such variation need not imply an absence of unity at the level of ritual action (or deep culture). Rather, as Maurice Freedman (1974) has argued, local and class variations in religious belief and practice represent transformations stemming from a shared underlying cultural system. If my analysis of pilgrimage ritual is not off the mark, it is possible to go beyond Freedman and argue that many local differentiations in religious belief and practice are meaningful precisely because they are produced in the very rituals (like pilgrimage) that transcend them. Thus pilgrimage rituals must be viewed in functional (if not historical) terms as producing more than a higher level of social and cultural inclusiveness; they are also one of the important arenas in which lower-order differentiations are reproduced (be they territorial-cult or class differences). Contrary to Marx's characterization of peasants, in China they are—culturally if not politically— more than a "sack of potatoes."

In sum, the iconography, myths, and rituals associated with pilgrimage suggest that, rather than escaping culture, pilgrims actively attempt to create, reify, or discover a consistency between a cultural construction of reality (e.g., the deity and all it stands for in the wider field of meaning) and their own knowledge and experience. The processes of social and cultural reproduction and those of individual socialization and discovery converge.

11

The Social Construction of Power

I have argued that from the point of view of established institutions and authority, orthodoxy amounts to recognition of the hegemony of yang in any cult's ideology. To understand the process by which orthodoxy is established, we must now probe more deeply into the relationships among history, legitimacy, and power in Chinese thought.

Votive Lamps and Ta-ch'i's Social Register

Anthropologists who set out to study local Chinese religion and ritual usually find themselves spending a great deal of time talking to people about local history. The reasons for this are easily discerned. Foremost among them is the fact that Taiwanese themselves view ritual organization as a product of history, so that many of the anthropologist's questions concerning current ritual practice are answered in historical terms. Both historical events (e.g., interethnic battles, patterns of migration and settlement, and competition among rival political factions) and events that an objectivist view would reject as "myth" (e.g., miracles) inform the native view of history. For example, inquiry into why a particular deity is worshiped often elicits an account of how the village's first settlers brought the deity's image with them from their native place on the mainland. Thus the Kuan-yin *t'ing* was built because Kuan Yin appeared on the site in an apparition and later performed miracles on behalf of local inhabitants in violent disputes with rivals from another ethnic faction.

Similarly, Ma Tsu is revered because she protected immigrants in their journey across the sea from Fukien.

Because the native view of history itself influences current ritual practice, the task of analysis cannot be reduced simply to separating "fact" from "fiction" in native accounts. Instead, the goal of the anthropologist must be to discover the "mythical realities" in what at first appear to be fabrications. This requires explicit attention to the connection between ritual and history in native thought. Chapter 4's analysis of the Kuan Kung procession provides one example of this connection. Here I shall examine a particularly revealing ritual in some detail. My aim is to show not only how history is embodied in present ritual form, but also how ritual, as an important producer of native historical consciousness, endows history with a particular kind of significance.

Much like the *chiao* ceremony, the *p'u-tu* ceremony at the Fu-jen *kung* requires a realignment of the temple's deity altar so that it faces inward, with the gods' backs toward the temple doors. The position normally occupied by the temple gods is taken up by votive lamps belonging to individual households and to groups of households set up especially for the *p'u-tu*. According to Liu (1967: 164):

> The votive lamp or *tou-teng* ("measure lamp") derives its name from the fact that hulled rice is placed in the *tou* ("rice measure") of the lamp. Other items, colored umbrellas, lanterns, swords, mirrors, balances, rules, scissors, and copper coins have the double function of warding off undesired influences from the convoked spirits and are a compilation of objects associated with curses in folk belief. The votive lamp is a combined symbol of human life and instrument of imitative magic; its object is to ward off evil, lengthen life, and maintain harmony.

People in Ta-ch'i believe that the flame of each oil-burning lamp symbolizes the life of its owner. At the conclusion of the *p'u-tu* ceremony, each lamp is taken to its owner's home, where the flame is carefully guarded until all the oil is consumed. Only then may the lamp be disassembled and stored away until the following year.

Tou-teng ceremonies are conducted at other temples (the P'u-ch'i *t'ang*, Hsiu-te *t'ang*, and Yüeh-mei-shan Kuan-yin *ssu*), usually in the first lunar month and in the twelfth lunar month. They are also part of the ritual associated with *chiao*. However, their worship at the Fu-jen *kung*'s *p'u-tu* is especially relevant to the present analysis because of the implications arising from lamp ownership.

In general, on all occasions where *tou-teng* are displayed, each lamp represents an honorary ritual office, and the larger a household's contribution to the ceremonies, the more prestigious its ritual office and the larger its votive lamp. Moreover, in the case of the *p'u-tu*, the Buddhist flavor of the proceedings means that greater merit (*kung-te*) accrues to generous contributors. In the annual *p'u-tu* ceremonies held at the Fu-jen *kung*, however, the ritual offices are held in perpetuity rather than reassigned each year on the basis of annual contributions. Thus, the same households that held them when the temple instituted the custom continue to hold them today. Annual payments to the temple are required to retain possession of the lamp offices, but only the lamp belonging to each year's *lu-chu* changes hands. The most prestigious and expensive lamps at the Fu-jen *kung* thus measure the relative wealth and status of households in Ta-ch'i about a century ago, rather than at present.*

The lamps themselves are elaborately carved of wood (in contrast to the usual coffee cans covered with red paper) and are prized family heirlooms. When the lamps are passed on to descendants, an eldest son may assume the office, or several descendants may share its rights and obligations in annual rotation.

The positioning of the lamps on the temple altar places the largest and most prestigious in the most honored position in yin/yang terms. Thus the temple altar temporarily becomes an iconic representation of community hierarchy (as it once was), modeled along the lines of the celestial hierarchy that normally occupies it. But two notions of the relationship between time and social order are condensed in the iconography of the Fu-jen *kung*'s votive lamps. The fact that the lamp offices are, in theory, held in perpetuity conveys the notion that this social hierarchy is an enduring one. However, the fact that some formerly wealthy families have descended and poor ones climbed Ta-ch'i's social register is subtly displayed by the inescapable comparison between present and past statuses that the lamps' hierarchical modeling evokes. It is important to emphasize that the idea of permanence dominates, is iconographically explicit, and in a sense "encompasses" the notion of change. Change, though recognized, is relatively superficial and subordinate to hierarchical structure.

This particular instance encapsulates more general traditional Taiwanese notions regarding the relationship between history and ritual organization. It is clear, for example, in the process of ritual intensification, that the structure of hierarchical relations is seen as permanent. This is so despite the fact that territories are continually added to the domain encompassed by cosmic bureaucracy, and hence by civilization (*t'ien-hsia*),

---

*Although most of the lamp offices are owned by households, some are owned by groups or corporations (*hui*) formed specifically for the purpose. In such cases, the rights and duties associated with the lamp are rotated annually among the shareholders. By forming a *hui*, relatively poor households could acquire the prestige of a high-ranking lamp, if only to enjoy its public recognition less frequently than wealthier households.

while existing domains subdivide and are upgraded in hierarchical position. One might even argue that for Taiwanese, while social relations are fluid, the hierarchical patterns that organize them are stable, conceptually speaking.

The point I wish to emphasize with this example is the recursive structure of the relationship between social organization and its historical representation in ritual. Although the particular arrangement of *tou-teng* at the Fu-jen *kung*'s *p'u-tu* models Ta-ch'i's past social hierarchy, this does not mean that social organization unidirectionally determines ritual or symbolic forms. In iconically representing past social organization in *tou-teng* arrangements, Ta-ch'i natives actively select what is to be defined as significant in their history (see also Rosaldo 1980: 31). In making this selection, they are guided by other ritually embodied models, including the *tou-teng* ceremony itself.

Moreover, the *tou-teng* ceremony is but one of many rituals whose meanings include implicit reference to history. Indeed, the entire edifice of territorial-cult structure conveys and embodies an emic vision of local history. The ritual intensification process outlined in Chapter 5 is one of which most informed natives are quite conscious. A culturally constructed model of history is literally mapped onto the landscape in the form of the territorial-cult hierarchy, and this model of history is simultaneously a model of and for social relations in the present.

The criteria for selecting the historically significant in local ritual differ a great deal from those of objectivist historical description, but as I argued at the outset, the former must be encompassed as a "social fact" in the latter. It is to these criteria that I now turn.

History, Miracles, and the Authentication of Power

Many observers of Chinese "folk" religion have noted the role of miracles in authenticating *ling*, and have gone on to attribute the historical rise and fall of deity cults to the frequency of such miracles. This argument is circular unless the idea that *ling* is primarily an aspect of individual belief is also abandoned. But if *ling* reproduces socially meaningful relations, as I have argued, the tautology of evoking *ling* (and miracles) to explain the historical development of cults disappears. Cults do not appear, grow, and disappear because deities' powers wax and wane, although this is what most Taiwanese informants will report; rather, cults wax and wane because social relations wax and wane.

The relationship of *ling* to social relations is best understood in historical terms. But "history" in this sense is itself culturally appropriated. With some notable exceptions, divinities in Taiwanese religion are not thought to stand outside history. Many of the most important—for example, K'ai Chang Sheng Wang, Kuan Kung, and Ma Tsu—are believed to have lived in specific historical periods.* Only after their deaths are they thought to have been rewarded for their exemplary lives by celestial "appointment" to divinity status and celestial office. Heaven is said to communicate such appointments and promotions by various miraculous means, including revelation, seances, spirit writing, and shamanic possession. Deities that became foci for very popular cults might also be appointed to celestial status or be promoted in the celestial hierarchy by the emperor.

When Taiwanese say they worship a deity because it is *ling*, the relevant issue is not whether one "believes" in a particular deity or not, but which deities are most *ling* in the relevant social context. Moreover, the degree of *ling* possessed is assigned not merely on the basis of personal experiences of prayers answered and ignored. As the analysis in preceding chapters demonstrates, the *ling* attributed to any entity is specified by a complex set of structurally interconnected contrasts. The pattern of these contrasts is the product of operations of an essentially symbolic or logical sort. In addition, deities—and particular images of them—must be authenticated as *ling* in local historical tradition. The kinds of historical events that provide this authentication pertain, broadly speaking, to social structure. *Ling*, or power, is thus a pivotal idiom; it is defined or constrained by both general cultural logic and by a historically unfolding logic of social relations in particular contexts.

For example, K'ai Chang Sheng Wang, patron of Chang-chou people, is said to have been the T'ang dynasty general who first pacified the Chang-chou area in Fukien. K'ai Chang Sheng Wang is one of the most popular territorial-cult deities among Taiwan's Chang-chou people, and every local temple embellishes his reputation with stories of local divine intervention. Typically, K'ai Chang Sheng Wang is said to have provided protection against specific natural disasters or the hostile attacks of aborigines, the Japanese, or other Chinese ethnic groups—that is, to have created or restored social order by vanquishing chaotic (*luan*) forces emanating from outside the community.

In Pai-chi village, I was told that K'ai Chang Sheng Wang's spirit-

---

*Even Kuan Yin, whom sophisticated Buddhists recognize as the Chinese form of the Indic Avalokiteśvara, is better known in popular imagination for her earthly incarnation as the Chinese princess Miao-shan, thought to have lived in the distant past (Dudbridge 1978; Sangren 1983).

soldiers defeated an aborigine raiding party about to attack unsuspecting villagers. Such stories not only authenticate K'ai Chang Sheng Wang's power, but also authenticate the boundaries of the community he represents. The miraculous historical events credited to territorial-cult deities emphasize precisely those contexts in which the community acts as a group vis-à-vis outsiders. The reason so many of the central myths associated with territorial-cults in Taiwan pertain to past conflicts with outsiders (aborigines, other ethnic groups, or the Japanese) is that it is only in contrast to outsiders that the community can define itself. In Chapter 8 I argued that mediation of this insider/outsider contrast underlies the magical power of the territorial-cult deity. From the vantage of an "objectivist" history purged of supernatural mythologizing, the occasions when communities have in fact acted most like corporate entities have been precisely those that are appropriated to the status of miracles.

Mythologized historical events thus simultaneously authenticate the power of territorial-cult deities and community boundaries. Culturally appropriated history is in this sense a charter for social relations in the present; but also, conversely, the present structure of social relations structures the cultural appropriation of events. Viewed historically, then, culture and social structure are part of a single process.

That informants unconsciously mystify the connection between *ling* and its social origin is yet another manifestation of the structural requirement that the cultural (i.e., arbitrary) origins of the legitimacy of social order and structures of authority be masked. If they were not so masked, appeal to *ling* as constituted in past social differences could not legitimate those same differences in the present. This mystification takes the form of granting an objectified entity external to society (the territorial-cult god) a kind of creative power (*ling*) that is in fact the process of society's reproduction of itself.

It is worth elaborating the differences between this line of reasoning and other kinds of functional explanation. For example, the fact that religious symbols legitimate such social solidarities as territorial communities, guilds, and native-place associations is a commonplace in sociological and anthropological studies of Chinese institutions. In other words, it is undeniable that religion has the effect of reinforcing social relations. But this effect does not itself explain religion. If religion is epiphenomenal to social relations, why is it necessary at all? And even if it is shown to be necessary, what produces it? Surely not the need to reinforce social relations itself.

In attempting to restore an appreciation of how Chinese religion is embedded in social institutions, I have been at pains to avoid the teleologies and tautologies of traditional functional explanations. To escape from these shortcomings requires conceiving *ling* as both a cultural logic of relations among symbolic categories and a material logic of relations among social collectivities. The dialectical functioning of *ling* as a material logic of social relations and as a cultural logic of religious meaning is perhaps clearest in the idiom of dividing incense (*fen-hsiang* or *fen-ling*).

Dividing Incense

If a new deity image is to be more than a mere doll, it must acquire *ling*. This it does by being passed through the smoke of the incense burned in an established image's censer. Through such a ritual division of the incense (*fen-hsiang*), accompanied by appropriate *k'ai-kuang* ("eye-opening") ceremonies, the branch image (and its temple) are made to share in the power and identity of the old. In this manner the cult of any Chinese deity can spread through "generations" of images and temples whose relationships are traced to a common origin (see also Baity 1977). These relationships among deity images, particularly images that are the foci of territorial cults, thus correspond to native conceptions of the historical relations among communities. Indeed, social identities that transcend social solidarities at each hierarchical level depend in part upon the ritual maintenance of *fen-hsiang* relations. As far as Taiwanese are concerned, should ritual *fen-hsiang* relations fade, there is no longer any relevant shared history or communal identity. *Fen-hsiang* is thus both a process and a statement of relationship.

These themes are clearest in pilgrimage rituals. Pilgrims routinely bring their branch image (*fen-shen*) to the founding temple, to worship and offer incense (*chin-hsiang*). This ritual is said to restore the efficacy of the branch image, much in the way that a battery is recharged. The relationship between deity images, temples, and communities is thus perpetuated in the process of restoring to the branch image its spiritual efficacy or power (*ling*). The structure of *fen-hsiang* ties is a model of historical relations among communities that are recreated synchronically in periodic rituals of rejuvenation of magical power.

The native exegesis of Taiwan's Ma Tsu pilgrimages provides the clearest example of how ritual acts as both a medium of local historical consciousness and an expression of contemporary relations among communities. Almost any Taiwanese can tell you that Ma Tsu lived long ago on

Mei-chou Island off the coast of Fukien.* Once, in a dream, she saw her father and two brothers drowning in the sea after their boat capsized. In the dream she managed to save her father and one of her brothers, but she was awakened before saving the second. Incredibly, the events in her dream proved actually to have occurred. Ma Tsu died young, but continued to intercede miraculously on behalf of imperiled seafarers. Consequently, people began to worship her, and native Fukienese carried her image wherever their merchant endeavors led them.

The same informant would also tell you that Ma Tsu protected Fukienese emigrants on the dangerous passage to Taiwan. The grateful immigrants quickly established branch temples in Taiwan's oldest ports, and it is to these ports that other branch images throughout Taiwan trace their origin. Recognizing Ma Tsu's virtue, the imperial government promoted her to higher and higher honors, conferring on her cult the prestige of official status. Few informants could say exactly when Ma Tsu lived, but most believe that an exact period can be identified.

Images in both old and new temples partake of the same spiritual essence (ling-ch'i), but older images are felt to be stronger or more efficacious (ling) in their responsiveness to devotees. Thus there is an explicit differentiation of Ma Tsu's power in spatial terms. Her manifestations are strongest at the point of the cult's founding in Mei-chou, still quite powerful in Taiwan's oldest Ma Tsu temples, and somewhat diminished in more recently established altars. It is the symbolic rejuvenation of these branch images that provides the rationale for pilgrimages to cult centers.

When pilgrims from all over Taiwan converge on Pei-kang and other Ma Tsu cult centers, they think of themselves as retracing part of their ancestors' journeys from the Chinese mainland. Moreover, their sense of common history is what marks such pilgrimages as quintessentially Taiwanese. Thus many of the authenticating miracles associated with cult centers involve Ma Tsu's intercession in defense of Taiwan's Chinese inhabitants. The Ma Tsu image at Lu-erh-men's T'ien-hou *kung*, for example, is credited with aiding Koxinga's defeat of the Dutch by providing an unusually high tide for his invading fleet (Lin 1961); Pei-kang's Ma Tsu received official citation from the Chia-ch'ing Emperor for helping suppress pirates in the Taiwan Straits and from the T'ung-chih Emperor for helping defeat rebels led by Tai Wan-sheng (Suzuki 1978: 382–88); more recently, Ma Tsu protected An-p'ing from American bombs during the Second World War; and, of course, Ma Tsu protected all the immigrants who crossed the Taiwan Straits. Although Ma Tsu's power is manifested

*For variants extant in Taiwan, see Saso (1968: 41–46).

in other contexts as well (particularly those defined earlier as appropriate to female deities), the special power associated with the pilgrimages is grounded in Taiwanese constructions of their collective history and social identity.*

That *ling* or magical power is grounded in a cultural construction of history is evident in the terms in which contending cult centers frame their claims to supremacy. Each temple's advocates argue either that their temple is Taiwan's oldest Ma Tsu center or that the temple's *fen-hsiang* ties to the founding temple in Mei-chou are the most direct. Although miracles are cited as evidence of authenticity, the major thrust in these claims is historical.[†] An unstated but fundamental assumption is that the historically authentic (*chen*) must necessarily also be the most powerful (*ling*).

The stakes in these disputes involve more than prestige. As noted in Chapter 6, pilgrimage is big business in Taiwan, and the competing temples spare no effort in marshaling historical argument to validate their claims to high status. What is historically relevant depends in part on the relationship between culture and social institutions in the process of social reproduction. If Taiwanese identity were to cease to be of social significance, it seems likely that the popularity of the Ma Tsu pilgrimages would diminish or that their meaning (and "history") would change.

The Reciprocal Authentication of State and Local Cults

The cultural logic that connected history, social relations, and magical power played an important role in the remarkable ability of the traditional Chinese state to incorporate and, to some degree, co-opt popular cults. By conferring titles and promotions upon their deities, the state not only overauthenticated deity cults, but also legitimized itself in local traditions.

---

*During my 1984 visits to Taiwan's Ma Tsu centers, I discovered what appear to be two distinct authenticating strategies. In one, the temple bases its claim on the intimacy of *fen-hsiang* ties to the cult's founding temple in Mei-chou, Fukien. Temples in Pei-kang and Hsin-kang, for example, dispute each other's status in these terms. The other strategy turns on the claim of official status. This was the crux of a dispute between Ma Tsu temples in T'u-ch'eng and Ma-tsu-kung (near Tainan), both of which claimed to be rightful continuators of a temple established by Koxinga at the point where his troops landed before their defeat of the Dutch in the seventeenth century. In both strategies, authenticity is buttressed by mythical/historical constructions of efficacy. Significantly, however, the largest pilgrimages are not to what were once official temples, but to Pei-kang, whose major claims are framed in terms of the *fen-hsiang* idiom.

[†]Lin Heng-tao (1961) documents a dispute between rival claimants to succeed a Ma Tsu temple destroyed by a flood. Both sides mentioned "history" as well as "efficacy" in their claims.

To achieve this wedding of state-legitimizing ideology and local religion, however, required ignoring subtle yet important differences in the structures of two rather different systems of thought.

As we saw in Chapter 8, similar differences are already present in local religion's notions about the ultimate sources of the power of territorial-cult deities, who are seen as exercising power by virtue of their appointment to celestial offices, but who also seem to have received these offices as a reward for the meritorious exercise of this power. In effect, in promoting deities to official office, the bureaucratic hierarchy indirectly validates the structure of the local social relations and the miracles that, in turn, invest local deities with magical power. Conversely, in accepting the idea that such validation is a source of power, local society indirectly acknowledges its place within a larger social order. The circular nature of this logic must be masked if legitimacy is to be preserved, for if order and the power that structures it do not stem from nature and the cosmos, they must be constructed by men in society. It is precisely the denial of this latter possibility—even at the cost of the logical flaw of tautology—that defines this epistemology as an ultimately ethical one, despite its naturalistic trappings. The problem of legitimizing a culturally constructed social order cannot be confronted directly, given the structure of value implicit in Chinese thought. Hence Chinese local religion, even as viewed through the notion of *ling*, is necessarily vague on the ultimate origins of power and order. This tension within local religion is replicated in a tension between the logic of efficacy apparent in local territorial cults and the legitimizing notion of virtue (*te* or *jen*) in official religion.

Perhaps the integrating theme in the historical development of Confucian ideology is the concept of the virtuous "gentleman" (*chün-tzu*; see W.-T. Chan 1963: 3–114; Watt 1972: 78–88). The notion of virtue (*te*) as a humanistic value legitimizing state authority emerged in tandem with the doctrine of the Mandate of Heaven (*t'ien-ming*) during the Chou dynasty. An emperor who lacks virtue will lose heaven's mandate and the power to order civilization. Confucius himself emphasized the notion of *jen* (transformed from a particular virtue of kindness to virtue in a broader sense) as the defining characteristic of the *chün-tzu*. More generally, *jen* is the virtue that superiors are supposed to exhibit toward subordinates. During the Ch'ing dynasty (1644–1912), official emphasis on virtue diminished in favor of a more managerial, legalistic doctrine, but its influence lived on in the classical education required of bureaucrats (Watt 1972: 89–98).

A contrastive, hierarchical yin/yang relationship informs Confucian notions of virtue and merit. According to the Han scholar Tung Chung-shu, for example, "The relationships between sovereign and subject, father and son, and husband and wife, are all derived from the principles of *yin* and *yang*. The sovereign is *yang*, the subject is *yin* the father is *yang*, the son is *yin* the husband is *yang*, the wife is *yin*. . . . The three cords of the Way of the [True] King may be sought in Heaven." (Quoted in Richard J. Smith 1983: 111.)

Like *ling*, virtue is a kind of magical power. Some Neo-Confucians, for example, defined *jen* as "the vital force in living things" (Watt 1972: 93; see also W.-T. Chan 1963: 16, 588–604). These ideas build on an ancient Chinese association between divine status and meritorious deeds, which are defined in terms of instituting order. According to K.-C. Chang (1983: 41), "Almost invariably, according to hero myths, the lineage ancestors had performed meritorious deeds, and it was precisely for their merits and deeds that ancestors were honored in the rites." He cites as a classic example, "The Great Yü, founder of the Ssu clan and the Hsia dynasty, [who] was credited with the containment and control of the Great Flood" (p. 42). In Confucian texts, mythical heroes like Yü are frequently cited as exemplars of merit or virtue.

As Figure 16 shows, virtue permeates the official religion much as *ling* permeates popular religion (compare Fig. 11). It is unnecessary to belabor the emperor's role as heaven's mediator; that role is generally acknowl-

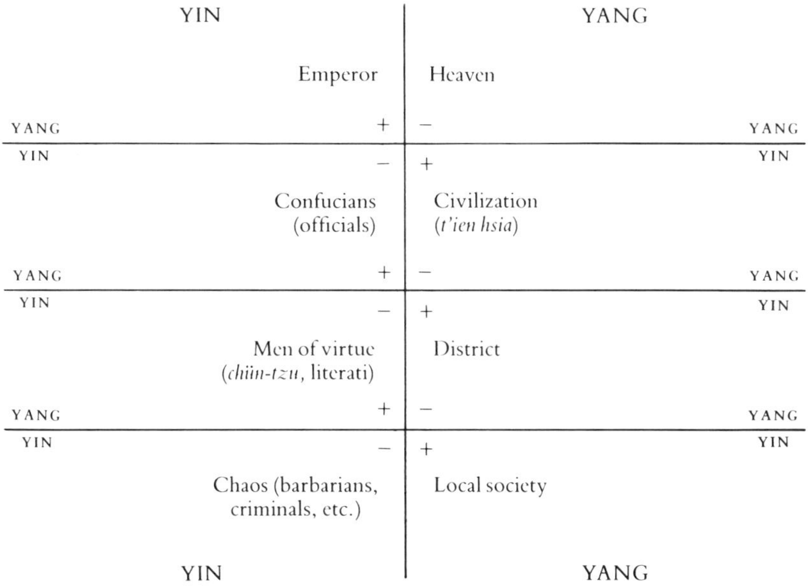

	YIN		YANG	
		Emperor	Heaven	
YANG		+	−	YANG
YIN		−	+	YIN
		Confucians (officials)	Civilization (*t'ien hsia*)	
YANG		+	−	YANG
YIN		−	+	YIN
		Men of virtue (*chün-tzu*, literati)	District	
YANG		+	−	YANG
YIN		−	+	YIN
		Chaos (barbarians, criminals, etc.)	Local society	
	YIN		YANG	

Fig. 16. The orthodox hierarchy of virtue

edged as the basis of imperial legitimacy. By analogy, then, the emperor, who is yang to all under heaven (*t'ien-hsia*), is yin to heaven (*t'ien*) itself.* By the same token, the Confucian bureaucrat, who is yin in relation to the emperor and the generalized notion of order condensed in the notion of *t'ien-hsia*, or "civilization," is an efficacious mediator between this order and the relatively undifferentiated yin of the district for which he is responsible.† Similarly, "men of virtue" (Confucian literati in official ideology; leaders of local society, lineages, and voluntary organizations; patriarchs) mediate hierarchically hegemonic abstract order and relatively yin local society (see, for example, Dardess 1983).

Note that this schematization represents Confucian ideology, not actual bureaucratic structures. As Watt (1972) argues, the bureaucracy, though manned by Confucian-educated officials, was structured along essentially legalist lines—especially during the Ch'ing dynasty. The legalist school emphasized methods and managerial expertise, but it provided no legitimizing ideology; authority and control were valued for their own sakes. Consequently, the state relied on a tenuous and contradictory wedding of Confucian values to legalist methods.

Citing Hsün-tzu, Watt (1972: 225) notes that "the preservation of order depended on getting the right men. While methods [the techniques developed by legalists] were the starting point to administrative order, the *chün-tzu* was its fundamental principle. No matter how well the methods were drawn up, if there were no *chün-tzu* to adapt and apply them, methods themselves would lead to disorder." The *chün-tzu*'s role as an efficacious, almost magical, mediator seems clear.

Figure 16 differs from Figure 11 ("The Efficacy of Territorial-Cult Gods") in two important respects. First, power and efficacy "trickle" down this hierarchy rather than up, as in Figure 11. This direction of action is very explicit in Confucian ideology: if the prince is a genuine man

---

*According to Stephan Feuchtwang (1977: 595), "The officials could believe in a *t'ien* (Heaven) that was the moral nature of the universe, a metaphysical category that was dominant over all other categories, being the arbiter of their and the world's destiny (*ming*). This *t'ien* was not substantial. As Lien, the historian of Taiwan, wrote: 'Good and evil depend on *t'ien*. What is *t'ien*? T'ien is something that has no voice and no smell, that you can see and yet cannot see, can hear and yet cannot hear. . . . Its meaning is naturalness [*tzu-jan*]. . . . This cannot be comprehended by the common people, who therefore resort to Shang-ti [supreme emperor].'" In other words, heaven in official religion amounts to immanent order and, implicitly, power.

†This structural role is consistent with the notion of Confucian bureaucrat as an exemplar of virtue, defined in a generalized way. In Confucian theory, such virtue ought to manifest itself in the effective management of people—that is, leadership was seen as a consequence of the leader's moral qualities, not of his technical expertise (Dardess 1983: 13–84). Defining leadership in narrow, technical terms would have divested it of its charisma and, hence, undermined the moral basis of legitimate authority.

of virtue, then all officials, fathers, and husbands will perforce follow his example and fulfill their roles as mediators of proper orderly relations. The source of power is similar to that of the "exemplary center" (Hocart 1970; Geertz 1980). In contrast, in local religion, ritual acts on the celestial bureaucrats; it is mainly in relation to the outside world (up in spatial-hierarchical terms) that the deity attains efficacy.

Second, because in the Confucian conception, legitimacy begins at the top, the emperor, as heaven's mediator, is constrained to occupy the top left position in my schematization. That this reverses the left/right relationships between entities conceived as individuals and those conceived as collectivities in Figures 16 and 11 strikes me as more than an arbitrary consequence of my schematizations. The relegation of social collectivities to the yang side of the diagram in Figure 16 precludes their occupying the yin/yin (lower left) position in any four-category set. Consequently, the notion of encompassed equality that seems crucial to Figure 11 is absent in Figure 16. The emperor, officials, and men of virtue do not democratically represent their districts, but hierarchically order them by inspiring all within their domains to order themselves internally in terms of the same hierarchical model (see also Feuchtwang 1977: 597). Thus in Figure 16 men, not social collectivities represented by gods, are the loci of power.

The most important implication of this analysis pertains to the nature of the relationship between the popular notion of *ling* and Confucianism's emphasis on merit and virtue. Efficacy in territorial cults derives from the active ritual mediation of conceptually egalitarian communities; expanding orders of community are defined as this efficacy shifts upward through the further mediation of tutelary deities. As I argued in Chapter 8, absolute distinctions between insiders and outsiders at any given level of community are not ordered into a nested hierarchy of such communities without contradiction. Because *ling* creates order by differentiating outsiders from insiders (yin from yang), community at any particular level can be asserted only by ignoring more encompassing levels (at least in cult rituals). But in official religion, efficacy and order are immanent in the most encompassing of categories, *t'ien* (heaven), and they are mediated ritually not upward by a collectivity of equals, but downward by a hierarchy of individual holders of ethical/magical authority. Both *ling* and merit/virtue are hierarchically ordered, but *ling* diminishes at the higher levels and virtue at the lower.

Virtue, like *ling*, requires the authentication of history. This is clear in ancient philosophical traditions, such as those regarding the Mandate of Heaven and the establishment of reputation (*shen-ming*), that carried the spirit of the man of virtue beyond the boundaries of his bodily existence. History's role in authenticating virtue followed from the conviction that heaven's order must inevitably be revealed in human events. Joseph Needham's (1965: 240–42) summation is worth quoting at length in this regard:

In China good history was considered (a) objective, (b) official, and (c) normative. Confucius himself, in his doctrine of the "rectification of names" (*cheng-ming*), had insisted on a spade being called a spade, no matter how powerful the interests which wanted it to be called a shovel; and it was the duty of the historian, even though he was what we should call a civil servant, an eater of the bread of authority, to render judgments on the acts of the past without fear or favour, "for the punishment of evil-doers, and the praise of them that do well." Government in China could and did bestow titles and honours on the dead as well as the living, . . . so it was natural that the making of a just and definitive record of the past should be its function also. Finally, history served an essential moral purpose "for aid in government," for guiding administrative action, encouraging virtue and deterring vice. Such was the basic "praise-and-blame" of Chinese historiography, a high endeavor of the human spirit. . . . Anything apparently paradoxical in this combination was resolved by a profound if tacit conviction which ran through all generations of Chinese historical writers, namely that the process of social unfolding and development had an intrinsic logic, an indwelling Tao, which rewarded "human-heartedness" with good social consequences in the long run and when all balances were struck, while its opposite brought irretrievable evil. This induction was felt to have overwhelming empirical justification. Thus history is the manifestation of the Tao, and has its origins in Heaven.

That both *ling* and virtue require historical authentication is the basis for the finessing of differences between elite and popular notions of the power needed to canonize popular deities. It is a mark of the genius of traditional Chinese civilization (and one of the factors that contributed to its remarkable scale and longevity) that the state managed to turn the culturally authenticating role of history to its advantage. When various emperors rewarded Ma Tsu for her services on behalf of Taiwan, for example, local events were asserted to manifest the same cosmic order upon which the state's claim to legitimacy was implicitly based. Of course, in selecting which miracles were to receive official recognition, the state consistently emphasized the loyal hierarchical subordination of local divine powers to the emperor—a notion somewhat at variance with local interpretations. Whether a deliberate ploy or not, in cases like the Ma Tsu cult, it seems to have worked.

In sum, the reciprocal legitimation of local social structure by official religion and of state authority by local religion depends on the similarities in the hierarchical structures of both systems of thought. But this crucial symbiosis depends equally on disguising the very different trajectories through which order permeates reality. In local religion, *ling* mediates up the hierarchy of social collectivities; in official religion, virtue mediates downward. Since both virtue and *ling* require historical authentication (the former mainly through ancient sacred texts,* the latter through divine revelation and miracles), the necessary obfuscation of their different trajectories is easily accomplished. In neither system of thought is the hegemony of order, yang, challenged. Thus ignoring the subtle differences in the trajectories of virtue and *ling* leaves intact essentially identical hierarchies of authority.† It is the nature of leadership and its legitimizing logic that differs from the two points of view: for the Confucian leadership is exemplary, for the peasant community it is representative.

In this regard, the relationship between virtue and *ling* brings to mind the M. C. Escher drawing in which a flock of birds flying to the left is just as easily perceived as a school of fish swimming to the right. The same orderly hierarchies of authority that, when viewed from the perspective of virtue, convert all under heaven into one household (*t'ien-hsia-i-chia*), from the perspective of *ling* divide society into a segmentary hierarchy of competing communities.

This analysis is consistent with official objections to the particularizing tendencies of local religion. Feuchtwang (1974a) documents a modern example of this official distrust of local religion in the emergence in Taipei of a new, somewhat puritan religious synthesis that emphasizes the worship of deities who have no ties to particular groups or localities. By minimizing the socially particularistic in cult ideology, this new religious synthesis presents itself as less threatening to the universalizing values of the state. The fact that the governments of both Taiwan and the People's Republic marshal similar arguments against popular "superstition," while remaining generally tolerant of the universal symbols of "great tradition" religion, suggests that these tensions persist despite the demise of imperial institutions and the wane of Confucian bureaucracy.

---

*Broadly speaking, history records the workings of heaven's mandate or moral order (K.-C. Chang 1963: 22–23), and the possession of this mandate is what authenticates the emperor's virtue. Should an emperor fail to be virtuous, he would lose the mandate, and disorder would result. Mencius concluded that once the emperor lost the mandate of heaven, it should pass to another, more virtuous prince. This controversial doctrine was evoked by newly triumphant dynasties to legitimate the rebellious overthrow of predecessors. (On the cyclical alternation of order and disorder in Confucian notions of history, see W.-T. Chan 1963: 72, 78.)

†Indeed, this conjuncture may replicate the transition from tribal-level epistemology to hierarchical epistemology. Future research may find a parallel "structure of conjuncture" (Sahlins 1981) in the historical process by which tribal societies have been aggregated, hierarchically, into Chinese civilization. Maspero (1981: 197–247) and Friedman and Rowlands (1978) present arguments that are consistent with this interpretation. And according to Berr (1930: xxi), Granet saw all of Chinese history as "a kidnapping of power, a utilizing of *virtue*, which is gradually individualized and concentrated."

Why, one might ask, would traditional officials permit *ling* to flourish in local practice at all? Why did Confucian officials and philosophers usually stop short of militant suppression? The answer, it seems to me, is that they recognized in peasant piety a legitimizing force that complemented their own concern for orderly social relations. The oft-noted ability of the Confucian establishment to co-opt peasant religion was more than a strategy pursued by condescending or even cynical elites. No less than the illiterate peasant, the Chinese bureaucrat/intellectual depended on a worldview that valued order by implicitly denying its cultural (i.e., arbitrary) origins. Why? Because to recognize that arbitrariness would undermine not only the legitimacy of secular order (both state and local), but also both officials' and common people's confidence in reality itself.

Moreover, it would be a mistake to map the two models of order and power too literally onto social classes or even particular social actors. As we have seen, the two trajectories of power are already present to some degree in local religion. Although *ling* is clearly predominant, a notion closely related to the Confucian conception of power or virtue pervades local culture in the notion of *hsiao*, usually translated as "filial piety." (In fact the *Lun-yü* finds the roots of *jen*, or virtue, in *hsiao* and *ti*; see Richard J. Smith 1983: 111–12.) Fathers should exhibit *jen* toward their sons, and sons should respond with *hsiao*.

In this construction, patriarchal authority is a downward extension of the virtue principle. But real patriarchs must be representative as well as exemplary leaders, and the mark of a successful patriarch is the ability to minimize occasional contradictions in his two roles. For example, in Confucian terms, a son's primary obligation is to honor his father; the son's own authority is hierarchically encompassed by that of the patriline. However, as leaders of their own lines, as opposed to those of their brothers, and particularly regarding the career prospects of their own sons, brothers must also act as representative leaders. Like territorial-cult deities, they are expected to mediate upward between their nuclear families and wider social groups. Obviously, these two sets of expectations may conflict, particularly in competition among brothers over the division of patrimony (see Wolf & Huang 1980; Cohen 1976; Freedman 1958, 1966).

Another example is found in the attitudes of Ta-ch'i people toward their "civilizing" influence on the Atayal aborigines. As Figure 17 indicates, the descendants of the ethnic Chinese settlers see their forebears as the efficacious actors through whom land was incorporated into civilization. The categorical relegation of aborigines to the domain of chaos (which of course is also where demons, monsters, and Westerners be-

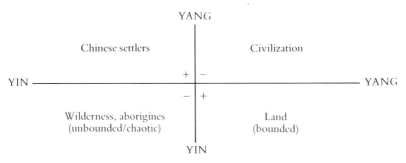

Fig. 17. The civilizing efficacy of settlers

long) may account for the savagery that characterized some episodes of
Han/Atayal relations in Ta-ch'i's history.

James W. Davidson (1903: 418) describes a particularly cruel incident in
which aborigine children were kidnapped and tortured by Chinese camphor merchants in Ta-ch'i. Elderly Ta-ch'i informants corroborate his
claims that cannibalism also occasionally took place in the nineteenth-
century campaigns against the Atayal (pp. 254–55):

> One horrible feature of the campaign against the savages was the sale by the Chi-
> nese in the open market of savage flesh. . . . After killing a savage, . . . the body
> was then divided among its captors and eaten, or sold to wealthy Chinese and
> even to high officials, who disposed of it in like manner. The kidney, liver, heart,
> and soles of the feet were considered the most desirable portions, and were or-
> dinarily cut up into very small pieces, boiled, and eaten somewhat in the form of a
> soup. . . . During the outbreak of 1819, savage flesh was brought in—in bas-
> kets—the same as pork, and sold like pork in the open market of Tokoham [the
> romanized version of the Japanese translation of Ta-k'o-k'an, Ta-ch'i's name be-
> tween about 1870 and 1920] before the eyes of all.

The outermost limits of *jen* did not encompass aborigines.*

For most Chinese, wilderness is not so much "natural" as chaotic. The
glorification of nature in such traditional Chinese arts as landscape painting always reveals an orderly balance of elements, of yin and yang. Consequently, the scenes are almost always imaginary. Whether in paintings
or in settling new land, man's role is to create or reveal order in chaos.

* See Taussig 1984 for an interesting analysis of a similar "culture of terror" in the early-
twentieth-century rubber boom in Colombia. To simplify a complex argument, Taussig's
point is that in the context of capitalist exploitation of Indian labor, the exploiters themselves converted their own "terrifying mythologies" about death, hell, and the jungle into
"fictional realities." But in the process, the savagery attributed to the forest and the Indians
was in fact realized in their own behavior. I suspect that some similar process accounts for
the Taiwanese savagery toward the Atayal.

This locating of order in an administered cosmos—and the associated idea that man should construct society in harmony with this order—may be a general property of "hierarchical" societies (in the sense developed by Louis Dumont). In contrast, tribal societies, broadly speaking, seem to conceive nature as chaotic and unordered (see, in addition to the works of Lévi-Strauss, Fajans 1983; T. Turner 1980).*

For Chinese sophisticates, order was thought to stem from abstract dialectical principles and the highly elaborated theories of essences, elements, *tao*, and merit—not *ling*. But even for those (probably relatively few) Chinese who doubted the existence of personalized divinities, cosmic order was taken as a given, independent of man's cultural construction of it. A major thrust of Chinese historical, religious, and social philosophy (if these can be distinguished) was to bring man's behavior and institutions into harmonious alignment with this order.

At this point I may appear to be neglecting the traditions of Taoist skepticism and monastic Buddhism—traditions that undeniably diluted confidence in the independent reality (and hence legitimacy) of particular orders and institutions. But the historical influence of this skepticism was confined primarily to introducing a degree of flexibility into order's institutional hegemony. There is little evidence that the ultimate heterodoxy of affirming the essentially arbitrary nature of human constructions of order (in contrast to the relatively intelligible heterodoxy of challenging legitimacy in particular contexts) ever achieved institutional hegemony in China. But as an ongoing counterpoint to orthodox ordering impulses, elements of Taoist and Buddhist skepticism did provide a kind of Hegelian antithesis to rigid positivisms and, by challenging these orthodoxies, contributed to their historical development (compare Mote 1971).

In sum, the essentially orthodox impulses that made order a dominant value in local religion were reconcilable with, if not identical to, similar tendencies toward orthodoxy in official ideology. This shared, underlying concern with order played an important role in the relatively seamless cultural integration of ritual and text, popular and elite expression into local, or "natural" (in Skinner's terms), and administrative institutions. The legitimacy of all institutions, both local and official, derived from the hegemonic position of yang and order; threats to the legitimacy of one were easily understood as threats to the legitimacy of the other. In short, the ordering ritual of the elite production of texts and the "text" inherent in peasant ritual were variant idiomatic expressions of an underlying process—the simultaneous reproduction of the administered, nested hierar-

---

*For a convincing if speculative theory on the role of ideology in transforming Asian tribal societies into stratified ones, see Friedman (1975) and Friedman and Rowlands (1978).

chical order of reality, social relations (including those of domination and hierarchy), and value.* This essential cultural resonance was a foundation of China's cultural integration and a necessary condition for the integration of China's many local traditions into a wider cultural and political system.

Ideology and the Social Order

Current anthropological writing on ideology and institutions can be aligned between two poles. At one extreme is an anti-Enlightenment (perhaps even Romantic) relativism insisting that every society embodies a particular structure of value fully understandable only in its own terms. A frequent correlate of this view is that there is no privileged perspective (e.g., science) from which an objective or generic understanding of culture can be achieved. At the other extreme is an antirelativist positivism insisting that value systems can be studied as social facts from a scientific point of view. A frequent correlate of this second stance is that these values are mapped directly onto particular interested actors of groups and are not properly ascribed to societies as wholes (e.g., Merquior 1979).

My analysis of the structure of value in Chinese culture and society suggests an alternative, one that remains positivist (in the sense that it assumes the reality of the object of analysis and the difference between that object and the discourse that the analysis constitutes), but that preserves a kind of holism in its view of culture. This alternative requires that ideology itself be conceived as hierarchically structured. Very broadly speaking, if a representative notion of authority such as *ling* embodies the interests of hierarchical subordinates, then an exemplary notion of leadership is more consistent with the interests of superiors. But I have argued that the different trajectories by which *ling* and virtue legitimate authority can be reconciled (though not entirely without contradiction) into a single structure. This reconciliation amounts to the holistic encompassment of ideologies embodying divergent sectional interests at an ascendant level. This encompassment, in turn, is accomplished mainly by the dependence of both *ling* and virtue on historical authentication.

In other words, the idea that sectional interests find ideological expression need not preclude an encompassing holism. Rather, what this analysis of *ling* and virtue suggests is that the stability of traditional Chinese social institutions depended in part on the construction of an idiom

---

*Again, note the dangers of assuming that texts embody the culture of an elite class and rituals the culture of the masses (Sangren 1984a). As leaders in their native localities, members of elite classes were often instrumental in organizing "peasant" rituals.

capable of encompassing divergent notions regarding the nature and sources of authority's legitimacy.

The construction of the encompassing idiom depended as much on a hierarchical compromise with egalitarian idiom as the converse. Insofar as this compromise validated the prestige and legitimacy of authority figures at all levels, it was consistent with their interests. This framework thus preserves the old Marxist adage that the ruling ideas of any historical age are those of its ruling class (if husbands, patriarchs, officials, and emperors can be said to constitute a class), but abandons crude determinism.

Nonetheless, the "solution" to the problem of legitimacy that this holistic system implies is only proximate, and the different trajectories of *ling* and virtue can give rise to conflicting expectations for people acting at the junctures between local social systems and administrative hierarchy. For example, Skinner (1971) notes that local elites in China have tended to subscribe to the Confucian ideal of leadership and have aligned themselves with state interests during dynastic heydays, but have withdrawn to become representatives of their own communities as local systems "closed" during periods of dynastic crisis.

Confucian ethics expected classically educated gentlemen to set good examples for their social inferiors and to promote harmony and loyalty to the emperor. At the same time, the status of these gentlemen in their own communities depended on their successful advocacy of local interests in competition with outsiders. Successful leaders in Chinese society were those who managed to balance these representative and exemplary expectations.

This inherent contradiction in the position of local degree-holders parallels the contradiction in the basis of territorial-cult deities' power. From the viewpoint of their communities, degree-holders were a boon because they could promote community interests at higher levels. From the viewpoint of the state, degree-holders were expected to ensure local loyalty to authoritarian hierarchy. In short, the legitimacy of their authority emanated both from above and from below.

This contradiction was latent as long as the interests of the state and the locality did not diverge too radically. However, should the state be perceived as a hostile outside force, local degree-holders and other elites would be forced to choose between the two. When, for example, members of Ta-ch'i's elite took it upon themselves to defy imperial officials and resist the Japanese takeover in 1896, they were clearly acting as representatives of their community in response to an outside threat. But during the prosperous years of the mid-eighteenth century, local elites identified more with the state, and great prestige was bestowed upon the handful of imperial degree-holders in Ta-ch'i.*

This contextual shifting from exemplary to representative leadership and power adds another dimension of political complexity to the shifting boundary between insiders and outsiders elaborated in previous chapters. Skill in the culture of Chinese politics—whether in the family, in the community, or in the circles of state—requires not only the exploitation of the potentials created by these shifts, but a successful encompassment (or finessing) of the contradictions they imply. Although the symbols and idioms have changed, I believe that recurrent political issues in the People's Republic reflect this same set of tensions. Do cadres represent or lead the masses? Does one owe primary allegiance to the state, the commune, or the family? And how, finally, can these tensions be reconciled?

---

* Even in the domain of kin relations, a similar contradiction is evident. Good fathers are expected to set examples for their sons (who are expected to respond with filial submission to their authority), and they are also expected to defend their sons' interests against those of outsiders. But when more than one son is involved, the obligation of each brother to defend the interests of his nuclear family may conflict with the exemplary value attached to patrilineal solidarity (Freedman 1966: 46–47; compare M. Wolf 1972: 164–67).

Conclusion

Summary

To make sense of history and social life in Ta-ch'i, I have attempted to incorporate the strengths of structuralist analyses of symbolic systems into an objectivist historical perspective. This endeavor has raised a number of issues regarding the nature of Ta-ch'i's social, economic, and cultural place in Taiwan and in Chinese civilization.

In Part I, I argued that our understanding of local history is significantly deepened by taking into account the nested structure of regional economic systems. The embeddedness of local communities in larger regional systems raised several questions about the explanatory claims of nondialectical theories of historical causation. My periodization of Ta-ch'i's economic history was intended to illustrate how attention to the embeddedness of the town's marketing community might incorporate insights from formalist, substantivist, and Marxist perspectives without necessarily adopting their theoretical assumptions whole cloth.

Part II shifted focus from the historical development of the local economy to the ritual construction of social relations. The description of local territorial-cult and pilgrimage organization paved the way for a study of the patterns of economic, ritual, and administrative interaction at the market-system level. I concluded that Ta-ch'i's culture, economy, and social institutions have interacted historically to produce a measure of spatial congruence at the market-system level. This congruence is a necessary condition for Ta-ch'i's continued viability as a community, but even "necessary" correspondences ought not be mistaken for historical causes.

Part III moved from a rejection of a single-cause interpretation to suggest that production, economic maximization, values, and the like are encompassed within a holistic process—what I term "social reproduction." To this end, I argued that the connection between Chinese social institutions and religious ideas is even more intimate than supposed in conventional functionalist treatments. I began with a broadly structuralist reinterpretation of the meaning of a variety of Chinese religious symbols. The most important thrust of my critique was that the power, or *ling*, attributed to supernatural entities is better understood as a function of their mediating order and disorder with reference to the entire set of cosmological categories than as a function of their resemblances to corresponding categories of people. Moreover, what I called the "contextual relativity" of community identity is specified in the structure of religious symbols through the idiom of magical power. In particular, the efficacy attributed to territorial-cult deities corresponds more closely to their roles as mediators of community than to their resemblances to real-world officials.

To the degree that *ling* corresponds to the structure of actual social relations, it is because these relations are in large part constituted in the very rituals that specify which "systems of truths become mutually convertible and therefore simultaneously acceptable to several different subjects" (Lévi-Strauss 1969a: 11). In other words, *ling* replicates both the structure of social relations and the structure of relations among supernatural entities because it is constituted in public rituals on the one hand, and in historical events culturally selected as significant on the other. Hence, the relationship between society and cosmology is even more intimate than conventional functional accounts presume, because relatively less must be assumed about the psychological dispositions of individuals. Instead, correspondences between the structure of social institutions and the structure of collective representations can be ascribed to their both being reproduced in the same social processes—among them, communal rituals and historical events as they are culturally appropriated. Insofar as ritual reproduces both community and religious symbols, it is constitutive, not mere display.

This perspective preserves the structuralist insight that social institutions (neighborhoods, villages, marketing communities, for example) embody the same categorical distinctions and values as those symbolically manifest in myths, iconography, and cosmology (nested hierarchy, insider/outsider distinctions, contextual relativity). The open-endedness and infinitely productive possibilities of culture (e.g., through such processes as Louis Dumont's "encompassing of the contrary") are vigorously affirmed. Moreover, as I have argued in my analysis of the symbolic logic of cosmological categories and magical power, what might be termed a "logic of the symbolic" imposes itself not only on collective representations, but also on the "objective" structures of social institutions. For example, the historical emergence of nested hierarchical structure in Ta-ch'i society (neighborhoods, villages, marketing community) was in part culturally predetermined by the pioneers' similarly structured models of what society is and ought to be. In short, Ta-ch'i's history cannot be fully understood without taking into account the culture of those who made it.

My analysis departs somewhat from conventional structuralist treatments, however, in insisting that the fit between collective representations or cultural logics and social institutions be viewed as a functional property of the hierarchically encompassing process of social reproduction. I have argued that historical and scientific understanding of society (and I mean to imply a philosophically fundamental identity) requires not only the demonstration that social institutions embody values, but also a theory about how these values are recursively created in the process of social reproduction. My discussion of the socialization of value in pilgrimage, hinging on the pivotal notion of power, was intended to show one way such reproduction occurs.

Both in Ta-ch'i's local tradition and more widely, in Chinese civilization in general, power as culturally constituted is thought to require the authentication of history. The relationship between history and power in Chinese thought, I argued, played an important role in the reciprocally legitimating relationship between local and state religion and institutions in imperial times. My comparison of the Confucian notion of virtue with local religion's notion of efficacy was intended to complement studies of China's economic and administrative integration by presenting a model of cultural integration. I argued that the partial reconciliation of elite and local notions of legitimate structures of authority was just as important in maintaining the impressive scale of Chinese civilization as were patterns of economic interaction and institutionalized central authority.

In this regard it is appropriate to reiterate a point made in Part I: that the spatially and temporally bounded character of case studies limits their ability to serve as tests of ultimate causes in history. Consider, for example, the fit between the structure of value in Chinese culture as I have outlined it and the nested-hierarchical structure of China's economy. In the relatively short course of Ta-ch'i's history, the emergence of nested hierarchy in social organization owes as much to culture as to a purely economic logic, although it is clear that the former has not been inconsistent with nor wholly unconstrained by the latter. But what of the longer course of Chinese history? Is it either possible or probable that the economic logic of the system determined the emergent forms of a corresponding cultural logic?

Although the limited nature of this case study prevents its being a test of this question, the general perspective developed here suggests the dialectical answer that all relevant logics and constraints (including the symbolic, economic, and ecological) are encompassed in a self-reproducing whole. Put in a somewhat simple-minded and only apparently paradoxical way, Chinese categorize the world the way they do in part because the world is the way they categorize it because they categorize it the way they do. Alternatively, as Peter Berger and Thomas Luckmann put it, "Society is a human product. Society is an objective reality. Man is a social product" (1967: 61).

Many of the key cultural distinctions that structure cosmology in Ta-ch'i today have clear antecedents in ancient China. Yin and yang, disorder and order, outsider and insider, and the power embodied in their respective mediations clearly antedate the full-blown emergence of integrated regional economic systems in China. Although it would be incorrect to argue that Chinese cultural logics directly caused the complex patterns of organization of China's late traditional economy (Skinner's arguments provide a much more plausible and compelling set of explanations), the persistence of the structure of value embodied in these ancient ideas just as clearly suggests that they were also no impediment to the development of those patterns. To borrow a metaphor from evolutionary theory, ancient Chinese epistemology may have been "preadapted" for the development of empire. Moreover, this structure of value gives the Chinese economy its uniqueness. Other agrarian civilizations developed marketing hierarchies as well, but the social meaning of these hierarchies is culturally mediated. In Ta-ch'i, as Skinner suggests, the standard marketing community is indeed an important locus of little tradition, but the content of what it means to be a member of the standard marketing community is culturally constituted.

Anti-Antipositivism

In writing this book, I have engaged in what Geertz (1973) terms "translation"—that is, in setting up a discourse between Western and Chinese cultures. If I may be allowed some license with Chinese categories, I have attempted to mediate the "order" constituted by Western social science and, from its point of view, the "disorder" represented by Chinese culture. Out of this mediation, a new order (the book) is created. Just as in the case of princely virtue or supernatural *ling*, however, this order must be historically authenticated. In other words, my arguments will inevitably be subject to evaluation and selection. Whether this selection will be based on, broadly speaking, scientific values, or whether some unacknowledged ideological thrust in the reproduction of our own institutions (the academy included) will render the ultimate judgments, is another question. The last observation may seem to be beside the point. However, the fact that this book is itself subject to some kind of selection in the process of cultural reproduction raises important questions for the status of the analytic endeavor itself. Western anthropologists, increasingly aware of the ideological (hence functional) role of history in legitimating and reproducing exotic cultures and institutions, have awakened to the mystifying potential of their own social science. This heightened sensitivity has resulted, in turn, in an ambivalence running through the writings of those anthropologists most cognizant of history's dialectical power. This ambivalence is evident in a seeming reluctance to choose between (1) viewing one's own account as a "truer" or more encompassing history than either narrowly positivist and ethnocentric Western accounts or ideologized native histories and (2) viewing all "histories" (including one's own account) as relative, so that none can claim an encompassing status.

I suspect that this ambivalence stems from a number of considerations. One of anthropology's long-standing commitments has been to defend the rationality of exotic cultures as a means of bringing our own relative rationality into question. Thus, in restoring a place for native historical consciousness in our conceptions of exotic cultures, we undermine confidence in our own sense of history and, not incidentally, the legitimacy of our own enterprise. At the same time, cultural anthropology has begun to take more note of trends in literary criticism that stress the ways ideology is constituted in discourse. Obviously, our own discourse does not escape scrutiny here. For example, the "other" that is inevitably created as the object in any social science analysis is thus subordinated to the discourse itself. Social science implicitly claims objectivity relative to the objects of its analysis, and in this claim there is an exercise of power.

I do not intend to dismiss the perplexing philosophical difficulties such insights raise. Nonetheless, it seems to me that our attempts to identify the role of history in culture and the role of culture in history are weakened by our ambivalence toward the epistemological status of "history." The proper anthropological endeavor may indeed be translation or interpretation, but we still need some criterion for deciding what distin-

guishes a good translation from a bad one. Consequently, let me acknowledge rather boldly an allegiance to a broadly positivist, scientific
view of history, but one that attempts to encompass the many culture-
specific histories it studies as important social facts. In other words, even
though I have argued that the historical consciousness of Ta-ch'i natives,
as evident in communal rituals and symbolic iconography, has structured
historical events, I have not abandoned the traditional "objectivist" voice
of the Western historian/ethnographer. I have already adduced arguments
consistent with this view; this concluding section restates them in somewhat different form, in order to underline the relevance of this study to a
wider field of theoretical and philosophical concerns.

Stated somewhat crudely, what follows amounts to a positivist defense
of cultural relativism—a position that, contrary to some principled philosophical arguments, does not seem to me to constitute any contradiction.
Culture viewed as a symbolic system constructs experiences and manifests social efficacy in varied and concrete ways. To defend a positivist
view of culture is to argue that culture is real and can be studied scientifically; it does not necessarily imply that causal paradigms or hypothesis-
testing methodologies borrowed from other sciences can be applied me-
chanically to explain cultural phenomena.

To study culture scientifically is to admit that both argument and evidence ought to inform theory and analysis. "Reality" as experienced may
always be culturally constructed, but science (itself a part of such a construction) is in essence a set of principles for selecting among alternative
"realities." The assumption that there is any reality independent of its
particular cultural constructions may elude philosophical proof, but to argue that this assumption should be abandoned in the study of culture or
history leads to equally unresolvable philosophical paradoxes. Let me
elaborate this last point by comparing positivist and relativist views of
history.

The insight that all worldviews are symbolically constructed is sometimes thought to overthrow any kind of objective history or transcendent
science. In brief, it is possible to argue that there are as many "histories"
or "realities" as there are cultures to construct them, so that our positivist/
objectivist history or science is no more "true" than any other. In my
view, this position is both internally inconsistent and practically undesir-
able. It is one thing to demonstrate that culture objectively informs behavior (and hence "reality"). But it is quite another to take this to mean
that there are no realities independent of these cultural systems, and that
all cultures must therefore be seen as equally capable of describing or
modeling their relative realities. Such a position implies that because sci-

ence is part of a Western cultural system, a "science" of culture is a delusion.

This conclusion is difficult to defeat in strictly logical terms. To be sure, one can turn the argument around and point out that a radically relativist position is itself a culturally constructed worldview, so that the claim that there are only relative realities and histories is itself a statement about reality. In other words, in the name of cultural relativism, an antipositivist stance holds that all criteria for choosing among differing worldviews are illegitimate because such criteria are necessarily culturally constructed and hence ideological. But the criterion for preferring this stance is itself unspecified; one must surmise that it enters argument as a value, and thus is no less arbitrary than values that define positivism. In practical terms, such a stance makes illegitimate any study of the functional connections between culture and social action/history. Anthropology and history are thus relegated to the realm of what Lévi-Strauss (1976: 275) terms coherent "deliriums"; by default, "good" writing is differentiated from "bad" not by scientific criteria, but by virtuosity and erudition (though scientific values often sneak back, unacknowledged, into such arguments).

An additional, although somewhat indirect, defense of positivist social science and history is best demonstrated by analogy. An antipositivist view of culture is also antireductionist; culture is not "caused" by or completely explainable in terms of biology, chemistry, or physics. Yet in the course of evolution these forces combined in ways necessary for culture's emergence. Once "under way," of course, culture generates its own dynamics of change—dynamics that, if not completely freed of the constraints of biology, chemistry, and physics, might be more properly understood as encompassing them (Geertz 1973; Sahlins 1976).

This line of argument is quite orthodox in cultural anthropology. Yet many who insist that culture transcends its material bases deny that culture could ever generate a transcendent, self-conscious science. One need not argue that science stands to culture in exactly the same relation as culture stands to its material preconditions to be open to the possibility of a science of culture. No less a champion of cultural anthropology than Emile Durkheim argued that history in the West (and to some degree elsewhere) has been marked by a progressive emancipation of thought from social experience. As Barry Schwartz (1981: 18) puts it, Durkheim's claim that modern science is objective does not mean that it is developed outside of a social context, any more than culture's transcendence of natural selection means that it developed outside of its material context (compare Douglas 1975). In other words, although there may be no proof that culture can generate transcendent science, there is no proof that it cannot. Moreover, the successes of both the natural and the social sciences—equally the products of culture—provide a considerable body of practical argument in favor of the view that it can.

Thus, even in interpretive historical and anthropological writing involving the most radically exotic worlds, positivist criteria must still obtain. Lévi-Strauss's *Mythologiques* and Clifford Geertz's "thick descriptions" are seminal works not because they display an impressive erudition, but because they explain cultural phenomena more exhaustively and parsimoniously than competing interpretations. Even the positivist insistence that scientific propositions be "falsifiable" is implicitly answered by such studies; evidence inconsistent with any theory of exotic culture is quite often and legitimately introduced in constructing better ones.* It is true that the complexities of the human element may prevent cultural anthropology from attaining the predictive rigor of physics or chemistry, but this in itself does not disqualify anthropology as a science. This point is strengthened when one considers natural selection; except in unusually controlled cases, the theory is incapable of predicting the course of biological evolution, yet few critics argue that it is thus not a scientific theory.

In the same vein (Marvin Harris's 1968 doubts notwithstanding), Lévi-Strauss's claim that his arguments are not antimaterialist is entirely justified. Culture as symbolic process must be understood first of all in terms of its internal logic, and culture affects the material world in the ways it informs people's perceptions and actions. However, in the process of social reproduction, material social/historical forces also affect culture. A radically antipositivist stance seems to me to limit historical and anthropological inquiry to a single dimension of this dialectic, thus impoverishing our understanding of cultural systems.

In asserting my faith in broadly scientific values, however, I wish to preserve certain valuable insights of relativist critiques. The most impor-

---

*Jean-Paul Dumont (1972: 163–64) defends structural analysis in explicitly positivist terms, arguing that "structural analysis can be tested from top to bottom, . . . from relative proof given by the coherence of the elicited structure to the absolute proof given by the experimental manipulation of the empirical data. Ultimately, the models proposed in the analysis are erroneous if their predictions are contradicted at the empirical level. . . . On the other hand, the model is wrong if all the same facts can be accounted for by a simpler model. Conversely, a model that integrates more elements is a better model than a model that integrates fewer elements. It goes without saying that the analyst attempts to integrate the maximum number of elements. However, the history of scientific knowledge suggests that humility is in order and that the investigator ought not be under any illusion that his ephemeral maximum is absolute." Lévi-Strauss (1976: 274–76) seems to take a similar position.

tant of these is the notion that all systems of thought tend to veil consciousness of their own arbitrariness. No analysis can claim to escape what might be termed "ideological pollution" completely. But even if analysis inevitably falls somewhere between scientific insight and ideological reification, this insight itself provides some hope for a kind of relative "purification." Thus we can forgo the claim of perfect knowledge of reality, but not that of proximate knowledge of it. Rather than rejecting relativist critiques of positivist social science, I propose that they be encompassed within a positivism that is broadly defined.

In sum, an awareness of the shortcomings of functionalist arguments should not preclude attention to the social efficacy of culture, and the shortcomings of historical treatments that ignore participants' understandings of events should not lead us to discount causal/functional relationships within a wider positivist (albeit Western) framework.

This stance informs my treatment of Ta-ch'i's history. Although I have attempted to demonstrate its advantages in illuminating particular cultural and historical conjunctures, it has entered the study as a premise rather than emerging from it as a conclusion. If the reader is convinced that attention both to history conceived objectively and to what Ta-ch'i's natives make of it provides a fuller understanding of local history and culture, then at the very least this premise will be shown to possess a certain degree of interpretative, perhaps magical, power.

Reference Material

Bibliography

I have chosen to omit notes on works dealing with the general economic and historical background of China and Taiwan. For the interested reader, let me recommend the following. The best general English-language history of Taiwan is Davidson (1903). For an analysis of the regional and ethnic dimensions of Taiwanese immigration, see Knapp (1976) and Chen Chi-lu (1972). On interethnic competition in Taiwan, see Ino (1928), TCS, and Lamley (1977a,b, 1981). On land tenure and Sino-aborigine relations, see Shepherd (1978, 1981), Wickberg (1970), Meskill (1979), R. Myers (1972a,b), and Okamatsu (1900). See C. Smith (1976: 32–44) and Kelley (1976: 219–54) for discussions of dendritic marketing systems, and Rawski (1972) for a study of economic development in Fukien during the Ming dynasty (especially pp. 10–30, 146–51).

The following abbreviations are used in the footnotes:

JD   Jimyo daichō (Register of Temples and Shrines). Unpublished records of township government. Ta-ch'i: Township government offices, ca. 1930.

RTKC   *Rihanshikō* (History of the Control of the Aborigines), Vol. 1. Taihoku: Taiwan Sotokufu Keisatsu Honsho, 1918.

SE   *Shinchikushū enkakushi* (History of Hsin-chu *chou*). Shinchiku: Yamanakadō Insatsujo, 1938.

SS   *Shinchikushō shōkōmeiran* (Hsin-chu *chou* Trade and Industry). Shinchiku: Tosho Kankokai, 1930.

TCKK   *Ta-ch'i kai k'uang* (Ta-ch'i Overview). Ta-ch'i: Ta-t'ung, 1955.

TCS   *Tōenchōshi* (T'ao-yüan *T'ing* Gazetteer). Tōenchō: Taiwan Nichinichi Shimposha, 1906.

TKS   *Taikeishi* (Ta-ch'i Gazetteer). Taikei: Taikeigun Yakusho, 1944.

TS   *Taiwan shihō* 1: *Fudōsun* (Private Law in Taiwan 1: Real Estate), ed. Daiichibu. Kobe: Rinji Taiwan Kyūkan chosakai, 1910.

TYHC   *T'ao-yüan hsien chih* (T'ao-yüan County Gazetteer): *Hsüan shou* (Intro-
ductory Vol), 1962; *Hsüan ssu, Ching chi* (Vol. 4, Economy), 1966;
Hsuan wei chih yü (Supplementary Vol.), 1969. T'ao-yuan: T'ao-yüan
hsien wen hsien wei yüan hui.

Ahern, Emily Martin. 1973. *The Cult of the Dead in a Chinese Village*. Stanford,
Calif.

———. 1975. "The Power and Pollution of Chinese Women," in Margery Wolf
and Roxane Witke, eds., *Women in Chinese Society*, pp. 193–214. Stanford,
Calif.

———. 1981a. *Chinese Ritual and Politics*. Cambridge, Eng.

———. 1981b. "The Thai Ti Kong Festival," in Emily Martin Ahern and Hill
Gates, eds., *The Anthropology of Taiwanese Society*, pp. 397–425. Stanford,
Calif.

Augé, Marc. 1982 (1979). *The Anthropological Circle: Symbol, Function, and History*. Cambridge, Eng.

Baity, Philip C. 1975. *Religion in a Chinese Town*. Asian Folklore and Social Life
Monographs 64. Taipei.

———. 1977. "The Ranking of the Gods in Chinese Folk Religion," *Asian Folklore Studies* 35: 75–84.

Baker, Dwight Condo. 1925. *T'ai Shan: An Account of the Eastern Peak of China*.
Shanghai.

Barclay, George W. 1954. *Colonial Development and Population in Taiwan*. Princeton, N.J.

Bateson, Gregory. 1958 (1936). *Naven: A Survey of the Problems Suggested by a
Composite Picture of the Culture of a New Guinea Tribe Drawn From Three Points
of View*. 2d ed. Stanford, Calif.

———. 1972. *Steps to an Ecology of Mind*. New York.

———. 1979. *Mind and Nature: A Necessary Unity*. New York.

Becker, Ernest, 1973. *The Denial of Death*. New York.

———. 1975. *Escape from Evil*. New York.

Berger, Peter L., and Thomas Luckmann. 1967. *The Social Construction of Reality:
A Treatise in the Sociology of Knowledge*. Garden City, N.Y.

Berr, Henri. 1930. "Preface," in Marcel Granet, *Chinese Civilization*, pp. xi–
xxiii. New York.

Bhardwaj, Surinder Mohan. 1973. *Hindu Places of Pilgrimage in India: A Study in
Cultural Geography*. Berkeley, Calif.

Bloch, Maurice, and Jonathan Parry. 1982. "Introduction: Death and the Regeneration of Life," in Maurice Bloch and Jonathan Parry, eds., *Death and the
Regeneration of Life*, pp. 1–44. Cambridge, Eng.

Boehmer, Thomas. 1977. "Taoist Alchemy: A Sympathetic Approach Through
Symbols," in Michael Saso and David W. Chappell, eds., *Buddhist and Taoist
Studies* 1: 55–78. Honolulu.

Bohannon, Paul. 1955. "Some Principles of Exchange and Investment Among
the Tiv," *American Anthropologist* 57: 60–70.

Boon, James A. 1973. "Further Operations of 'Culture' in Anthropology: A Synthesis of and for Debate," in Louis Schneider and Charles M. Bonjean, eds.,
The Idea of Culture in the Social Sciences, pp. 1–32. Cambridge, Eng.

———. 1982. *Other Tribes, Other Scribes: Symbolic Anthropology in the Comparative
Study of Cultures, Histories, Religions, and Texts*. New York.

Bourdieu, Pierre. 1977 (1972). *Outline of a Theory of Practice*, tr. Richard Nice. Cambridge, Eng.

Brenner, R. 1977. "The Origins of Capitalist Development: A Critique of Neo-Smithian Marxism," *New Left Review* 104: 29–93.

Brook, Timothy. 1981. "Guides for Vexed Travelers: Route Books in the Ming and Qing," *Ch'ing-shih wen-t'i* 4: 32–76.

Burn, D. C. 1926. *A Guide to Lunghwa Temple: With Brief Notes on Chinese Buddhism*. Shanghai.

Chan Lien. 1973. "Taiwan in China's External Relations, 1683–1874," in Paul K. T. Sih, ed., *Taiwan in Modern Times*, pp. 87–170. Philadelphia.

Chan, Wing-tsit, trans. and comp. 1963. *A Source Book in Chinese Philosophy*. Princeton, N.J.

Chang Han-yu and Ramon H. Myers. 1963. "Japanese Colonial Development Policy in Taiwan, 1895–1906: A Case of Bureaucratic Entrepreneurship," *Journal of Asian Studies* 22: 433–49.

Chang Hsiao-mei. 1978. *O-Mei Shan*. Taipei.

Chang, K. C. 1983. *Art, Myth, and Ritual: The Path to Political Authority in Ancient China*. Cambridge, Eng.

Chen Cheng. 1961. *Land Reform in Taiwan*. Taipei.

Chen, Cheng-siang [Ch'en Cheng-hsiang]. 1961. *A Geography of Taiwan* (T'ai-wan ti-chih), Vol. 3. Fu-min Geographical Institute of Economic Development Research Report 94. Taipei.

Chen Chi-lu. 1972. "History of Immigration into Taiwan," *Bulletin of the Institute of Ethnology, Academia Sinica* 33: 119–34.

Chen Ching-chih. 1967. "The Police and *Hoko* Systems in Taiwan Under Japanese Administration (1895–1945)," in *Papers on Japan* 4: 147–76. Cambridge, Mass.

Ch'en Jui-t'ang. 1971. *T'ai-wan ssu-miao fa-lü kuan-hsi chih yen-chiu* (Study of the Legal Status of Temples and Shrines in Taiwan). Taipei: Ssu-fa Hsing-cheng Pu.

Ch'en, Kenneth. 1964. *Buddhism in China: A Historical Survey*. Princeton, N.J.

Christian, William A. 1972. *Person and God in a Spanish Valley*. New York.

———. 1981. *Local Religion in Sixteenth-Century Spain*. Princeton, N.J.

Chu, Samuel C. 1963. "Liu Ming-ch'uan and the Modernization of Taiwan," *Journal of Asian Studies* 23: 37–54.

Cohen, Myron L. 1976. *House United, House Divided: The Chinese Family in Taiwan*. New York.

Crissman, Lawrence W. 1976. "Specific Central-Place Models for an Evolving System of Market Towns on the Changhua Plain, Taiwan," in Carol A. Smith, ed., *Regional Analysis* 1: *Economic Systems*, pp. 183–218. New York.

Croll, Elisabeth. 1981. *The Politics of Marriage in Contemporary China*. Cambridge, Eng.

Culler, Jonathan. 1979. "Jacques Derrida," in John Sturrock, ed., *Structuralism and Since: From Lévi-Strauss to Derrida*, pp. 154–80. Oxford.

Dardess, John W. 1970. "The Transformation of Messianic Revolt and the Founding of the Ming Dynasty," *Journal of Asian Studies* 29: 539–58.

———. 1983. *Confucianism and Autocracy: Professional Elites in the Founding of the Ming Dynasty*. Berkeley, Calif.

Davidson, James W. 1903. *The Island of Formosa: Historical View from 1430 to 1900: History, People, Resources, and Commercial Prospects: Tea, Camphor, Sugar, Gold, Coal, Sulphur, Economical Plants, and Other Productions*. New York.

Day, Clarence Burton. 1940. *Chinese Peasant Cults: Being a Study of Chinese Paper Gods*. Shanghai.

DeGlopper, Donald R. 1974. "Religion and Ritual in Lukang," in Arthur P. Wolf, ed., *Religion and Ritual in Chinese Society*, pp. 43–70. Stanford, Calif.

———. 1977. "Social Structure in a Nineteenth-Century Taiwanese Port City," in G. William Skinner, ed., *The City in Late Imperial China*, pp. 633–50. Stanford, Calif.

Derrida, Jacques. 1978 (1967). *Writing and Difference*. Chicago.

Doolittle, Justus. 1865. *Social Life of the Chinese*, 2 vols. New York.

Doré, Henri. 1914–33. *Researches on Superstition in China*, tr. M. Kennelly, Vols. 1–10, 13. Shanghai.

Douglas, Mary. 1966. *Purity and Danger: An Analysis of the Concepts of Pollution and Taboo*. London.

———. 1975. *Implicit Meanings*. London.

Dudbridge, Glen. 1978. *The Legend of Miao-Shan*. Oxford Oriental Monographs 1. London.

Dumont, Jean-Paul. 1972. *Under the Rainbow: Nature and Supernature Among the Panare Indians*. Austin, Tex.

———. 1984. "A Matter of Touristic 'Indifference,'" *American Ethnologist* 11: 139–51.

Dumont, Louis. 1972. "A Structural Definition of a Folk Deity of Tamil Nad: Aiyanar, the Lord," in L. Dumont, ed., *Religion, Politics and History in India, Collected Papers in Indian Sociology*. The Hague. Reprinted in William A. Lessa and Evon Z. Vogt, eds., *A Reader in Comparative Religion: An Anthropological Approach*, 3d ed. (New York, 1972), pp. 189–95.

———. 1980a. *Homo Hierarchicus: The Caste System and Its Implications*, rev. ed., tr. Mark Sainsbury, Louis Dumont, and Basia Gulati. Chicago.

———. 1980b. "On Value: Radcliffe-Brown Lecture," *Proceedings of the British Academy* 66: 207–41.

———. 1982. "A Modified View of Our Origins: The Christian Beginnings of Modern Individualism," *Religion* 12: 1–27.

Durkheim, Emile. 1915. *The Elementary Forms of the Religious Life*, tr. Joseph Ward Swain. New York.

Durkheim, Emile, and Marcel Mauss. 1963. *Primitive Classification*, tr. Rodney Needham. Chicago.

Edkins, Joseph. 1893. *Chinese Buddhism: A Volume of Sketches, Historical, Descriptive, Critical*, 2d ed. London.

Eliade, Mircea. 1962 (1956). *The Forge and the Crucible: The Origins and Structures of Alchemy*, tr. Stephen Corrin. Chicago.

———. 1963. *Myth and Reality*. New York.

Eto, Shinkichi. 1963. "An Outline of Formosan History," in Mark Mancall, ed., *Formosa Today*, pp. 43–58. New York.

Evans-Pritchard, E. E. 1965. *Theories of Primitive Religion*. Oxford.

Fajans, Jane. 1983. "Shame, Social Action and the Person Among the Baining," *Ethos* 11: 166–80.

Feuchtwang, Stephan. 1965. "An Anthropological Analysis of Chinese Geomancy," M.A. thesis, University of London.

———. 1974a. "City Temples in Taipei Under Three Regimes," in Mark Elvin and G. William Skinner, eds., *The Chinese City Between Two Worlds*, pp. 263–302. Stanford, Calif.

———. 1974b. "Domestic and Communal Worship in Taiwan," in Arthur P. Wolf, ed., *Religion and Ritual in Chinese Society*, pp. 105–30. Stanford, Calif.

———. 1977. "School-Temple and City God," in G. William Skinner, ed., *The City in Late Imperial China*, pp. 581–608. Stanford, Calif.

Fitch, Robert Ferris. 1929. *Pootoo Itineraries*. Shanghai.

Foster-Carter, Aidan. 1978. "The Modes of Production Controversy," *New Left Review* 107: 47–77.

Freedman, Maurice. 1958. *Lineage Organization in Southeastern China*. London School of Economics Monographs on Social Anthropology 18. London.

———. 1966. *Chinese Lineage and Society: Fukien and Kwangtung*. London School of Economics Monographs on Social Anthropology 33. London.

———. 1974. "On the Sociological Study of Chinese Religion," in Arthur P. Wolf, ed., *Religion and Ritual in Chinese Society*, pp. 19–42. Stanford, Calif.

———. 1975. "Sinology and the Social Sciences: Some Reflections on the Social Anthropology of China," *Ethnos* (Stockholm) 40: 194–211.

Friedman, Jonathan. 1975. "Tribes, States, and Transformations," in Maurice Bloch, ed., *Marxist Analyses and Social Anthropology*. Association of Social Anthropologists of the Commonwealth Studies 2, pp. 161–202. London.

Friedman, Jonathan, and M. J. Rowlands. 1978. "Notes Toward an Epigenetic Model of Evolution of 'Civilization,'" in J. Friedman and M. J. Rowlands, eds., *The Evolution of Social Systems*, pp. 201–76. Pittsburgh.

Gabel, Joseph. 1975. *False Consciousness: An Essay on Reification*, tr. Margaret A. Thompson. New York.

Gallin, Bernard. 1963. "Social Effects of Land Reform in Taiwan," *Human Organization* 22: 109–12.

———. 1966. *Hsin Hsing, Taiwan: A Chinese Village in Change*. Berkeley, Calif.

Gates, Hill. 1983. "Money for the Gods," paper prepared for the annual meeting of the American Anthropological Association, Chicago, Ill., Nov. 17.

Geertz, Clifford. 1960. *The Religion of Java*. New York.

———. 1973. *The Interpretation of Cultures*. New York.

———. 1980. *Negara: The Theatre State in Nineteenth-Century Bali*. Princeton, N.J.

Geil, William Edgar. 1926. *The Sacred 5 of China*. London.

Girardot, N. J. 1983. *Myth and Meaning in Early Taoism: The Theme of Chaos*. Berkeley, Calif.

Golas, Peter J. 1977. "Early Ch'ing Guilds," in G. William Skinner, ed., *The City in Late Imperial China*, pp. 555–80. Stanford, Calif.

Gordon, Leonard H. D. 1970. "Taiwan and the Powers, 1840–1895," in L. H. D. Gordon, ed., *Taiwan: Studies in Chinese Local History*, pp. 93–116. New York.

———. 1972. "Interpretations on the Cession of Taiwan," paper presented at the conference on Taiwan in Chinese History, Asilomar, Calif., Sept. 24–29.

Gough, Kathleen. 1972. "Nuer Kinship: A Re-examination," in T. L. Beitelman, ed., *The Translation of Culture*, pp. 79–121. London.

Granet, Marcel. 1930. *Chinese Civilization*. New York.

———. 1973 (1933). "Right and Left in China," tr. Rodney Needham, in R. Needham, ed., *Right and Left: Essays on Dual Symbolic Classification*, pp. 43–58. Chicago.

———. 1975 (1922). *The Religion of the Chinese People*, tr., ed., and with an introduction by Maurice Freedman. New York.

deGroot, J. J. M. 1885. "Buddhist Masses for the Dead at Amoy," extract from the Sixth International Congress of Orientalists (Leiden, 1883), *Actes* 4: 1–120.

Bibliography

————. 1892–1910. *The Religious System of China*, 6 vols. Leiden.

————. 1903–4. *Sectarianism and Religious Persecution in China*. Amsterdam.

Hamilton, Peter. 1974. *Knowledge and Social Structure: An Introduction to the Classical Argument in the Sociology of Knowledge*. London.

Harrell, Stevan C. 1974a. "Belief and Unbelief in a Taiwan Village," Ph.D. dissertation, Stanford University.

————. 1974b. "When a Ghost Becomes a God," in Arthur P. Wolf, ed., *Religion and Ritual in Chinese Society*, pp. 193–206. Stanford, Calif.

Harris, Marvin. 1968. *The Rise of Anthropological Theory: A History of Theories of Culture*. New York.

Hart, Virgil C. 1888. *Western China: A Journey to the Great Buddhist Centre of Mount Omei*. Boston.

Hocart, A. M. 1970 (1936). *Kings and Councillors: An Essay in the Comparative Anatomy of Human Society*. Chicago.

Houdous, Lewis. 1924. *Buddhism and Buddhists in China*. New York.

Howard, M. C., and J. E. King. 1975. *The Political Economy of Marx*. London.

Hsien-ch'eng Ju-hai. 1827. *Ts'an-hsüeh chih-chin* (Knowing the Fords on the Way to Knowledge). Hangchow: Chen-chi Monastery.

Inō Kanori. 1928. *Taiwan bunkashi* (A Cultural History of Taiwan). Tokyo.

Johnston, R. F. 1913. *Buddhist China*. London.

Jordan, David K. 1976. "The Jiaw of Shigaang (Taiwan): An Essay in Folk Interpretation," *Asian Folklore Studies* 35: 81–107.

Kelley, Klara Bonsack. 1976. "Dendritic Central-Place Systems and the Regional Organization of Navaho Trading Posts," in Carol A. Smith, ed., *Regional Analysis 1: Economic Systems*, pp. 219–54. New York.

Kendall, Elizabeth. 1913. *A Wayfarer in China: Impressions of a Trip Across West China and Mongolia*. New York.

Keyes, Charles F. 1975. "Buddhist Pilgrimage Centers and the Twelve-Year Cycle: Northern Thai Moral Orders in Space and Time," *History of Religions* 15: 71–89.

Kleinman, Arthur. 1980. *Patients and Healers in the Context of Culture: An Exploration of the Borderland Between Anthropology, Medicine, and Psychiatry*. Berkeley, Calif.

Knapp, Ronald G. 1971. "Marketing and Social Patterns in Rural Taiwan," *Annals of the Association of American Geographers* 61: 131–55.

————. 1976. "Chinese Frontier Settlement in Taiwan," *Annals of the Association of American Geographers* 66: 43–59.

Koo, Anthony Y. C. 1968. *The Role of Land Reform in Economic Development: A Case Study of Taiwan*. New York.

————. 1973. "Economic Development of Taiwan," in Paul K. T. Sih, ed., *Taiwan in Modern Times*, pp. 397–433. Philadelphia.

Kublin, Hyman. 1973. "Taiwan's Japanese Interlude, 1895–1945," in Paul K. T. Sih, ed., *Taiwan in Modern Times*, pp. 317–57. Philadelphia.

Kumata, Senson. 1897. *Taiwan rekishi kō* (Investigation into the History of Taiwan). Tokyo.

Kung, Lydia. 1976. "Factory Work and Women in Taiwan: Changes in Self-Image and Status," *Signs* 2: 35–58.

Kuo Ting-yee. 1973. "The Internal Development and Modernization of Taiwan, 1863–1891," in Paul K. T. Sih, ed., *Taiwan in Modern Times*, pp. 171–240. Philadelphia.

Kupfer, Carl F. 1911. *Sacred Places in China*. Cincinnati: Western Methodist Book Concern.

Laclau, Ernesto. 1971. "Feudalism and Capitalism in Latin America," *New Left Review* 67: 19–38.

Lamley, Harry J. 1970. "The 1895 Taiwan War of Resistance: Local Chinese Efforts Against a Foreign Power," in L. H. D. Gordon, ed., *Taiwan: Studies in Chinese Local History*, pp. 23–76. New York.

———. 1973. "A Short-Lived Republic and War, 1895: Taiwan's Resistance Against Japan," in Paul K. T. Sih, ed., *Taiwan in Modern Times*, pp. 241–316. Philadelphia.

———. 1977a. "The Formation of Cities: Initiative and Motivation in Building Three Walled Cities in Taiwan," in G. William Skinner, ed., *The City in Late Imperial China*, pp. 155–210. Stanford, Calif.

———. 1977b. "Hsieh-tou: The Pathology of Violence in Southeastern China," *Ch'ing-shih wen't'i* 3: 1–39.

———. 1981. "Subethnic Rivalry in the Ch'ing Period," in Emily Martin Ahern and Hill Gates, eds., *The Anthropology of Taiwanese Society*, pp. 282–318. Stanford, Calif.

Leach, Edmund R. 1961. *Rethinking Anthropology*. London School of Economics Monographs on Social Anthropology No. 22. London.

———. 1962. "Pulleyar and the Lord Buddha: An Aspect of Religious Syncretism in Ceylon," *Psychoanalysis and Psychoanalytic Review* 49: 80–102. Reprinted in abridged form in William A. Lessa and Evon Z. Vogt, eds., *A Reader in Comparative Religion: An Anthropological Approach*, 3d ed. (New York, 1972), pp. 302–13.

———. 1983. "The Gatekeepers of Heaven: Anthropological Aspects of Grandiose Architecture," *Journal of Anthropological Research* 39: 243–63.

LeBar, Frank M., ed. and comp. 1975. *Ethnic Groups of Insular Southeast Asia 2: Philippines and Formosa*. Human Relations Area Files Press.

Lévi-Strauss, Claude. 1962. *Totemism*, tr. Rodney Needham. Boston.

———. 1966. *The Savage Mind*, tr. George Weidenfeld and Nicholson, Ltd. Chicago.

———. 1969a (1964). *The Raw and the Cooked*, tr. John Weightman and Doreen Weightman. New York.

———. 1969b (1949). *The Elementary Structures of Kinship*. Boston.

———. 1976. *Structural Anthropology*, Vol. 2. Chicago.

Li Hsien-chang. 1979. *Matsu shinko no kenkyu* (Studies on Ma-tsu Belief). Tokyo.

Li I-yüan [Li Yih-yuan]. 1963–64. *Nan-ao ti t'ai-ya jen* (The Atayal of Nan-ao: An Ethnological Investigation), *Chung yang yen chiu yüan, min tsu hsüeh yen chiu so chuan k'an*, 5 and 6. Nan-kang, Taiwan.

Lin Heng-tao. 1961. "Lu-erh-men T'ien-hou kung chen wei lun-chan chih chieh-chüeh" (The Result of the Dispute over the Authenticity of the T'ien-hou Temple at Lu-erh-men), *T'ai-wan feng-wu* 11: 3–5.

Liu Chih-wan [Liu Chi-wan]. 1967. *T'ai-pei shih Sung-shan ch'ü an chien-chiao ssu-tien* (Great Propitiary Rites of Petition for Beneficence, Sung-shan, Taipei, Taiwan). Institute of Ethnology, Academia Sinica, Special Publication 14. Nan-kang, Taiwan.

———. 1974. *Chung-kuo min chien hsin-yang lun-chi* (Essays on Chinese Folk Belief and Folk Cults). Institute of Ethnology, Academia Sinica, Special Publication 22. Nan-kang, Taiwan.

Loewe, Michael. 1979. *Ways to Paradise: The Chinese Quest for Immortality*. London.

Lukes, Steven. 1973. *Emile Durkheim: His Life and Work*. London.

MacCannell, Dean. 1976. *The Tourist: A New Theory of the Leisure Class*. New York.

MacCormack, Carol P. 1980. "Nature, Culture and Gender: A Critique," in Carol P. MacCormack and Marilyn Strathern, eds., *Nature, Culture and Gender*, pp. 1–24. Cambridge, Eng.

Mancall, Mark. 1963. "Introduction," in M. Mancall, ed., *Formosa Today*, pp. 1–42. New York.

Maspero, Henri. 1981. *Taoism and Chinese Religion*, tr. Frank A. Kierman. Amherst, Mass.

Meillassoux, Claude. 1981. *Maidens, Meal and Money: Capitalism and the Domestic Community*. Cambridge, Eng. Originally published as *Femmes, greniers et capitaux* (Paris, 1975).

Merquior, J. G. 1979. *The Veil and the Mask: Essays on Culture and Ideology*. London.

Meskill, Johanna M. 1979. *A Chinese Pioneer Family: The Lins of Wu-feng, Taiwan, 1729–1895*. Princeton, N.J.

Meyer, Jeffrey F. 1976. *Peking as a Sacred City*. Asia Folklore and Social Life Monographs 81. Taipei: The Orient Cultural Service.

Moore, Sally F., and Barbara G. Myerhoff. 1977. "Introduction: Secular Ritual: Forms and Meanings," in Moore and Myerhoff, eds., *Secular Ritual*, pp. 3–24. Amsterdam.

Morse, Hosen Ballon. 1909. *The Guilds of China, with an Account of the Guild Merchant or Co-hong of Canton*. London.

Mote, Frederick W. 1971. *Intellectual Foundations of China*. Clinton, Mass.

Moulder, Frances. 1977. *Japan, China, and the Modern World Economy: Toward a Reinterpretation of East Asian Development ca. 1600 to ca. 1918*. New York.

Mullikin, Mary Augusta, and Anna M. Hotchkis. 1973. *The Nine Sacred Mountains of China: An Illustrated Record of Pilgrimages Made in the Years 1935–1936*. Hong Kong.

Myers, Fred R., and Donald L. Brennis. 1984. "Introduction: Language and Politics in the Pacific," in Brennis and Myers, eds., *Language and Politics in the Pacific*, pp. 1–29. New York.

Myers, Ramon H. 1971. "The Research of the Commission for the Investigation of Traditional Customs in Taiwan," *Ch'ing-shih wen-t'i* 2: 24–54.

———. 1972a. "Taiwan Under Ch'ing Imperial Rule, 1684–1895: The Traditional Economy," *Journal of the Institute of Chinese Studies of the Chinese University of Hong Kong* 5: 373–409.

———. 1972b. "Taiwan Under Ch'ing Imperial Rule, 1684–1895: The Traditional Society," *Journal of the Institute of Chinese Studies of the Chinese University of Hong Kong* 5: 413–51.

———. 1972c. "Some Reflections on Taiwan Economic History," paper presented at the conference on Taiwan in Chinese History. Asilomar, Calif., Sept. 24–29.

Myers, Ramon H., and Adrienne Ching. 1964. "Agricultural Development in Taiwan Under Japanese Colonial Rule," *Journal of Asian Studies* 23: 555–70.

Naquin, Susan. 1976. *Millenarian Rebellion in China: The Eight Trigrams Uprising of 1813*. New Haven, Conn.

Needham, Joseph. 1956. *Science and Civilization in China* 2: *History of Scientific Thought*. Cambridge, Eng.

————. 1965. *Time and Eastern Man*. London. Henry Myers Lecture, Royal Anthropological Institute, 1964. Reprinted in J. Needham, *The Grand Titration:
Science and Society in China and the West* (London, 1969), pp. 218–98.

Needham, Rodney. 1973. "Introduction," in R. Needham, ed., *The Right and the
Left: Essays on Dual Symbolic Classification*, pp. xi–xxxix. Chicago.

Obeyesekere, Gananath. 1963. "The Great Tradition and the Little in the Perspective of Sinhalese Buddhism," *Journal of Asian Studies* 22: 139–54.

————. 1966. "The Buddhist Pantheon in Ceylon and Its Extensions," in Man-
ning Nash, ed., *Anthropological Studies in Theravada Buddhism*, pp. 1–26. Cultural Report Series No. 13. New Haven, Conn.

Okamatsu, Santaro. 1900. *Provisional Report on Investigation of Laws and Customs in
the Island of Formosa*. Kobe.

Ortner, Sherry P. 1984. "Theory in Anthropology Since the Sixties," *Comparative
Studies in Society and History* 26: 126–66.

Overmyer, Daniel L. 1974. "The Tz'u-hui T'ang: A Contemporary Religious
Sect on Taiwan: An Introduction to Its History, Organization and Beliefs,"
paper presented at the annual meeting of the Canadian Society for Asian Studies, Toronto, June 2.

————. 1976. *Folk Buddhist Religion: Dissenting Sects in Late Traditional China*.
Cambridge, Eng.

————. 1980. "Dualism and Conflict in Chinese Popular Religion," in Frank E.
Reynolds and Theodore M. Ludwig, eds., *Transitions and Transformations in the
History of Religions: Essays in Honor of Joseph M. Kitagawa*. Supplements to
Numen, Studies in the History of Religions (Leiden) 39: 153–84.

Pang, Duane. 1977. "The *P'u-tu* Ritual," in Michael Saso and David W. Chappell,
eds., *Buddhist and Taoist Studies* 1: 95–122. Honolulu.

Parish, William L., and Martin King Whyte. 1978. *Village and Family in Contemporary China*. Chicago.

Pasternak, Burton. 1968. "Some Social Consequences of Land Reform in a Taiwanese Village," *Eastern Anthropologist* 21: 135–54.

Pfaffenberger, Bryan. 1979. "The Kataragama Pilgrimage: Hindu-Buddhist Interaction and Its Significance in Sri Lanka's Polyethnic System," *Journal of
Asian Studies* 38: 253–70.

Polanyi, Karl. 1957. "The Economy as Instituted Process," in K. Polanyi, C. W.
Arensberg, and H. W. Pearson, eds., *Trade and Market in the Early Empires*,
pp. 243–70. New York.

Pratt, James Bissett. 1928. *The Pilgrimage of Buddhism and a Buddhist Pilgrimage*.
New York.

Pye, Lucian W. 1968. *The Spirit of Chinese Politics: A Psychocultural Study of the
Authority Crisis in Political Development*. Cambridge, Mass.

Radcliffe-Brown, A. R. 1952. *Structure and Function in Primitive Society*. London.

Rawski, Evelyn Sakakida. 1972. *Agricultural Change and the Peasant Economy of
South China*. Harvard East Asian Series 66. Cambridge, Mass.

Redfield, Robert. 1956. *Peasant Society and Culture*. Chicago.

Reichelt, K. L. 1934. *Truth and Tradition in Chinese Buddhism*. Shanghai.

Rey, Pierre-Philippe. 1971. *Colonialisme, néo-colonialisme, et transition au capi-
talisme*. Paris.

————. 1973. *Les Alliances de classes*. Paris.

Rosaldo, Renato. 1980. *Ilongot Headhunting, 1883–1974: A Study in Society and History*. Stanford, Calif.

Sahlins, Marshall D. 1965. "On the Sociology of Primitive Exchange," in Michael Banton, ed., *The Relevance of Models for Social Anthropology*. Association of Social Anthropologists of the Commonwealth Monographs 1, pp. 139–236. London.

———. 1976. *Culture and Practical Reason*. Chicago.

———. 1981. *Historical Metaphors and Mythical Realities*. Association for Social Anthropology in Oceania Special Publications 1. Ann Arbor, Mich.

———. 1982 (1979). "The Apotheosis of Captain Cook, in Michel Izard and Pierre Smith, eds., *Between Belief and Transgression: Structuralist Essays in Religion, History, and Myth*, tr. John Leavitt, pp. 73–102. Chicago.

———. 1983. "Other Times, Other Customs: The Anthropology of History," *American Anthropologist* 85: 517–44.

Salaff, Janet W. 1981. *Working Daughters of Hong Kong: Filial Piety or Power in the Family?* Cambridge, Eng.

Sangren, P. Steven. 1980. "A Chinese Marketing Community: An Historical Ethnography of Ta-ch'i, Taiwan," Ph.D. dissertation, Stanford University.

———. 1983. "Female Gender in Chinese Religious Symbols: Kuan Yin, Ma Tsu, and the 'Eternal Mother,'" *Signs* 9: 4–25.

———. 1984a. "Great Tradition and Little Traditions Reconsidered: The Question of Cultural Integration in China," *Journal of Chinese Studies* 1: 1–24.

———. 1984b. "Traditional Chinese Corporations: Beyond Kinship," *Journal of Asian Studies* 43: 391–415.

Saso, Michael R. 1968. *Taiwan Feasts and Customs*, 3d ed. Hsinchu: Fu Jen University Language School Press.

———. 1972. *Taoism and the Rite of Cosmic Renewal*. Pullman, Wash.

———. 1977. "Buddhist and Taoist Notions of Transcendence: A Study in Philosophical Contrast," in Michael Saso and David W. Chappell, eds., *Buddhist and Taoist Studies* 1: 3–22. Honolulu.

———. 1978. *The Teachings of Taoist Master Chuang*. New Haven, Conn.

Schipper, Kristofer M. 1974. "The Written Memorial in Taoist Ceremonies," in Arthur P. Wolf, ed., *Religion and Ritual in Chinese Society*, pp. 309–24. Stanford, Calif.

———. 1977. "Neighborhood Cult Associations in Traditional Tainan," in G. William Skinner, ed., *The City in Late Imperial China*, pp. 651–76. Stanford, Calif.

Schwartz, Barry. 1981. *Vertical Classification: A Study in Structuralism and the Sociology of Knowledge*. Chicago.

Seaman, Gary. 1978. *Temple Organization in a Chinese Village*. Taipei: The Chinese Association for Folklore.

———. 1981. "The Sexual Politics of Karmic Retribution," in Emily Martin Ahern and Hill Gates, eds., *The Anthropology of Taiwanese Society*, pp. 381–96. Stanford, Calif.

Shepherd, John R. 1978. "Land Reform and Land Grants in Heng-chi Valley," unpublished manuscript.

———. 1981. "Plains Aborigines and Chinese Settlers on the Taiwan Frontier in the Seventeenth and Eighteenth Centuries," Ph.D. dissertation, Stanford University.

Shih Chen-min [Chinben See]. 1973. Chi-ssu ch'üan yü she-hui tsu-chih: Chang-hua p'ing-yüan lo fa-chan mo-shih ti t'an-t'ao (Religious Sphere and Social

Organization: An Exploratory Model on the Settlement of the Chang-hua Plain). Institute of Ethnology, Academia Sinica, Special publication 36. Nankang, Taiwan.

Siegel, James T. 1969. *The Rope of God*. Berkeley, Calif.

Silin, Robert H. 1976. *Leadership and Values: The Organization of Large-Scale Taiwanese Enterprises*. Cambridge, Mass.

Singer, Milton. 1961. "Text and Context in the Study of Contemporary Hinduism," *Adyar Library Bulletin* 25: 274–303.

Skinner, G. William. 1964–65. "Marketing and Social Structure in Rural China," 3 parts, *Journal of Asian Studies* 24: 3–43, 195–228, 363–99.

———. 1971. "Chinese Peasants and the Closed Community: An Open and Shut Case," *Comparative Studies in Society and History* 13: 270–81.

———. 1976. "Mobility Strategies in Late Imperial China: A Regional Systems Analysis," in Carol A. Smith, ed., *Regional Analysis* 1: *Economic Systems*, pp. 327–64. New York.

———. 1977a. "Introduction: Urban Development in Imperial China," in G. William Skinner, ed., *The City in Late Imperial China*, pp. 3–31. Stanford, Calif.

———. 1977b. "Introduction: Urban and Rural in Chinese Society," in G. William Skinner, ed., *The City in Late Imperial China*, pp. 253–73. Stanford, Calif.

———. 1977c. "Cities and the Hierarchy of Local Systems," in G. William Skinner, ed., *The City in Late Imperial China*, pp. 275–352. Stanford, Calif.

———. 1977d. "Introduction: Urban Social Structure in Ch'ing China," in G. William Skinner, ed., *The City in Late Imperial China*, pp. 521–53. Stanford, Calif.

———. 1977e. "Regional Systems in Late Imperial China," paper prepared for the second annual meeting of the Social Science History Association, Ann Arbor, Mich., Oct. 21–23.

———. 1985. "The Structure of Chinese History," *Journal of Asian Studies* 44: 271–92.

Smith, Arthur H. 1970 (1899). *Village Life in China: A Study in Sociology*. Boston.

Smith, Carol A. 1975. "Examining Stratification Systems Through Peasant Marketing Arrangements: An Application of Some Models from Economic Geography," *Man* 10: 95–122.

———. 1977. "How Marketing Systems Affect Opportunity in Agrarian Societies," in Rhoda Halperin and James Dow, eds., *Peasant Livelihood: Studies in Economic Anthropology*, pp. 117–46. New York.

———. 1978. "Beyond Dependency Theory: National and Regional Patterns of Underdevelopment in Guatemala," *American Ethnologist* 5: 574–617.

———, ed. 1976. *Regional Analysis* 1: *Economic Systems*. New York.

Smith, Richard J. 1983. *China's Cultural Heritage: The Ch'ing Dynasty, 1644–1912*. Boulder, Colo.

Smith, Robert J. 1974. *Ancestor Worship in Contemporary Japan*. Stanford, Calif.

Solomon, Richard H. 1971. *Mao's Revolution and the Chinese Political Culture*. Berkeley, Calif.

Sopher, David E. 1968. "Pilgrim Circulation in Gujarat," *The Geographical Review* 58: 392–425.

———. 1973. "Place and Location: Notes on the Spatial Patterning of Culture," in Louis Schneider and Charles M. Bonjean, eds., *The Idea of Culture in the Social Sciences*, pp. 101–17. Cambridge, Eng.

Speidel, William M. 1976. "The Administrative and Fiscal Reforms of Liu Ming-ch'uan in Taiwan, 1884–1891: Foundations for Self-Strengthening," *Journal of Asian Studies* 35: 441–59.

Speidel, William M., and Wang Shih-ch'ing. 1974. "Lin Wei-yüan hsien sheng shih chi" [Biography of Lin Wei-yüan], *T'ai-wan feng-wu* 24: 161–75.

Srinivas, M. N. 1966. *Social Change in Modern India*. Berkeley, Calif. (Chap. 1, "Sanskritization," reprinted in Thomas R. Metcalf, ed., *Modern India: An Interpretive Anthology*, London, 1971, pp. 113–42.)

Statler, Oliver. 1983. *Japanese Pilgrimage*. New York.

Stein, Rolf A. 1979. "Religious Taoism and Popular Religion from the Second to Seventh Centuries," in Holmes Welch and Anna Seidel, eds., *Facets of Taoism*, pp. 53–81. New Haven, Conn.

Strickmann, Michel. 1980. "History, Anthropology, and Chinese Religion," *Harvard Journal of Asiatic Studies* 40: 201–48.

Sturrock, John, ed. 1979. *Structuralism and Since: From Lévi-Strauss to Derrida*. Oxford.

Sun Sen-yen. 1969. "Shen-ming-hui" (Deity Cults), in *T'ai-wan min-shih hsi-kuan tiao-ch'a pao-kao* (Report on Investigation of Customs of Taiwan's People), pp. 605–92. Ssu-fa Hsing-cheng-pu, Taipei.

Suzuki Seiichirō. 1934. *Taiwan kyūkan: Kankonsōsai to nenjū gyōji* (Taiwanese Customs: Coming-of-Age, Marriage, Funerals, and the Annual Round of Festivities). Taipei: Taiwan Nichinichi Shimpōsha. Translated into Chinese as *T'ai-wan chien kuan hsi su hsin yang* by Kao Hsien-chih and Ma Tso-min (Taipei, 1978).

Takekoshi Yosaburo. 1907. *Japanese Rule in Formosa*. New York.

Tambiah, S. J. 1970. *Buddhism and the Spirit Cults of Northeast Thailand*. Cambridge, Eng.

Taussig, Michael. 1980. *The Devil and Commodity Fetishism in South America*. Chapel Hill, N.C.

———. 1984. "Culture of Terror—Space of Death: Roger Casement's Putumayo Report and the Explanation of Torture," *Comparative Studies in Society and History* 26: 467–97.

Taylor, Romeyn. 1973. "Social Origins of the Ming Dynasty, 1351–1360," *Monumenta Serica* 22: 1–78.

Terray, Emmanuel. 1972. "Historical Materialism and Segmentary Lineage-Based Societies," in *Marxism and "Primitive" Societies: Two Studies by Emmanuel Terray*, tr. Mary Klopper, pp. 93–106. New York.

———. 1978. "Event, Structure and History: The Formation of the Abron Kingdom of Gyaman (1700–1780)," in J. Friedman and M. J. Rowlands, eds., *The Evolution of Social Systems*. Pittsburgh.

Thompson, Laurence G. 1973. "The Cult of Matsu," in Thompson, ed., *The Chinese Way in Religion*, pp. 195–201. Encino, Calif.

———. 1980. "Taiwanese Temple Arts and Cultural Integrity," *Bulletin of the Society for the Study of Chinese Religions* 8: 70–78.

———. 1981. "Popular and Classical Modes of Ritual in a Taiwanese Temple," *Bulletin of the Society for the Study of Chinese Religions* 9: 106–22.

Topley, Marjorie. 1954. "Chinese Women's Vegetarian Houses in Singapore," *Journal of the Malayan Branch of the Royal Asiatic Society* 27: 51–67.

———. 1963. "The Great Way of Former Heaven: A Group of Chinese Secret Religious Sects," *Bulletin of the School of Oriental and African Studies* 26: 362–92.

————. 1975. "Marriage Resistance in Rural Kwangtung," in Margery Wolf and Roxane Witke, eds., *Women in Chinese Society*, pp. 67–88. Stanford, Calif.

Tsurumi, E. Patricia. 1967. "Taiwan Under Kodama Gentaro and Goto Shimpei," in *Papers on Japan* 4: 95–146. Cambridge, Mass.

Tu Wei-ming. 1979. "Shifting Perspectives on Text and History: A Reflection on Shelly Errington's Paper," *Journal of Asian Studies* 38: 245–51.

Turner, Terence S. 1977a. "Narrative Structure and Mythopoesis: A Critique and Reformulation of Structuralist Concepts of Myth, Narrative and Poetics," *Arethusa* 10: 103–63.

————. 1977b. "Transformation, Hierarchy and Transcendence: A Reformulation of Van Gennep's Model of the Structure of Rites de Passage," in Sally F. Moore and Barbara G. Myerhoff, eds., *Secular Ritual*, pp. 53–72.

————. 1979a. "Kinship, Household, and Community Structure Among the Kayapo," in David Maybury-Lewis, ed., *Dialectical Societies: The Ge and Bororo of Central Brazil*, pp. 179–214. Cambridge, Mass.

————. 1979b. "The Ge and Bororo Societies as Dialectical Systems: A General Model," in David Maybury-Lewis, ed., *Dialectical Societies: The Ge and Bororo of Central Brazil*, pp. 147–78. Cambridge, Mass.

————. 1980. "The Social Skin," in J. Cherfas and R. Lewin, eds., *Not Work Alone*. Beverly Hills, Calif.

————. 1984. "Dual Opposition, Hierarchy and Value: Moiety Structure and Symbolic Polarity in Central Brazil and Elsewhere," in Jean-Claude Galey, ed., *Différences, Valeurs, Hiérarchie: Textes Offerts à Louis Dumont*, pp. 335–70. Paris: Éditions de l'École des Hautes Études en Sciences Sociales.

Turner, Victor W. 1969. *The Ritual Process: Structure and Anti-Structure*. Chicago.

————. 1974. *Dramas, Fields, and Metaphors: Symbolic Action in Human Society*. Ithaca, N.Y.

————. 1977. "Variations on a Theme of Liminality," in Sally F. Moore and Barbara G. Myerhoff, eds., *Secular Ritual*, pp. 36–52. Amsterdam.

Turner, Victor W., and Edith Turner. 1978. *Image and Pilgrimage in Christian Culture: Anthropological Perspectives*. New York.

United States, Office of Naval Operations. 1944. *Taiwan (Formosa): Shinchiku Province*. Washington, D.C.

Wallerstein, Immanuel. 1974. *The Modern World-System*. New York.

————. 1975. "The Rise and Future Demise of the World Capitalist System," *Comparative Studies in Society and History* 16: 387–415.

Wang Shih-ch'ing. 1974. "Religious Organization in the History of a Chinese Town," in Arthur P. Wolf, ed., *Religion and Ritual in Chinese Society*, pp. 71–92. Stanford, Calif.

Ward, Barbara E. 1977. "Readers and Audiences: An Exploration of the Spread of Traditional Chinese Culture," in Ravindra K. Jain, ed., *Text and Context: The Social Anthropology of Tradition*, pp. 181–204. Philadelphia.

————. 1979. "Not Merely Players: Drama, Art and Ritual in Traditional China," *Man* 14: 18–39.

Warner, W. Lloyd. 1961. *The Family of God: A Symbolic Study of Christian Life in America*. New Haven, Conn.

Watson, James L. 1976. "Anthropological Analyses of Chinese Religion," *The China Quarterly* 66: 355–64.

————. 1982. "Of the Flesh and Bones: The Management of Death Pollution in

Cantonese Society," in Maurice Bloch and Jonathan Parry, eds., *Death and the Regeneration of Life*, pp. 155–86. Cambridge, Eng.

———. 1985. "Standardizing the Gods: The Promotion of T'ien Hou ('Empress of Heaven') Along the South China Coast, 960–1960," in David Johnson, Andrew J. Nathan, and Evelyn S. Rawski, eds., *Popular Culture in Late Imperial China*, pp. 292–324. Berkeley, Calif.

Watt, John R. 1972. *The District Magistrate in Late Imperial China*. New York.

Weber, Max. 1951. *The Religion of China: Confucianism and Taoism*, tr. Hans H. Gerth. Glencoe, Ill.

Wei, Yung. 1973. "Taiwan: A Modernizing Chinese Society," in Paul K. T. Sih, ed., *Taiwan in Modern Times*, pp. 435–505. Philadelphia.

Welch, Holmes. 1967. *The Practice of Chinese Buddhism, 1900–1950*. Cambridge, Mass.

Whitney, Joseph B. R. 1970. *China: Area, Administration, and Nation Building*. University of Chicago, Department of Geography Research Paper 123.

Wickberg, Edgar B. 1970. "Late Nineteenth Century Land Tenure in North Taiwan," in L. H. D. Gordon, ed., *Taiwan: Studies in Chinese Local History*, pp. 78–92. New York.

Wolf, Arthur P. 1974a. "Gods, Ghosts, and Ancestors," in Arthur P. Wolf, ed., *Religion and Ritual in Chinese Society*, pp. 131–82. Stanford, Calif.

———. 1974b. "Introduction," in Arthur P. Wolf, ed., *Religion and Ritual in Chinese Society*, pp. 1–18. Stanford, Calif.

Wolf, Arthur P., and Chieh-shan Huang. 1980. *Marriage and Adoption in China, 1845–1945*. Stanford, Calif.

Wolf, Eric. 1957. "Closed Corporate Peasant Communities in Mesoamerica and Central Java," *Southwestern Journal of Anthropology* 13: 1–18.

———. 1982. *Europe and the People Without History*. Berkeley, Calif.

Wolf, Margery. 1968. *The House of Lim: A Study of a Chinese Farm Family*. New York.

———. 1972. *Women and Family in Rural Taiwan*. Stanford, Calif.

Wolpe, Harold. 1980. "Introduction," in Wolpe, ed., *Articulation of Modes of Production: Essays from Economy and Society*, pp. 1–43. London.

Yang, Ch'ing-k'un. 1961. *Religion in Chinese Society*. Berkeley, Calif.

Yang, Martin M. C. 1970. *Socio-Economic Results of Land Reform in Taiwan*. Honolulu.

Character List

Entries are categorized as follows:

A   Agencies, sectarian cults, and other organizations
D   Deities
F   Physical features
O   Organizational types and categories
P   Place names and administrative districts
S   Terms and titles indicating status, official position, ethnicity, or occupation
T   Temples and altars

Names of county- and higher-level administrative units are excluded, as are the names of major cities. Glosses are provided for nonspecific statuses, organizational types, and miscellaneous terms.

A-mu-p'ing (P) 阿母坪
Chai-ming *ssu* (T) 齋明寺
Chang-chou (P. S) 漳州
Chang-hua (P) 漳化
ch'ang-wu li-shih (S) [executive committee member] 常務理事
ch'ang-wu wei-yüan-hui (O) [executive committee] 常務委員會
chen (O) [urban township] 鎮
chen [authentic, real] 真
chen-min tai-piao (O) [township-council representative] 鎮民代表

Chen-nan *kung* (T) 鎮南宮
Ch'eng Huang Yeh (D) 城隍爺
ch'eng-shou [mature] 成熟
Chi-lung (P) 基隆
chi-ssu-kung-yeh (O) [lineage corporation] 祭祀公業
Ch'i-chou (P) 溪洲
ch'i-tou [opening votive-lamp ceremonies] 起斗
chia [household] 家
chia [land measure, 0.97 hectare] 甲
chia [100 households] 甲

chia-t'ou (or *chia-chang*) (S) [household head] 家頭

chiao [rite of cosmic renewal] 醮、

chiao [corner, hamlet] 角

chiao-chü (O) [ceremonial committee] 醮,居

Ch'iao-ai (P) 僑愛

Ch'iao-t'ien *kung* (T) 朝天宮

chieh (O) [administrative township under Japanese] 街

chieh [street] 街

chieh-pai-hui (O) [sworn brotherhood] 結拜會

chien teng-kao [lamp-pole dedication ceremony] 建燈篙

ch'ien [heaven, yang, male] 乾

chih-hsing wei-yüan-hui (O) [steering committee] 執行委員會

chin-hsiang [offer incense, go on pilgrimage] 進香

chin-hsiang t'uan (O) [pilgrimage group] 進香圍

Ching-mei (P) 景美

Ch'ing Shui Tsu Shih (D) 清水祖師

Ch'ing-ming [Spring Festival] 清明

Chiu-hua Shan (P) 九華山

ch'iu-kuei [request a turtle] 求龜

chou (O) [administrative county under Japanese] 州

chu-chi-che (S) [master of ceremonies] 主祭者

chu-ch'ih (S) [manager] 主持

chu-hsi (S) [chairman] 主席

chu-jen wei-yüan (S) [committee chairman] 主任委員

chu-kung [sacrificial pig] 豬公

Chu-t'ou-chiao (P) 竹頭角

Chu-tung (P) 竹東

chu-wen (M) [celestial petition] 祝文

chuang (O) [village, hamlet; also administrative village under Ch'ing and Japanese] 庄

Chung-chuang (P) 中庄

Chung-hsin (formerly Chung-chuang) (P) 中新

Chung-li (P) 中壢

Chung-liao (P) 中寮

chung-yüan [middle calendrical festival] 中元

chü-jen (S) [provincial-level degree-holder] 舉人

Ch'üan-chou (P, S) 泉州

chün (O) [administrative subcounty under Japanese] 郡

chün-tzu (S) [gentleman, man of virtue] 君子

fa-tou [contest of magical power] 法鬥

fan (S) [barbarian, aborigine] 番

fan-ta-tsu (S) [aborigine landlord] 番大租

fan-tsu [rent paid to aborigine landlord] 番租

Fan-tzu-liao (P) 番仔寮

fang shui-teng [water-lamp ceremony] 放水燈

fen-chia [divide the household] 分家

fen-hsiang, fen-ling, or *fen-huo* [divide incense in temple branching] 分靈，分火

fen-shen [branch deity image] 分神

feng-chien [ancient system of land tenure, feudal] 封建

Feng-ling *ta-mu-kung* (D, T) 峰靈大墓公

feng-shui [geomancy] 風水

fo [buddha, bodhisattva] 佛

Fo-kuang-shan (P, T) 佛光山

fu [magic charm] 符

fu lu-chu (S) [assistant ritual officeholder] 副爐主

Fu Te Cheng Shen (D) 福德正神

Fu-an *kung* (T) 福安宮

Fu-hsing (P) 復興

Fu-hsing *kung* (T) 復興宮

Fu-hsing *kung* (T) 福興宮
Fu-jen *kung* (T) 福仁宮
Fu-k'en *chü* (A) 撫墾局
Fu-shan *yen* (T) 福山巖
Fu-te *kung* (T) 福德宮
Hai-shan *pao* (P) 海山保
hao-hsiung-ti [good brothers, ghosts]
   好兄弟
hsia-yüan [ending calendrical festival]
   下元
hsiang (O) [rural township] 鄉
hsiang-huo [incense fire] 香火
hsiang-yu ch'ien [contributions to
   a temple] 香油錢
Hsiang-yün *ssu* (T) 香雲寺
hsiao [filial piety] 孝
Hsiao-li *she* (S) [Hsiao-li plains
   aborigines] 霄裡社
hsiao-tsu [small rent] 小租
hsiao-tsu-hu (S) [small landlord] 小租戶
hsieh [heterodox] 邪
hsien (O) [county] 縣
hsien i-yüan (S) [county-assembly
   representative] 縣議員
hsien-t'ien [prior heaven] 先天
Hsin-chu (P) 新竹
Hsin-chuang (P) 新莊
Hsin-kang (P) 新港
hsin-ting-kao [cake in honor of
   newborn son] 新丁糕
hsin-t'u (S) [believer, follower] 信徒
hsiu-chien wei-yüan-hui (O) [reconstruc-
   tion committee] 修建委員會
Hsiu-te *t'ang* (T) 修德宮
hsiu-ts'ai (S) [county-level degree-holder]
   秀才
hsüeh-pao [study secret sect teachings]
   學寶
hu [household] 戶
hu-k'ou (O) [household registration] 戶口
Hua Shan (P) 華山
Hua-lien (P) 花蓮

hui [association] 會
hun [yang spirit] 魂
hun-tun [primal chaos] 混沌
i-min (S) [martyrs] 義民
I-te *li* (P) 義德里
jen [virtue] 仁
Jen-an *kung* (T) 仁安宮
Jen-ho *kung* (T) 仁和宮
ju-tao-chiao [Confucian/Taoist religion]
   儒道教
Jui-yüan *kung* (T) 瑞源宮
K'ai Chang Sheng Wang (D) 開漳聖王
k'ai-k'en [open land for settlement] 開墾
k'ai-kuang [spirit-giving ceremony] 開光
kao-t'a [cake tower] 糕塔
k'o-chia-jen (S) [guest people, Hakkas]
   客家人
k'o-t'ing [living room] 客廳
ku-hun [lonely ghost] 孤魂
Kuan Kung (D) 關公
Kuan Yin (D) 觀音
Kuan-hsi (P) 關西
kuan-hsi [relationship] 關係
kuan-li wei-yüan-hui (O) [governing
   committee] 管理委員會
kuan-li-jen (S) [manager] 管理人
Kuan-yin *t'ing* (T) 觀音寺
kuei [ghost] 鬼
kuei-hua [ghost language] 鬼話
k'un [earth, yin, female] 坤
kung [temple] 宮
Kung-kuan (P) 公館
kung-te [Buddhist merit] 公德
kuo-huo [fire walk] 過火
Lao Mu (D) 老母
li (O) [administrative village] 里
li-chang (S) [administrative village head]
   里長
li-chien-shih-hui (O) [censorial
   committee] 理監事會
li-shih-hui (O) [executive committee]
   理事會

lin (O) [administrative neighborhood] 鄰

lin-chang (S) [administrative neighborhood head] 鄰長

ling [alive, efficacious, powerful] 靈

ling-ch'i [spiritual essence, spiritual power] 靈氣

ling-hun [spirit, spiritual essence] 靈魂

Lo-tu (P) 羅浮

lu-chu (S) [ritual officeholder] 爐主

Lu-erh-men (P) 鹿耳門

Lu-kang (P) 鹿港

luan [chaos] 亂

lun-liu [take turns in rotation] 輪流

Lung-t'an (P) 龍潭

Ma Tsu (D) 媽祖

Mei-chou (P) 湄洲

Meng-chia (P) 艋舺

miao-kung (S) [temple custodian] 廟公

Miao-shan (D) 妙善

Min-nan-hua [Southern Min dialect] 閩南話

Mu Lien (D) 木蓮

Nan-hsing (P) 南興

Nan-tzu-kou (P) 南仔溝

Nan-ya *kung* (T) 南雅宮

Nei-chia (P) 內柵

O-mei Shan (P) 峨嵋山

Pai-chi (P) 百吉

pai-pai [worship, religious festival] 拜拜

pan-chang (S) [broker for opera troupes] 班長

pao [1,000 households] 保

pao (O) [township-level administrative district during Ch'ing] 堡

pao-chia (O) [administrative organization of households] 保甲

Pei-kang (P) 北港

p'ing-an [peace and prosperity] 平安

p'ing-an-hsi [festival of peace and harmony] 平安戲

p'ing-p'u-tsu (S) [plains aborigines] 平埔族

p'o [yin spirit, ghost] 魄

pu lo-chia (S) [women who marry, but refuse to cohabit with their husbands] 不落家

P'u Hsien (D) 普賢

P'u-ch'i *t'ang* (T) 普濟堂

P'u-ting (P) 埔頂

P'u-t'o Shan (P) 普陀山

p'u-tu [Buddhist ceremony of universal salvation] 普渡

San Chieh Kung (D) 三界公

San Kuan Ta Ti (D) 三官大帝

San-chiao-yung (P) [old name for San-hsia] 三角勇

San-hsia (P) 三峽

san-hsien-li [a Confucian ceremony] 三獻禮

San-min (P) 三民

San-ts'eng (P) 三層

San-yüan *kung* (T) 三元宮

Shan-chu-hu (P) 山豬湖

shang-yüan [beginning calendrical festival] 上元

she-t'uan (O) [social/religious club] 社團

shen [deity] 神

shen-ming [bright, yang spirits] 神明

shen-ming-hui (O) [deity association] 神明會

sheng [raw, unassimilated, uncivilized] 生

sheng-fan (S) [unassimilated barbarians] 生番

sheng-yüan (S) [county-level degree-holder] 生員

Shih-men (P) 石門

shou-shih (S) [assistant] 首事

shu (*shou*) [cooked, assimilated, civilized] 熟

shu-fan (S) [assimilated aborigines] 熟番

Shu-lin Hsin-ts'un (P) 樹林新村

Shui-liu-tung (P) 水流東

shui-t'ou [upstream end] 水頭

shui-wei [downstream end] 水尾

ssu [Buddhist temple] 寺

ssu-ta-ming-shan (P) [four famous
    Buddhist mountains] 四大名山

Ta Shih Yeh (D) 大士爺

Ta-ch'i (P) 大溪

Ta-han (F) 大漢

Ta-k'o-k'an (P) [old name for Ta-ch'i]
    大嵙崁

Ta-ku-k'an (P) [old name for Ta-ch'i]
    大姑崁

ta-mu-kung [mass-grave spirit] 大墓公

Ta-tao-ch'eng (P) 大稻埕

ta-tsu [large rent] 大租

ta-tsu-hu (S) [large landlord] 大租戶

ta-t'ung [great unity, great equality] 大同

t'ai-chi tao [immanent tao] 太極道

T'ai-wan *jen* (S) [Taiwanese] 台灣人

T'ai-ya *tsu* (S) [Atayal] 泰雅族

Tan-shui (P) 淡水

tang-ki (S) [spirit medium, Hokkien
    pronunciation] 童乩

t'ang [temple, hall] 堂

tao-shih (S) [Taoist priest] 道士

T'ao-chien *pao* (P) 桃澗堡

T'ao-yüan (P) 桃園

te [virtue] 德

t'e-ch'an [local specialty] 特產

ti [fraternal submission] 弟

ti-fang-shen [local god] 地方神

ti-li-shih (S) [geomancer] 地理師

Ti-tsang (D) 地藏

t'ien [heaven] 天

T'ien Hou (D) 天后

T'ien Kung (D) 天公

T'ien-hou *kung* (T) 天后宮

t'ien-hsia [all under heaven, the
    Chinese empire] 天下

t'ien-hsia-i-chia [all under heaven
    is one family] 天下一家

t'ien-ming [mandate of heaven, fate] 天命

t'ing (O) [county under Japanese] 廳

t'ing [temple, pavilion] 亭

tou [measure of rice] 斗

tou-fu-kan [dried bean cake] 豆腐乾

tou-teng [votive lamp] 斗燈

ts'an-fang [wander, visit the four
    quarters] 參方

Tsao Shen (Tsao Chün, or Tsao Wang
    Yeh) (D) 竈神，竈君，竈王爺

tsu (O) [group, organization] 組

tsu-hsien [ancestors] 祖先

tsung-wu (S) [administrative secretary]
    總務

T'u Ti Kung (D) 土地公

T'u-ch'eng (P) 土城

Tung-hsing *kung* (T) 東興宮

t'ung-hsiang-hui (O) [native-place
    association] 同鄉會

t'ung-hsüeh-hui (O) [alumni association]
    同學會

T'ung-jen *she* (A) 同仁社

tzu-ti-hsi [opera performed by
    children] 子弟戲

Tz'u-hu (P) 慈湖

Tz'u-hui *t'ang* (T, A) 慈惠堂

wan-tou [closing votive-lamp ceremony]
    完斗

Wang Mu Niang Niang (D) 王母娘娘

Wei-liao (P) 尾寮

wei-yüan-hui (O) [committee] 委員會

Wen Shu (D) 文殊

Wu Ku Hsien Ti (D) 五穀仙帝

Wu Sheng Lao Mu (D) 無生老母

Wu Sheng Sheng Mu (D) 無生聖母

wu-chi tao [eternal tao] 無極道

wu-sheng [not subject to life and death]
    無生

Wu-t'ai Shan (P) 五台山

wu-wei tao [changeless tao] 無 為道

wu-yü (P) [five famous pilgrimage
  mountains] 五 嶽

Yao Ch'ih Chin Mu (D) 瑤 池 金 母

Ying-ko (P) 鶯 歌

yu-ching [to tour the boundaries] 遊 境

yu-wei tao [changeable tao] 有 為道

yu-ying-kung [mass-grave spirit] 有 應 公

yung (S) [militia, braves] 勇

Yung-an kung (T) 永 安 宮

Yung-ch'ang kung (T) 永 昌 宮

Yung-fu (P) 永 福

Yü Huang Shang Ti (D) 玉 皇 上 帝

Yüan Shuai Yeh (D) 元 帥 爺

Yüan-shu-lin (P) 圓 樹 林

Yüeh-mei (P) 月 眉

Yüeh-mei-shan Kuan-yin ssu (T) 月 眉 山
  觀 音 寺

Index

Library of Congress Cataloging-in-Publication Data

Sangren, Paul Steven.
    History and magical power in a Chinese community.

    Bibliography: p.
    Includes index.
    1. Ta-hsi chen (T'ao yüan hsien, Taiwan)—History.
    2. Ta-hsi chen (T'ao yüan hsien, Taiwan)—Social life and
    customs. I. Title.
    DS799.9.T24S36 1987   951'.249   86-23199
    ISBN 0-8047-1344-8 (alk. paper)